OECD Environmental Performance Reviews: Norway 2022

OECD
BETTER POLICIES FOR BETTER LIVES

Please cite this publication as:
OECD (2022), *OECD Environmental Performance Reviews: Norway 2022*, OECD Environmental Performance Reviews, OECD Publishing, Paris, https://doi.org/10.1787/59e71c13-en.

ISBN 978-92-64-18200-4 (print)
ISBN 978-92-64-44926-8 (PDF)
ISBN 978-92-64-76547-4 (HTML)

OECD Environmental Performance Reviews
ISSN 1990-0104 (print)
ISSN 1990-0090 (online)

Photo credits: Cover © VladOrlov/Shutterstock.com; Pawel Uchorczak/Shutterstock.com.

Corrigenda to OECD publications may be found at: https://www.oecd.org/en/publications/support/corrigenda.html.

Foreword

The principal aim of the OECD Environmental Performance Review programme is to help member and selected partner countries improve their individual and collective performance in environmental management by:

- helping countries assess progress in achieving their environmental goals
- promoting continuous policy dialogue and peer learning
- stimulating greater accountability from governments towards each other and public opinion.

This report reviews the environmental performance of Norway since the previous review in 2011. Progress in achieving domestic objectives and international commitments provides the basis for assessing the country's environmental performance. Such objectives and commitments may be broad aims, qualitative goals or quantitative targets. A distinction is made between intentions, actions and results. Assessment of environmental performance is also placed within the context of Norway's historical environmental record, present state of the environment, physical endowment in natural resources, economic conditions and demographic trends.

The OECD is indebted to Norway's Ministry of Climate and Environment for its co-operation in providing information, for the organisation of the virtual review mission (20-24 September 2021) and policy mission (7 December 2021) as well as for facilitating contacts inside and outside government institutions. Thanks are also due to all government ministries and agencies, as well as to the non-government organisations, that participated in the virtual missions and/or provided information and comments. Due to the COVID-19 pandemic, most of the review was conducted remotely engaging close to 150 stakeholders.

The OECD is grateful to the representatives of the two examining countries: Veli Auvinen and Kaarle Kupiainen (Finland), and Megan Barnhart, Daniel Gogal, Chris Hartley, Eva Kreisler, Karen Maguire, Hope Bigda-Peyton, Steve Wolfson and Lia Yohannes (United States).

The authors of this report are Julia Wanjiru Nikiema (Chapter 1, OECD Environment Directorate) and Roger Martini (Chapter 2, OECD Trade and Agriculture Directorate). The review process was co-ordinated by Julia Wanjiru Nikiema. Ivana Capozza and Nathalie Girouard provided oversight. Valuable inputs were provided by Ivana Capozza, Eugene Mazur and Nils Axel Braathen. Carla Bertuzzi provided statistical support and research assistance; Fiona Smyth and Annette Hardcastle provided administrative support and Mark Foss copy-edited the report. Natasha Cline-Thomas provided communications support. Preparation of this report also benefited from inputs and comments from Enrico Botta, Ben Conigrave, Lara Fleischer, Gregoire Garsous, Guillaume Gruère, Håvard Halland, Philip Hemmings, Katia Karousakis, Krzysztof Michalak, Sarah Miet, Mark Mateo, Daniel Nachtigall, Edward Perry, Anasuya Raj, Jonas Teusch, Konstantinos Theodoropoulos, Kurt van Dender and Frédérique Zegel of the OECD Secretariat.

The OECD Working Party on Environmental Performance discussed the draft Environmental Performance Review of Norway at its meeting on 16 February 2022 and approved the Assessment and Recommendations.

Table of contents

Tables

Figures

Boxes

Reader's guide

Signs

The following signs are used in figures and tables:

..	: not available
–	: nil or negligible
.	: decimal point

Country aggregates

OECD Europe: This zone includes all European member countries of the OECD, i.e. Austria, Belgium, the Czech Republic, Denmark, Estonia, Finland, France, Germany, Greece, Hungary, Iceland, Ireland, Italy, Latvia, Lithuania, Luxembourg, the Netherlands, Norway, Poland, Portugal, the Slovak Republic, Slovenia, Spain, Sweden, Switzerland, Turkey and the United Kingdom.

OECD: This zone includes all member countries of the OECD, i.e. the countries of OECD Europe plus Australia, Canada, Chile, Colombia, Costa Rica, Israel*, Japan, Korea, Mexico, New Zealand and the United States.

Country aggregates may include Secretariat estimates.

Currency

Monetary unit: NOK

In 2021, USD 1 = NOK 8.599
In 2020, USD 1 = NOK 9.419
In 2019, USD 1 = NOK 8.800

In 2021, EUR 1 = NOK 10.163
In 2020, EUR 1 = NOK 10.723
In 2019, EUR 1 = NOK 9.851

Cut-off date

This report is based on information and data available up to December 2021, including some updated information received in January 2022.

Disclaimer

* The statistical data for Israel are supplied by and under the responsibility of the relevant Israeli authorities. The use of such data by the OECD is without prejudice to the status of the Golan Heights, East Jerusalem and Israeli settlements in the West Bank under the terms of international law.

This document and any map included herein are without prejudice to the status of or sovereignty over any territory, to the delimitation of international frontiers and boundaries and to the name of any territory, city or area.

Basic statistics of Norway

2020 or latest available year (OECD values in parentheses)[a]

PEOPLE AND SOCIETY					
Population (million)	5		Population density per km²	9	(36)
Share of population by type of region:			Population compound annual growth rate, latest 5 years	0.8	(0.6)
Predominantly urban (%)	24	(48)	Income inequality (Gini coefficient)	0.26	(0.33)
Intermediate (%)	50	(28)	Poverty rate (% of pop. with less than 50% median income)	8	(12)
Rural (%)	26	(24)	Life expectancy	83	(81)
ECONOMY AND EXTERNAL ACCOUNTS					
Total GDP (National currency, billion)	3 413		Imports of goods and services (% of GDP)	33	(29)
Total GDP (USD, billion, current prices and PPPs)	340		Main exports (% of total merchandise exports)		
GDP compound annual real growth rate, latest 5 years	0.9	(0.7)	Petroleum and related products	32	
GDP per capita (1 000 USD current PPPs)	63	(45)	Gas, natural and manufactured	17	
Value added shares (%)			Fish, crustaceans, molluscs	13	
Agriculture, forestry and fishing	2	(2)	Main imports (% of total merchandise imports)		
Industry including construction	33	(24)	Road vehicles	11	
Services	65	(74)	Electrical machinery and transport equipment	6	
Exports of goods and services (% of GDP)	38	(29)	Other industrial machinery	5	
GENERAL GOVERNMENT					
Percentage of GDP					
Expenditure	58.4	(40.8)	Education expenditure	5.6	(5.0)
Revenue	55.0	(37.7)	Health expenditure	8.7	(7.8)
Gross financial debt	53.6	(109.2)	Environment protection expenditure	0.9	(0.5)
Fiscal balance	-3.4	-(3.2)	Environmental taxes: (% of GDP)	2.0	(1.5)
			(% of total tax revenue)	5.1	(5.0)
LABOUR MARKET, SKILLS AND INNOVATION					
Unemployment rate (% of civilian labour force)			Patent applications (% of all technologies)[b]		
	4.4	(7.1)	Environment-related technologies	12	(11)
Tertiary educational attainment of 25-64 year-olds (%)	45	(40)	Environmental management	5	(3)
Gross expenditure on R&D, % of GDP	2.2	(2.5)	Climate change mitigation technologies	10	(10)
			Climate adaptation technologies	7	(1)
ENVIRONMENT					
Total energy supply (TES) intensity:					
TES per capita (toe/cap.)	5.3	(3.7)	Road vehicle stock (vehicles./100 inhabitants)	76	(67)
TES per GDP (toe/1 000 USD, 2015 PPPs)	0.09	(0.09)	Water stress (abstraction as % of available resources)	..	(8.6)
Renewables (% of TPES)	51	(12)	Water abstraction per capita (m³/cap./year)	..	(696)
Carbon intensity (energy-related CO_2):			Municipal waste per capita, (kg/capita)	772	(538)
Emissions per capita (t/cap.)	6.7	(8.3)	Material productivity (USD, 2015 PPPs/DMC, kg)	2.0	(2.9)
Emissions per GDP (t/1 000 USD, 2015 PPP)	0.11	(0.19)	Land area (1 000 km²)	365	
GHG intensity: [c]			% of arable land and permanent crops	2	(11)
Emissions per capita (tCO_2-eq/cap.)	9.4	(11.3)	% of permanent meadows and pastures	0	(23)
Emissions per GDP (tCO_2-eq/cap. USD, 2015 PPP)	0.15	(0.26)	% of forest area	33	(33)
Mean population exposure to air pollution ($PM_{2.5}$), µg/m³	6.7	(13.9)	% of other land (built-up and other land)	64	(32)

a) Values earlier than 2014 are not taken into consideration. OECD value: where the OECD aggregate is not provided in the source database, a simple OECD average of the latest available data is calculated where data exist for a significant number of countries.

b) Higher-value inventions that have sought protection in at least two jurisdictions. Average of latest three years.

c) Excluding emissions/removals from land use, land-use change and forestry.

Source: Calculations based on data extracted from databases of the OECD, IEA/OECD, EUROSTAT and the World Bank.

Executive summary

The fourth Environmental Performance Review of Norway provides an independent, evidence-based evaluation of the country's environmental performance over the past decade. Drawing on a broad range of expertise and analysis of cross-country economic and environmental data, it provides 30 country-tailored recommendations to help Norway further improve its environmental performance in line with its national and international commitments.

The first chapter summarises key environmental trends and assesses the environmental effectiveness and economic efficiency of the policy mix, including fiscal, economic, regulatory and voluntary instruments. Norway has made progress on the path towards green growth over the past decade. The country is a frontrunner in many environmental areas and invests heavily in technological development and innovation to support its green transition. It has set many ambitious national environmental targets across all sectors. Indeed, its national targets on climate mitigation are among the most ambitious worldwide, and the country aims to achieve climate neutrality by 2030. Norway has a well-functioning environmental management system, with a high level of co-operation, vibrant civic engagement in decision making and strong advisory bodies.

The second chapter offers an in-depth analysis of Norway's land use and biodiversity management. The topic was chosen by the Ministry of Climate and Environment, which saw the need for a critical, independent assessment of the country's land-use policy in a context of increased pressure on land and biodiversity. Norway is clarifying its vision of sustainable land use, even as it adopts new tools for assessment and new means of co-operation to achieve its goals. The situation remains a work in progress but is moving in the right direction. If the government implements all its plans, it could generate positive outcomes for the health of biodiversity and ecosystems and in benefits for Norwegians.

The report also examines actions taken to implement recommendations from the previous review and the results achieved. While Norway has addressed most of the previous recommendations, some of the identified challenges require sustained effort to achieve lasting results. Norway's experience offers many practical lessons for other OECD members and partner countries.

Key findings

The environmental impact of Norway's recovery measures was mixed

The health and economic impacts of COVID-19 have been less severe in Norway than in other European countries. While its economy was initially hit hard by slumping oil prices, Norway will reach pre-pandemic per capita levels of gross domestic product (GDP) in 2022. Economic measures included a mix of time-limited compensation and subsidy schemes, temporary changes in tax rules, income protection, investments in key infrastructure sectors, increased funding in technology development and a green transition package. The cost of these measures was NOK 230 billion in 2020 and 2021 (about USD 26.7 billion), including substantial support for the oil and gas industry and the aviation sector. Thanks to the rebound in oil prices, policy makers can now turn more fully to structural challenges.

Norway is on track to achieve many but not all Sustainable Development Goals

Norway ranked seventh on the 2021 index of countries' progress towards achieving the Sustainable Development Goals. Norway has fully achieved six goals and is making good progress towards another four. Like many other OECD countries, Norway still faces "significant" or "major" challenges for several goals, including climate action, sustainable consumption patterns and biodiversity protection. Most of the remaining challenges are related to increased environmental pressures.

Norwegians enjoy good overall air quality

Norway's four major cities rank in the top 20 of the European City Air Quality Index. Premature death attributed to fine particulate matter ($PM_{2.5}$) exposure is less than one-third the OECD average. Norway complies with EU directives on air quality standards. Its pollutant emissions and intensities of $PM_{2.5}$, nitrogen oxide, sulphur oxide and black carbon have all decreased over the past decade. Except for ammonia and non-methane volatile organic compounds, Norway reached its air emission targets.

Norway has abundant water resources but needs to tackle water losses

The country is endowed with a large number of lakes and river habitats. Nearly 90% of drinking water is withdrawn from surface water, and about 90% of Norwegians have access to treated drinking water from waterworks with high quality standards. However, up to 30% of abstracted water is estimated to leak from the drinking water supply system. The country needs to upgrade its ageing sewage and drinking water infrastructure, and adjust to new climate challenges, such as increased precipitation, floods and rising sea levels.

Significant challenges remain to achieve a circular economy

Norway is not on track to decouple waste generation from economic growth. Waste generation reached 12.2 million tonnes in 2019, a record high and up 3% from 2018. The average Norwegian produced 772 kg of municipal waste, among the highest amounts in Europe (OECD Europe average = 499 kg per capita). Norway reduced food waste by close to 10% between 2015 and 2020. Recycling remained fairly stable overall. Norway has one of the world's highest material consumption rates, a high material footprint per capita and low material productivity. Only a small share of products is cycled back into the economy.

Like many other countries, Norway has a way to go to reach its 2030 climate targets

Norway has decoupled greenhouse gas (GHG) emissions from GDP growth. Since 1990, emission levels have varied between 47.5 million (1992) and 56.9 million tonnes of CO_2-equivalent (CO_2-eq) (2007). Norway is expected to emit around 41.2 million tonnes of CO_2-eq annually by 2030, 20% below the 1990 level. These estimates do not include measures of the Climate Action Plan 2021-30 or the effects of Norway's participation in the EU Emissions Trading System (ETS). Outside of agriculture, climate measures are broad-based and should bring proportionate reductions in all sectors. As a small and open economy, Norway's focus on national GHG emissions provides only a partial picture of its global carbon footprint.

The electrification of the vehicle fleet is on track, but further efforts are needed for sustainable transport systems

Norway is a world leader in Zero Emission Vehicle (ZEV) adoption and made good progress towards achieving its policy targets to electrify its vehicle fleet. Thanks to generous incentives, the market share of newly registered ZEVs reached 64.5% in 2021. For a long time, the rapidly growing demand for mobility has outpaced progress in decarbonising the transport sector. Despite its great achievements, Norway needs to redouble efforts and make more structural changes to establish sustainable transport systems (e.g. Urban Growth Agreements).

The share of green taxes has declined due to tax incentives for electric vehicles

Norway's share of environment-related taxes in total tax revenue and GDP is below the OECD Europe average and has decreased over time. These taxes are a victim of their own success: reducing environmentally harmful activities has undercut the tax base. This is most clearly seen through forgone tax revenues in relation to ZEVs. While energy- and pollution-related taxes have increased since 2012, transport-related taxes have declined continuously since 2004 due to the uptake of ZEVs and related decline in internal combustion vehicles. As the electric vehicle market is maturing, it makes economic sense to reduce tax incentives gradually. Norway should prioritise preparation of a place-based road-pricing system. This should cover all passenger and light-duty vehicle categories, while considering the needs of people in remote areas.

Norway taxes a high share of CO_2 emissions

Norway ranks among the top OECD countries in carbon pricing. The country aims to provide a long-term perspective on carbon pricing. To that end, it provides a strong price signal to encourage increased investments in renewable energy and low-carbon technologies. Norway's Climate Action Plan 2021-30 proposes to raise the carbon tax from NOK 590 (USD 69) per tonne of CO_2-eq in 2021 to NOK 2 000 (about USD 233) by 2030. Norway's nominal carbon tax rate is among the highest in Europe and covers more than 80% of national emissions. Norway has also introduced a carbon tax on waste incineration and abolished the exemption for use of natural gas and liquefied petroleum gas in the greenhouse industry in 2022. The country has participated in the EU ETS since 2008.

Further reduce fossil fuel support and set time-bound targets

Total fossil fuel support has been declining over the past decade and represents about 0.2% of tax revenue. In 2020, the lion's share supports petroleum and the rest natural gas. Most support measures are related to exemptions from the tax on mineral oil used for domestic shipping and fishing. Norway should set time-bound targets and systematically screen actual or proposed subsidies, including those unjustified on economic, social and environmental grounds. It should develop a plan to phase out support to fossil fuel and other environmentally harmful forms of support.

Land-use change has exerted growing pressures on Norway's diverse and pristine landscapes

While Norway has one of the most diverse and pristine landscapes in Europe, trends in ecosystem status are unfavourable in many parts of the country. Land use and land-use change in forestry and agriculture, as well as for housing and roads, exerts substantial pressure on Norwegian biodiversity. Nearly all threatened species are affected by factors related to land use in some way.

Norway made good progress on objective setting for ecosystem protection and related knowledge systems

Norway is clarifying its vision of sustainable land use, even as it adopts new tools for assessment and new means of co-operation to achieve its goals. The Biodiversity Action Plan and the Nature Index for Norway are important tools in this regard. Government guidance to communities has improved overall. Norway needs to continue developing a management system for ecosystem types as foreseen in the Biodiversity

Action Plan and set aggressive timelines for implementation. It can build momentum for success by regularly assessing ecological status and set specific, measurable, achievable, realistic and time-bound objectives accordingly.

Better horizontal and vertical co-ordination can improve outcomes

Norway has used many different approaches for planning and decision making, embracing good practices that could help make land-use planning more holistic. Developing highly capable institutions that represent all stakeholders and handle conflict constructively can smooth the inevitable disagreements in land-use planning. Improved information on the cumulative effects of local land planning on the value of ecosystem services and national objectives will help county governors do their jobs better and help municipalities better reflect these concerns in their plans.

The share of threatened species is increasing

Despite activity to protect important habitats and increasing expenditures on recovery, threatened species face slow and steady decline. Habitat loss, degradation or fragmentation as a result of human activity remain key drivers of this decline. Threatened species are found mainly in the southern regions where species diversity is high and human activity widespread. Of the nearly 3 000 threatened species in the Red List 2021, nearly 10% are critically endangered, about one-third are endangered and half are vulnerable. In 2021, about one-quarter of mammals, bird species, mosses and plants were threatened.

The protected area system is expanding but incomplete

Protected areas make up 17% of Norway's mainland area, which is in line with the 2020 Aichi target and above the OECD average. Considerably larger portions of land area in Svalbard (65%) and Jan Mayen (nearly all) have been protected for several decades. However, protected areas do not represent all landscape types, and forest protection is about half the national target of 10%. Most areas needing additional protection are in the south. Moreover, nearly one-third of protected areas are at risk of degradation and require additional action to secure their conservation values. Norway is well below the OECD average for marine protected areas and failed to meet the Aichi target.

More is needed to promote climate-smart agriculture

Agricultural land suitable for arable crops is limited and benefits from many subsidies, among the highest in the OECD. Agricultural land use is largely determined by the small share of land that is technically feasible for farming combined with national policies to maintain and distribute production. Farmers remain exempt from GHG emission taxes and agriculture is not part of the EU ETS. Norway's levels of nitrogen and phosphorus surpluses, which place pressure on soil water and air quality, are among the highest in the OECD. It should redirect support from income and production objectives towards stronger incentives for farmers to improve agri-environmental outcomes and develop climate-smart agriculture. In this way, farmers would help restore the ecosystem value of agricultural landscapes.

Assessment and recommendations

The Assessment and recommendations present the main findings of the OECD Environmental Performance Review of Norway. They identify 30 country-tailored recommendations to help Norway make further progress towards its environmental objectives and international commitments. The OECD Working Party on Environmental Performance discussed and approved the Assessment and recommendations at its meeting on 16 February 2022.

1. Towards sustainable development

Norway has made progress on the path towards green growth over the past decade. The country is a frontrunner in many environmental areas and invests heavily in technological development and innovation to support its green transition. Norway's low-carbon transition is comparatively well advanced. The country has a low-carbon energy mix thanks to its widespread use of renewables. It is a world leader in electric vehicle adoption, and is advancing the decarbonisation of all transport sectors. However, the country still faces multiple challenges, including sustainable consumption patterns and biodiversity protection.

Norway set ambitious national environmental targets across all sectors. Its national targets on climate mitigation are among the most ambitious worldwide. The country aims at achieving climate neutrality by 2030 and enshrined in law the target of becoming a low emission society by 2050. While Norway is a climate mitigation and adaptation forerunner at home, it is also one of the world's largest energy exporters, thereby contributing indirectly to greenhouse gas (GHG) emissions abroad. Norway has the capabilities and financial means to accelerate a just transition within its own borders and abroad. The country already supports developing and emerging economies through the Norwegian International Climate and Forest Initiative, which is the largest single element in Norway's public climate finance. The government intends to double its total climate finance to NOK 14 billion (USD 1.6 billion) by 2026.

While not a member of the European Union, Norway is part of the EU internal market through the Agreement on the European Economic Area. As such, it implements large parts of EU environment and climate policies. The country also has a long tradition of applying a wide range of economic instruments to green its economy. Norway has a well-functioning environmental governance and management system with a high level of co-operation, vibrant civic engagement in decision making and strong advisory bodies. Citizens have generally free, open access to high-quality environmental information. The short distance between research and policy-making bodies is an asset of the Norwegian system. The integration of environmental concern into other policy areas has been at the core of policy making for several decades.

Norway is a frontrunner in many environmental areas, but there is still room for improvement.

Norway's energy transition is well advanced and the country is a leader in renewables

Norway has increasingly decoupled energy demand and related environmental effects from growth. Over the past decade, it has accelerated deployment of renewables and improved energy efficiency thanks to enhanced technology and the electrification of the transport and residential sectors. Nevertheless, Norway's energy consumption per capita, which historically has been among the highest in the OECD, is still above the OECD average. This is due notably to high energy consumption in the industry sector, as well as households' heating needs due to the cold Scandinavian climate. Improving energy efficiency thus needs to remain a priority for such an energy-intense economy.

Norway has one of the most decarbonised power sectors in the OECD area (Figure 1). It builds on widespread use of renewable electricity, primarily hydropower and more recently wind power. The country is energy self-sufficient with a surplus of renewable electricity in normal years, and has become Europe's largest energy exporter. Norway has reduced the share of fossil fuels in energy consumption since 2013 and decided to phase out its only coal-fired power plant in Svalbard. In 2020, it became the first country that formally prohibited use of fossil oil for heating in existing buildings and in new buildings altogether.

Figure 1. Norway's energy mix is much more decarbonised than the OECD average

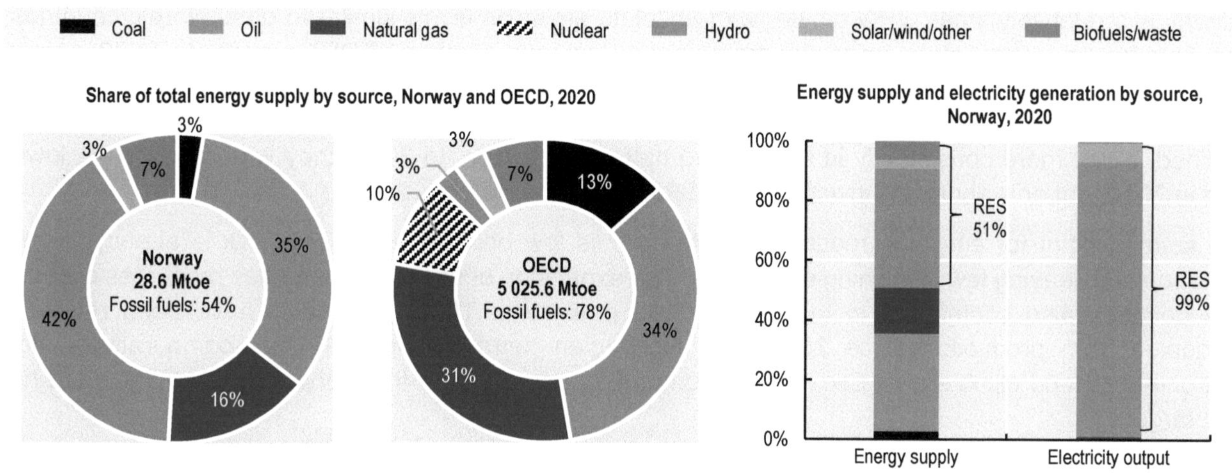

Note: The breakdown of energy supply excludes heat and electricity trade but percentages shown reflect ratios calculated on total energy supply. Biofuel and waste include negligible quantities of non-renewable waste.
Source: IEA (2021), *IEA World Energy Statistics and Balances* (database).

StatLink https://stat.link/9xogqj

Following Iceland, Norway has the second largest share of renewables, representing 51% in its energy mix and 99% of its electricity output (Figure 1). It overachieved its national target of 67.5% share of renewable energy in gross final energy consumption in 2020 in line with the EU Directive on renewable energy. Norway's renewables sector is rapidly growing. The country has a competitive advantage in large-scale deployment of offshore renewables, particularly wind.

Norway has ambitious climate targets…

The 2017 Climate Change Act, the 2020 Nationally Determined Contribution (NDC) under the Paris Agreement and the Climate Action Plan 2021-30 lay out the framework of Norway's climate action. Norway also adopted its Climate Adaptation Strategy 2021. The government provides annual reporting on both mitigation and adaptation efforts to Parliament.

Norway has raised ambition on legally binding climate targets. Within its NDC 2020, Norway aims to reduce GHG emissions by at least 50% and towards 55% by 2030 compared to 1990 levels, including through international emissions trading, such as the EU Emissions Trading System (EU ETS). The 2017 Climate Change Act sets the long-term target of becoming a low-emission society by 2050. Moreover, in 2016, Norway's Parliament pledged to become climate neutral by 2030 (previously 2050). This means it must offset remaining emissions through emissions trading systems or international co-operation.

Norway plans to fulfil its climate commitment in close collaboration with the European Union. Its objectives are aligned with the enhanced ambition of the new EU-wide 2030 Climate and Energy Framework under the EU Green Deal. Emission taxation and participation in the EU ETS are the main elements of the government's climate policy. The Climate Action Plan outlines economy-wide and sector-specific measures for reducing emissions, as well as its policy for increasing CO2 sequestration and reducing emissions from forestry and land use. The government committed to applying the no-debit rule under the EU Regulation on Land, Land-Use Change and Forestry and intends to enhance climate sinks.

... but reducing domestic emissions will be challenging

Norway is a relatively small GHG emitter with absolute emission levels similar to other Nordic countries. The country has decoupled emissions from gross domestic product (GDP) growth. In 2020 energy industries, including oil and gas production, contributed to 30% of the country's GHG emissions, followed by transport, industry, agriculture and buildings. After peaking in 2007, domestic GHG emissions have declined, albeit more consistently in the second half of the 2010s. In 2020, they were about 10% lower than in 2010, but only about 4% lower than in 1990 (Statistics Norway, 2021[1]).

The starting point for emission reductions in Norway is low because its energy mix is already largely decarbonised, leaving few remaining quick wins. The expansion of offshore oil and gas resources over the past decades also contributed to increasing GHG emissions. These emissions have been relatively decoupled from production since 2016. The Norwegian petroleum industry has comparatively high environmental and climate standards. Many companies operating on the Norwegian shelf have set net zero targets.

Figure 2. Norway has a way to go to reach its 2030 climate targets

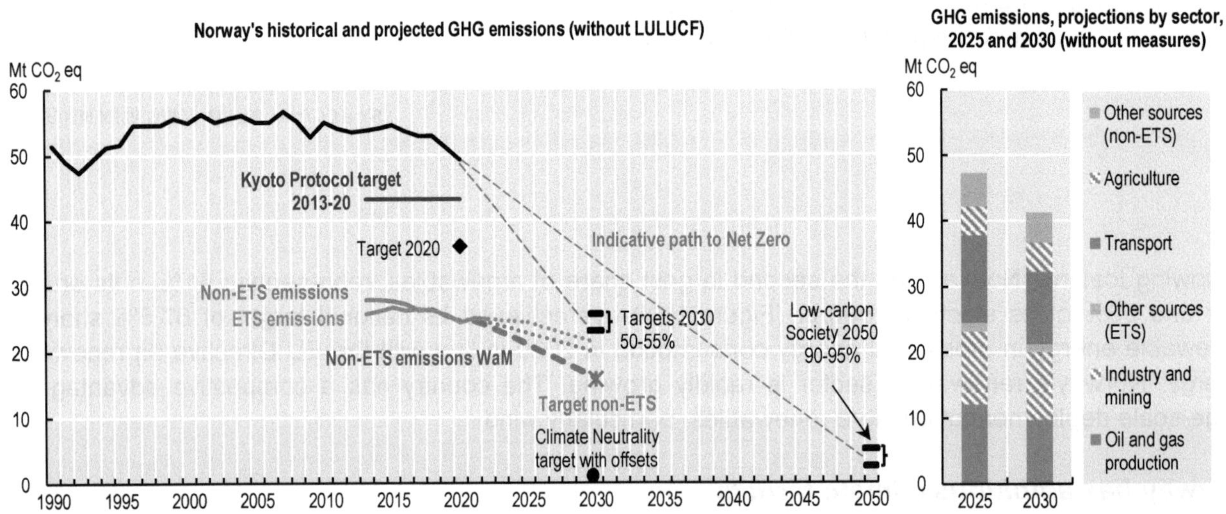

Note: IPCC = Intergovernmental Panel on Climate Change; LULUCF = land use, land-use change and forestry. The projections and effort sharing target apply different metrics (Global Warming Potential of IPCC's fourth and fifth Assessment Reports, respectively). The dotted line shows GHG emissions projections with existing measures. The dashed line (with additional measures - WaM) shows projections for the non-ETS sector, including the measures of the Climate Action Plan 2021-30. Data exclude emissions trading. Norway co-operates with the European Union to fulfil the 2030 climate target. The impact of this co-operation, especially Norway's participation in the EU Emissions Trading System, must be considered in assessing progress towards this target. Thus, reduction in domestic emissions cannot be used as the sole indicator to assess Norway's progress.
Source: EEA (2021), *Member States' greenhouse gas emission projections* (database); ESA (2021), *Climate Progress Report 2021*; Statistics Norway (2021), "Table 08940", *StatBank* (database).

StatLink https://stat.link/lzfota

Meeting the enhanced climate target through domestic emission cuts will be challenging (Figure 2). According to projections of the 2022 National Budget, Norway will emit around 41.2 million tonnes of CO_2 equivalent (CO_2-eq) by 2030, which represents a reduction of 19.5% of emissions compared to the 1990 level. These estimates do not yet include measures of the Climate Action Plan 2021-30 or the effects of Norway's participation in the EU ETS. However, the government still expects a gap to achieve the 2030 emissions reduction target.

With high marginal costs of reducing domestic GHG emissions, the purchase of foreign emission credits often makes economic sense. Emissions trading within the EU ETS was a major factor in achieving Norway's commitments under the Kyoto Protocol (2008-12 and 2013-20), along with carbon credits under the Clean Development Mechanism and domestic measures. Moreover, many counties, cities and municipalities have set net zero goals and contribute to fulfilling Norway's national ambitions. The city of Oslo has an ambitious climate action plan and climate budget covering all relevant sectors.

Norway is a world leader in electric vehicle adoption and is decarbonising transport

Norway has by far the largest share of electric vehicles (EVs) worldwide. In 2021, about two-thirds of new passenger vehicles sold were fully electric. The country is making progress towards its goal of registering all new passenger cars and light vans as zero emission vehicles by 2025. While the charging infrastructure is increasingly dense, Norway needs to pursue public financial support with a view to establishing and maintaining public charging stations in areas that lack a commercial market, particularly in the north. Norway electrified a third of its domestic ferries. Norway is also a pioneer in electric aviation, which could help address growing concerns about the large number of short-distance flights.

The government's transport goals, strategies and priorities are detailed in the National Transport Plan 2022-33. This plan aims to halve the non-quota emissions from the transport sector by 2030 compared with 2005 levels (representing about a quarter of total emissions in 2020). A broad range of economic instruments and regulatory instruments is used to decarbonise all transport sectors. The state-owned enterprise Enova supports technology development and early market introduction.

The implementation of the zero growth goal through Urban Growth Agreements has helped reduce car traffic volumes in Norway's major cities. This has contributed to reducing GHG emissions, air and noise pollution, and congestion, as well as to improving quality of life in cities. Such agreements should be rapidly extended to medium-sized cities and smaller urban areas. Norway's small and medium-sized cities could largely benefit from lessons learnt in major urban areas.

Norway needs to redouble its efforts and make more structural changes to establish sustainable transport systems to meet the 2030 target. This involves promotion of behavioural changes, a stronger focus on shared mobility services and a shift from increased mobility towards improved accessibility. The rail system needs to be further modernised and become a cheap alternative to road and air transport. Airport expansion is counterproductive to reducing GHG emissions and environmental concerns need to be better reflected in any new plans. It is an opportune moment to rethink mobility and develop a socially fair and spatially balanced transport system.

Air quality is among the best within the OECD, but some seasonal challenges in urban areas remain

Norwegians enjoy good air quality. Norway's pollutant emissions and intensities of fine particulates ($PM_{2.5}$), nitrogen oxide (NO_x), sulphur oxide (SO_x) and black carbon have all decreased over the past decade. Norway complies with the EU directives on air quality standards and will continue to follow the EU zero pollution agenda closely. In addition, the country has set more ambitious local and national targets, supported by excellent nationwide air quality monitoring services. Premature death attributed to $PM_{2.5}$ exposure in Norway is less than one-third the OECD average. Norway's 4 major cities rank in the top 20 of the European City Air Quality Index.

Nevertheless, nearly all larger cities in Norway face localised air pollution problems and periodic worsening of air quality with high peak PM_{10} concentrations during winter and into spring. Thanks to proactive measures (zero growth goal, EVs, replacement of wood stoves), local air quality in urban areas is expected to improve in the coming years. Fees for studded tyres, an important source of airborne particulates, helped considerably reduce their use in urban areas.

Norway needs to expedite the replacement of ageing water infrastructure

While Norway has abundant water resources, total freshwater withdrawal has increased over the past decade, notably due to higher consumption by households and significant water losses. Leakage from the drinking water supply system is estimated at 30% (Environment Norway, 2021[2]). This represents not only a significant loss of water resources but also a potential risk for microbiological contamination in drinking water. Water supply systems are often more vulnerable in small municipalities, notably in terms of water supply stability and the ability of drinking water utilities to prepare and respond to emergencies (bedreVANN and Norsk Vann, 2020[3]). Information on drinking water quality could be made accessible directly on websites of municipalities. This would enable consumers to easily consult relevant information on their drinking water sources, as well as inspection reports.

Most people are connected to municipal wastewater systems. However, only 60% of Norway's population is connected to advanced wastewater treatment plants, which is one of the lowest shares in the OECD area. According to national statistics from 2020, more than half of the population was connected to wastewater facilities, which do not comply with pollution permits. This calls for regular inspections and the use of coercive fines. As noted in the previous OECD EPR of Norway (OECD, 2011[4]), the country's ageing water infrastructure requires urgent upgrades. It also needs to adjust to new climate challenges, such as increased precipitation, floods and rising sea levels. The rate of infrastructure improvement has been slow despite substantial investment. Norway has invested by far the largest share in infrastructure renewal in Europe: EUR 225 (about USD 255) per inhabitant per year compared to EUR 82 (about USD 93) in other EU member states (five-year average) (EurEau, 2021[5]).There is scope for improving operational efficiency of water services and co-ordination between different administrative levels.

Accelerated action is needed to reduce waste

Norway is not on track to meet its objective of decoupling waste generation from economic growth. Waste generation in Norway reached a record high in 2019. The average Norwegian produced 772 kg of municipal waste, one of the highest amounts in Europe (OECD Europe average = 499 kg per capita). However, the definition of municipal waste has been changing over the years, which makes it difficult to compare data. The Waste Management Plan for 2020-25 includes a waste prevention programme and proposals for changes in waste infrastructure to prepare for tightened directives within the EU zero waste strategy.

Nearly half of Norway's municipal waste is treated by incineration with energy recovery, while landfilling has almost disappeared. The country will need to significantly increase its recycling capacity. Norway has excellent waste treatment facilities, with cutting edge technology for waste sorting. While more flexible regulations are needed, extended producer responsibility schemes and better incentives are key to creating demand for secondary raw material, notably in the construction sector. Technical building standards would need to be adjusted to enable increased use of recycled building materials.

Thanks to voluntary commitments by the food industry, Norway reduced food waste by 12% (2015-18) and aims to halve food waste by 2030. However, NOK 22 billion (about USD 2.6 billion) in food is still wasted each year, representing about 1.3 million tonnes of CO_2-eq emissions. Collected food waste is increasingly used for biogas production. Awareness campaigns to promote better consumer choices and better understanding of best-before dates need to be pursued. Binding measures to reduce food waste may be needed.

Norway still has a way to go towards achieving a circular economy

Promoting sustainable consumption patterns is a key challenge for Norway. The country has one of the world's highest material consumption rates, a high material footprint per capita and a declining material productivity (Figure 3). The government released its first strategy for developing a green, circular economy in July 2021, which sees the transition to a circular economy as an opportunity to foster value creation and sustainability. The strategy has broad scope, and largely applies the new EU Circular Economy Action Plan 2020.

The linear pattern of "take-make-use-dispose" does not provide producers with sufficient incentives to make their products more circular. Only a small share of products is cycled back into the Norwegian economy (Circular Norway, 2020[6]). As the European Union sets global standards in product sustainability, Norway could benefit from a stronger focus on life cycle thinking, eco-design, "the right to repair", etc. Policy makers need to create an enabling environment to facilitate the circular transition.

As typical for many other developed economies, material footprint originates in part from outside of Norway. A more holistic strategy would allow Norway to better understand and consider embedded emissions of imported goods and related global environmental impacts. Actions should not only tackle all economic areas to reduce Norway's material footprint (e.g. construction, forestry and wood products, energy transition, circular food systems, green transportation) but also focus on reducing its absolute levels of resource consumption. This involves further educating and empowering consumers to make informed decisions (e.g. use of sustainability labels).

Figure 3. Domestic material consumption productivity is decreasing

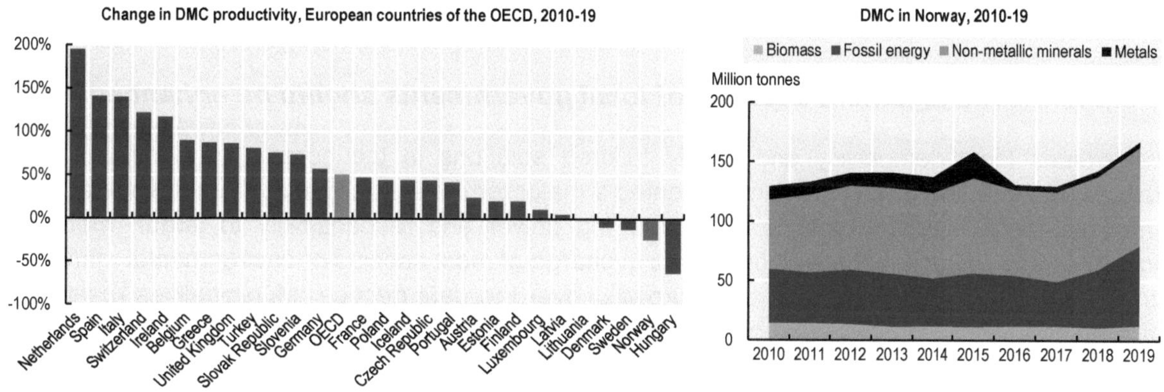

Note: Domestic material consumption (DMC) equals the sum of domestic extraction of raw materials used by an economy and their physical trade balance (imports minus exports of raw materials and manufactured products). DMC productivity designates the amount of GDP generated per unit of materials used. GDP at 2015 prices and purchasing power parities.
Source: OECD (2021), "Material resources", *OECD Environment Statistics* (database).

StatLink https://stat.link/o20sei

Norway has a well-functioning environmental management system.

The implementation of the SDGs is making good progress but needs to be strengthened throughout the country

Norway ranked seventh on the 2021 index of countries' progress towards achieving the SDGs (Sachs et al., 2021[7]). Despite good progress, Norway still faces "significant or major challenges" for several goals, including climate action, sustainable consumption patterns and biodiversity protection. The 2021 National Action Plan for implementation of the SDGs promotes a whole-of-government approach. It establishes measures to ensure better horizontal and vertical co-ordination, as well as stronger co-operation with the private sector, academia and civil society. In 2020, the Ministry of Local Government and Modernisation, which is also in charge of regional development, became the national co-ordinating body for implementing the SDGs with a view to promoting local ownership and increasing cross-sectoral co-operation.

While nearly all municipalities have started working with the SDGs (Hjorth-Johansen et al., 2021[8]), implementation varies greatly across the country. Large, central and network-oriented municipalities have done better overall, thanks to stronger political commitment and better knowledge sharing and co-operation with other levels of government (Hjorth-Johansen et al., 2021[8]). Counties and municipalities need to be fully involved in national decision making from early planning to monitoring and evaluation. They must also strengthen their capacity to work with the SDGs strategically and systematically (OECD, 2020[9]).

The national government needs to further promote policy coherence, multi-level governance and multi-stakeholder partnerships to move beyond a goal-by-goal approach rooted in specific sectors. As in all countries, inter-ministerial co-ordination between different policy areas could still be improved. Specifically, ministerial departments should invest more in interdisciplinary expertise (e.g. internal mobility) and pay more attention to cross-sectoral spillovers to better integrate policies across sectors.

Environmental management capacity of local governments should be enhanced

Norway values local democracy and locally tailored solutions in the context of significant regional differences. In 2020, the government implemented a major territorial reform that merged several counties and municipalities. The reform aims at transferring power and responsibility to larger, more robust municipalities and regions. Local authorities are in charge of most aspects of environmental management and their level of responsibilities has been growing over the past decade. Municipalities manage local pollution control, while County Governors and the Norwegian Environment Agency control pollution at the regional and national levels, under the guidance of the Ministry of Climate and Environment. This can contribute to a more efficient and user-friendly public administration. However, differences in implementation capacity, the influence of local interests and greater institutional autonomy have led to uneven application of environmental regulations and national guidelines. Therefore, it is crucial to further strengthen the capacity of small municipalities, particularly in remote areas. They often face trade-offs between economic, social and environmental objectives. A stronger focus on learning from peers, sharing of good practices and more frequent opportunities for policy dialogue could help build institutional knowledge on good environmental management practices and inspire specialised support services.

Efforts to promote a meaningful engagement with minority groups need to be pursued

Evidence from recent surveys (SDWG, 2019[10]) suggests the government has improved overall communication with the Sami community. The right of Indigenous peoples to participate in decision-making processes was formalised in 2005. Beyond mandatory consultations, the government also consults with other Sami interest groups, particularly in matters that directly affect Sami land use. This has contributed over time to enhancing awareness and knowledge of Sami issues in ministries and agencies. In addition, the government has set up dedicated mechanisms to better include minority groups' perspectives at municipality and county levels (e.g. councils for youth, seniors and persons with disabilities).

Nonetheless, there is still a way to go to better consider Sami-specific concerns in national policies and better protect minority rights. A research project (Ahlness, 2020[11]) found that "Members of the 'Nordic' majority population tend to view minority groups as less capable of ecological commitment." Reindeer herders' associations suspect consultation processes are undermined by asymmetric information, unequal negotiation power and lack of transparency. Promoting effective and meaningful engagement and incorporating indigenous knowledge remains a common challenge in the Arctic region. Dialogue has to be seen to help find better solutions and more strongly influence project design at an early stage.

Conflict of interest at local level can undermine the effectiveness of environmental assessment procedures

Since 2013, the Ministry of Climate and Environment and the Ministry of Local Government and Modernisation have shared responsibility for environmental impact assessment (EIA) and strategic environmental assessment (SEA). These processes are primarily integrated into the ordinary procedure for land-use planning and applications for licences and permits. In 2017, Norway incorporated the two EU directives on EIA and SEA in its legal system as one common system.

While environmental assessments are conducted at national level for major projects (e.g. national infrastructure, renewable energy projects), local municipalities are responsible for EIA in most cases. As a result, the local authority may be the applicant and the competent authority at the same time. This double role creates a potential conflict of interest, particularly in smaller municipalities, as there is no independent authority in the approval process. Local interests may sometimes lead to sub-optimal decisions as regards environmental outcomes and EIAs may address only direct and immediate on-site effects. This risks underestimating cumulative environmental effects that may occur in the medium and long term or beyond the spatial boundaries of municipalities. Limited local capacity can also undermine the quality of the EIA process. Every municipality should benefit from the expertise of a dedicated environmental officer. More room should be given to independent, critical, inter-disciplinary voices in local decision-making processes.

High non-compliance calls for continued compliance promotion

Norway has a solid legal and regulatory framework for compliance assurance using a combination of compliance promotion, monitoring and enforcement tools. Inspections are conducted by the Norwegian Environment Agency and the county governors. They have a joint monitoring strategy for 2016-20 and share a corporate database of inspection results across all sectors. However, as in all OECD countries, there is still an implementation gap. The country has a high rate of non-compliance (60-70% of the checks, including 10% of serious violations). About two-thirds of breaches are related to weaknesses of self-monitoring systems. Approximately 30% of site inspections are conducted without prior notice. Compliance monitoring also includes desk verification of self-monitoring reports and online checks of products. E-commerce non-compliance is particularly high and requires continued attention.[1]

Norway's strong focus on risk-based targeting leads to higher levels of non-compliance detection, which does not reflect the general compliance behaviour of the regulated community. Norway's inspection results also need to be interpreted in light of more in-depth compliance monitoring. Such monitoring checks the performance of company-internal environmental management systems whose elements are mandated by law. This makes the Norwegian system unique in the OECD area. However, the requirements are challenging for smaller companies; many have not sufficiently invested to meet them. They still lack routine checks and knowledge about safety standards and environmental requirements, including for chemical management of imported products. This underlines the importance of inspection campaigns and compliance promotion efforts, which need to be pursued. The impact of current compliance promotion activities could be more systematically monitored, beyond the annual reporting of the Norwegian Environment Agency.

Norway is well positioned to promote a just, green transition within its own borders and abroad.

Norway's recovery has an environmental and climate focus

The health and economic impacts of the global COVID-19 pandemic have been lower in Norway than in other European countries. As elsewhere, local pollution and GHG emissions declined in line with the lower level of activity. While its economy was initially hit hard by slumping oil prices, Norway has so far been recovering quickly from the economic impacts of the global pandemic. In 2021, it already reached close-to-pre-pandemic GDP per capita levels (OECD, 2021[12]).

Economic rescue packages included time-limited income protection measures and business support schemes. These funded investments in key infrastructure sectors such as green maritime transport projects. In addition, they increased funding in technology development and several green conversion packages; the largest of them were channelled through its state-owned enterprise Enova. However, the country also provided substantial support to rescue the oil and gas industry (USD 15.2 billion) and the aviation sector (USD 0.9 billion) (OECD, 2021[13]). Tax concessions to the petroleum sector allow the immediate tax deduction of current and projected investment spending from 2020 to 2024. Thanks to the rebound in oil prices, the petroleum industry recovered more quickly than initially expected. Tax concessions in the early months of the pandemic may have been more generous than necessary (OECD, 2022[14]).

Norway supported implementation of existing green restructuring measures and plans. The government set-up a Green Platform worth NOK 1 billion (about USD 116 million, 2020-22). This aims to stimulate "bigger and more rapid investments from companies in green sustainable solutions and products" (Green Platform Initiative). The initiative is cross-cutting and involves the participation of five ministries. As in other OECD countries, monitoring and evaluation are needed to ensure that funds are spent in an economically efficient, environmentally sustainable and publicly supported manner (OECD, 2021[15]).

Norway invests heavily in development of new technology to support its green transition

Norway invests heavily in research and development (R&D) of energy and climate technology with a view to supporting lasting market changes for climate-friendly solutions. Enova has been strengthened and provides funding for new technology development in all sectors (NOK 3.7 billion – about USD 393 million in 2020, 3 850 projects). The 2021-24 framework agreement defines new priorities to help achieve Norway's climate commitments and support the transition to a low-emission society.

Launched in 2020, Norway's carbon capture and storage project (CCS) known as "Longship" is the country's largest ever industrial climate project (total cost of NOK 25 billion – about USD 2.9 billion, including NOK 16.8 billion – close to USD 2 billion in government funding, 2021-34) (Ministry of Petroleum and Energy, 2019[16]). The project has the potential to create jobs. Longship aims at kick-starting CCS development both in Norway and Europe, as well as enabling other countries to replicate technological solutions. In addition, Norway supports the development of hydrogen production with CCS and hydrogen production using electrolysis with renewable electricity, material recycling from car batteries, etc. A Green Platform encourages investment and innovation in all sectors (NOK 1 billion – about USD 116 million for 2020-22). A new research centre – the Norwegian Research Centre on Wind Energy (NorthWind) – aims to create export opportunities for Norwegian business and industry over the next eight years and to minimise the environmental impacts from future wind power development. Other Norwegian energy research centres focus on CCS, hydropower, solar energy, biofuels, low emission industry, zero emission neighbourhoods, intelligent electricity distribution and zero emission energy systems for transport.

Norway counts heavily on technological developments to achieve its climate goals and strives to reap the gains from innovation and new technology. While strong government support for innovation will further boost Norway's green transition, technical solutions alone may not be sufficient. Norway's green transition will also need to involve behavioural changes and require adjustment to consumption patterns.

Green public procurement needs to be better monitored and assessed

A greener and more efficient use of public procurement is a powerful policy instrument for aligning public expenditure with green objectives and promoting greener consumption patterns. Norway's general government procurement spending has more than doubled over the past decade. It was 17% of GDP in 2020 (OECD, 2020[17]). Norway has a strong regulatory framework for sustainable public procurement. According to the 2016 Public Procurement Act, contracting authorities have a legally binding duty to develop and implement sustainable procurement practices. A stronger focus on life cycle costs is encouraged. The Act calls for the entire procurement cycle to consider sustainability criteria.

However, there is still room for improvement when it comes to implementation. Norway also needs to enhance countrywide uptake and strengthen the accountability framework. Audit and control are weak points in relation to sustainable public procurement in Norway (OECD, 2020[17]). Some good practices to follow up on sustainability considerations are available. However, as noticed by the previous OECD Environmental Performance Review (OECD, 2011[4]), there is no systematic approach for monitoring outcomes of sustainable procurement. Availability of data for monitoring purposes also remains a challenge. Data on the share of green spending in public procurement could usefully inform decisions, but they are not yet systematically available. Preliminary findings of the Norwegian Agency for Public and Financial Management indicate an increase in the share of green public procurement spending in food purchases and meal services as well as in the construction sector in 2021. A new action plan for 2021-30 proposes to increase the share of green public procurement.

Norway aims to provide a long-term perspective on carbon pricing

Norway is a pioneer in using economic instruments for environmental protection, one of the first countries to introduce a carbon tax in 1991. To date, CO_2 taxes and emissions trading (EU ETS) cover approximately 85% of Norway's GHG emissions, including offshore production. Norway is also among the few countries that tax non-road emissions at more than EUR 30 per tonne of CO_2.

Norway's Climate Action Plan 2021-30 proposes to raise the carbon tax from NOK 590 (USD 69) per tonne of CO_2-eq in 2021 to NOK 2 000 (about USD 233) by 2030. Compensation measures may be used to ensure that specific groups or regions are not affected disproportionally. Households in Norway's northern regions already benefit from some tax exemptions for the use of electricity and energy from alternative sources or are charged a reduced rate for various excise taxes on energy products. The precise arrangements to operationalise the required tax shift will be part of a negotiation process and approved by Parliament within its annual budget cycle. By 2030, the scheduled increase in carbon prices is expected to reduce emissions by an estimated 8 million tonnes of CO_2-eq. This gradual carbon tax increase would provide a long-term perspective on carbon pricing and a strong price signal to encourage increased investments in renewable energy and low-carbon technologies. The next step is to ensure an effective and socially-balanced implementation over the next eight years.

Figure 4. Norway taxes a high share of CO_2 emissions from energy use

Share of energy-related CO_2 emissions priced in OECD countries, 2018

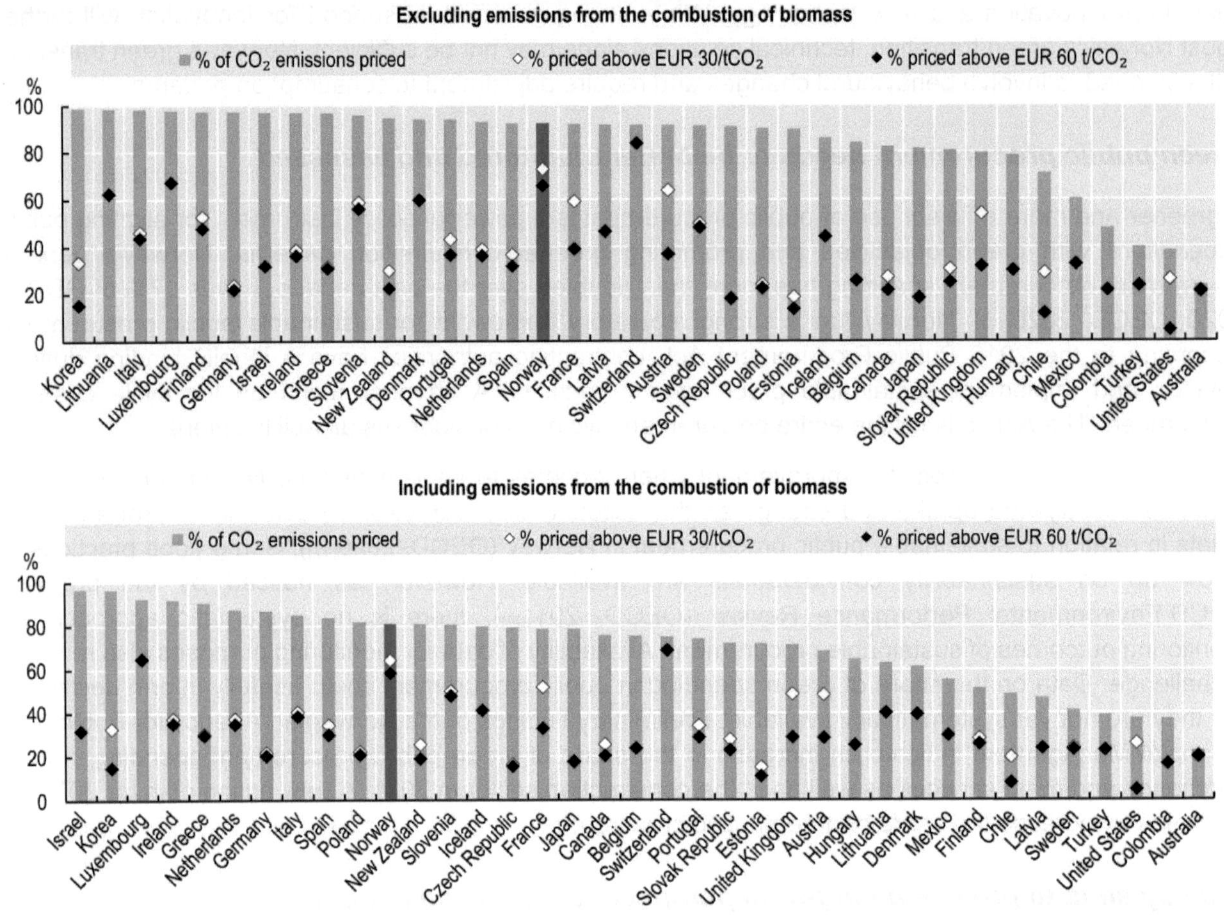

Note: The Effective Carbon Rate (ECR) is the sum of taxes (excise and carbon taxes) and tradeable permits that effectively put a price on carbon emissions. EUR 60 per tonne of CO_2 is a midpoint estimate for carbon costs in 2020, and a low-end estimate for 2030. Energy use data from IEA (2020), *World Energy Statistics and Balances*.
Source: OECD (2022), "Environmental policy: Effective carbon rates", *OECD Environment Statistics* (database).

StatLink https://stat.link/l9an4m

Norway should further reduce fossil fuel support and set time-bound targets

Norway's support to fossil fuels declined over the past decade, thanks to the gradual phase-out of several energy and carbon tax exemptions and reduced consumption of transport fuels with the uptake of EVs. Direct budgetary transfers to the oil and gas sector also declined over the decade. Most support measures are related to fiscal taxes (e.g. exemptions from the tax on mineral oil used for domestic shipping and fishing). Norway reports on tax expenditures diligently; debate is underway whether it makes sense to consider some of these expenditures as fossil fuel subsidies. Norway should systematically screen actual or proposed subsidies, including tax provisions to identify those that are not justified on economic, social and environmental grounds, and develop a plan to phase out fossil fuel and other environmentally harmful support. The government should also strengthen transparency by disclosing fossil fuel production and support plans in its commitments under the Paris Agreement (SEI et al., 2021[18]).

Furthermore, it would be useful for Norway to engage in a self-review and/or peer review of inefficient fossil fuel subsidies. Such reviews, similar to the ones within the G20, could help identify scalable good practices. Norway has been supporting various global initiatives to phase out fossil fuel support. The country is a member of the informal grouping of non-G20 countries known as the "Friends of Fossil-Fuel Subsidy Reform". In line with its international commitments, Norway should further reduce fossil fuel support and set quantified, time-bound targets.

Norway is working towards a sustainable vehicle taxation system

Having more vehicles that are fully electric generates important environmental benefits in relation to emissions of CO_2 and local air pollution. However, it has also strongly reduced revenues stemming from taxes on motor vehicles and motor-vehicle fuels. Responding to this loss of tax revenue, the government presented principles for a vehicle-taxation system that would be both environmentally and fiscally sustainable. The current taxation of vehicles and transport fuels has two main challenges. First, the tax largely does not apply to zero-emission vehicles. Second, it does not reflect differences in externalities depending on where and when the driving takes place. The government therefore plans to explore if it can reform the current system. An introduction of a time and place-based road use tax would be a welcome development.

Moreover, the government recently aligned the traffic insurance tax for EVs with the amount charged for motorcycles (70% of the traffic insurance tax for gasoline and diesel cars) and will apply the full rate as of March 2022. The government is also considering introduction of VAT on the most expensive EVs. These are first steps towards sharing the financial burden of road maintenance, infrastructure development and other externalities. As EV uptake becomes stronger, other measures (e.g. gradual removal of VAT exemption for EVs) may become necessary.

Norway has a well-developed road toll system. All major cities established toll rings using environmentally differentiated rates to discourage urban traffic and reduce related congestion problems. A recent road toll reform reduced the number of road toll companies from 60 to 5. It also simplified the price and discount schemes through an electronically managed AutoPass; some tolls serve as congestion pricing. The city of Oslo intends to transform the central area into a zero-emissions zone (ZEZ). Bergen is planning to implement a pilot ZEZ in 2023. Congestion charges are powerful tools that can address many externalities from road transport more effectively than fuel taxes (van Dender, 2019[19]).

The activities of the Government Pension Fund Global could become more consistent with Norway's international climate commitments

Norway needs to better consider emissions associated with foreign investments. The equity-portfolio carbon emissions of Norway's Government Pension Fund Global (GPFG) are estimated to be twice the country's total emissions (OMFIF, 2021[20]). The GPFG, which invests the surplus revenues of the petroleum sector, is the world's largest sovereign wealth fund. It pioneered ethical guidelines for investment decisions based on active ownership and the exclusion of firms from its portfolio. While climate risk is not explicitly anchored in its mandate, the fund has started incorporating some climate risks in its strategy.

The government should follow through on recommendations from an expert group that propose to base the responsible investment of the GPFG on the Paris Agreement's goals. At the COP26 in November 2021, Norway's prime minister announced government plans to make the GPFG "the leading fund in responsible investment and the management of climate risk".[2] This would help make the fund's activities more consistent with Norway's goals under international climate agreements. To date, despite its huge potential, the GPFG plays almost no role in the domestic or global green transition (Kattel et al., 2021[21]).

Norway is well positioned to prepare for a low-carbon future without oil and gas

Norway ranks number one on the Net Zero Readiness Index (KPMG, 2021[22]). It has a better track record than most other oil exporters in diversifying its economy. The country has many comparative advantages in other industries (e.g. low-carbon manufacturing in electricity-intensive industries, offshore wind, aquaculture, CCS). Building on its human capital with high education levels, well-functioning institutions, effective tax system and robust fiscal policy framework, Norway has the capabilities and financial means to accelerate a just transition within its own borders and abroad.

The transition to a less petroleum-dependent economy is already underway. The share of the petroleum sector within national GDP shrank from a peak of 25% in 2008 to 15% in 2021.[3] Employment in the petroleum sector dropped following the oil price plunge in 2014-16 and is set to decline in the long term; a more circular economy could create many new job opportunities. Shifting employment will require strategic planning and co-ordination.

According to the OECD Economic Survey of Norway 2022, the speed of the transition will determine any critical macroeconomic consequences for the Norwegian economy. If labour and capital resources can be reallocated from the oil and gas sector at a speed that avoids massive unemployment or stranded assets, then the transition will be comparatively benign (OECD, 2022[14]). While reduced oil and gas activities will create important economic and societal repercussions, the impact will probably be less than previously feared (Government of Norway, 2021[23]).

Beyond Norway's general system of workers' rights, the government has not yet developed an action plan for a "just and equitable transition" from fossil fuel production (SEI et al., 2021[18]). More clarity about the "just and equitable" transition in the Norwegian context would be useful. The government also needs to show it will address economic, social, spatial and gender inequalities beyond traditional support for affected communities or unemployment relief for workers. This involves a reflection on root causes to address structural changes and avoid replicating the same inequality patterns in new green industries. Equity issues concern uneven exposure to risk, uneven ability to capture the benefits and uneven responsibility for damage. Transformative change necessarily impacts lifestyle and consumption patterns.

The role of the private sector could be further leveraged by better integrating sustainability into business models. Civil society groups, communities and – more broadly – citizens are important sources of creativity and innovation, which policy makers could engage more strategically (Bruyninckx, 2021[24]). Today's children can drive the behavioural and lifestyle changes of tomorrow. Environmental education is of paramount importance.

Recommendations on sustainable development

Improving environmental governance

- Improve the understanding of local needs and provide adequate support for municipalities and counties to help them integrate the SDGs into local and regional planning; strengthen the capacity of small municipalities through peer learning, more systematic knowledge exchange and targeted support services.
- Develop inter-disciplinary expertise within ministerial departments (e.g. internal mobility) and a stronger focus on cross-sectoral spillover to better integrate policies across sectors and move beyond a goal-by-goal approach.
- Promote meaningful engagement of local communities and effective use of indigenous knowledge at an early stage of the decision-making process.
- Place stronger focus on cumulative environmental impacts in strategic and environmental impact assessments; ensure a clear separation of administrative roles in the validation process of environmental assessment at municipal level and develop local capacity (e.g. dedicated environmental officer); provide more room for independent, critical and inter-disciplinary voices to support the decision-making process.
- Enhance compliance promotion to reduce the high rate of non-compliance; improve the understanding of regulatory implementation gaps and better monitor the results of compliance promotion efforts, with a focus on small companies.

Greening the tax and subsidy system

- Implement the gradual increase in the CO_2 tax up to NOK 2 000 (USD 233) per tonne of CO_2 by 2030 as outlined in the Climate Action Plan 2021-30; if exemptions are needed, ensure these are limited in number and time-bound, while providing well-targeted support measures to households and firms particularly hit by the tax increase.
- Prepare the introduction of a placed-based road use tax system, with tax rates depending on where and when the driving takes place, and on the type of vehicle being used.
- Reduce the tax preferences given to EVs, by gradually removing their VAT exemption and by including these vehicles in the vehicle purchase tax.
- Systematically screen actual or proposed subsidies, including tax provisions to identify those that are not justified on economic, social and environmental grounds; develop a plan to gradually phase out support to fossil fuel consumption and use, as well as other environmentally harmful subsidies and define quantified, time-bound targets; assess the distributional and economic implications of removal of fossil fuel support and design alternative policies to achieve the same objectives in line with climate and environmental goals.

Promoting a green and just transition

- Place a stronger emphasis on promoting behavioural changes when providing support for businesses and households to meet environment- and climate-related goals; monitor and evaluate outcomes to ensure that support is spent in an economically efficient, environmentally sustainable and publicly supported manner.
- Create stronger incentives to reverse the trend of growing waste generation (e.g. expand and optimise the use of pay-as-you-throw schemes and central sorting capacity for municipal waste); increase significantly Norway's recycling capacity, and create incentives to increase demand for secondary raw materials, notably in the construction sector.

- Expedite the replacement of ageing water supply and wastewater pipes and the modernisation of sewerage systems; improve operational efficiency of water services and co-ordination between different administrative levels.
- Create an enabling environment and implement rapidly economy-wide measures to facilitate the circular transition; account for consumption-based emissions and promote more sustainable consumption patterns (e.g. educating and empowering consumers' choices, right to repair, sustainability labels) with a view to reducing Norway's global material footprint.
- Enhance countrywide uptake of green public procurement; encourage local authorities to make more use of green public procurement and strengthen the accountability framework (e.g. data on the share of green spending in public procurement).
- Make strategies related to Norway's exports, imports and foreign assets more consistent with its national and international climate goals (e.g. consider CO_2 emissions embodied in international trade and promote responsible investment and the management of climate risk within the GPFG).
- Develop analytical capacity to better understand Norway's global environmental and carbon footprints; use this information in environmental assessment.
- Ensure externalities relating to climate change and other environmental considerations are fully incorporated in policy towards the oil and gas extraction sector, including in decisions for new licensing rounds; provide support to businesses and regions to help them diversify in the context of decline in the petroleum-sector activity.

2. Land use and biodiversity management

Land-use change has exerted growing pressures on Norway's diverse and pristine landscapes

Norway has one of the most diverse landscapes in Europe. While the country is dominated by forest and bare mountains, it has a wide range of climatic conditions, landscapes, vegetation and land use in close proximity. In addition to its diversity, Norway contains the largest or most pristine representations of many European landscape types. Thus, Norway plays an important role in landscape and species conservation for the whole continent (Ciglič and Perko, 2013[25]).

Land use and land-use change place the greatest pressure on Norwegian biodiversity, negatively impacting 90% of threatened species (Norwegian Biodiversity Information Centre, 2018[26]) (OECD, 2020[9]). Climate change adds to the pressure, and is considered to have an increasingly negative effect (Ministry of Climate and Environment, 2015[27]). Development is the most important factor, but commercial forestry operations alone put pressure on 41% of threatened species (Norwegian Biodiversity Information Centre, 2018[26]); (Miljoverndepartementet, 2011[28]). According to the Nature Index for Norway, ecosystem quality has declined in several important ecosystem types since the early 2010s (Lier-Hansen et al., 2013[29]). From 2000 onwards, the Nature Index shows a weak positive development for forests and freshwater, while the impact of development is slightly negative for mountains. For open lowlands, there is a clear decline. The other ecosystems have been fairly stable but with smaller fluctuations between years and regions.

Almost a quarter of the endangered species live in agricultural landscapes. Populations of farmland bird species are declining at a faster rate than other Nordic countries. The area suitable for farming is scarce, with cultivated land accounting for less than 4% of the country's surface. Agricultural activity creates a cultural landscape that is valued for its own sake and for the biodiversity it supports. The most productive areas are often near fast-growing towns, which has led to the conversion of agricultural land to housing, roads, industry and other purposes. Norway set an annual target to convert no more than 400 hectares of cultivated land, which it has met in the last several years.

Norway has set the stage for continued improvement in management of landscapes and biodiversity

Norway is clarifying its vision of sustainable land use even as it adopts new tools for assessment and new means of co-operation to achieve its goals. The situation remains a work in progress but is moving in the right direction. If the government implements all its plans, it could generate positive outcomes for the health of biodiversity and ecosystems in Norway and in benefits for its people.

The Nature for Life Biodiversity Action Plan 2015, adopted by Parliament in 2016, sets out ambitious goals for biodiversity preservation with clear direction on how to achieve them (Ministry of Climate and Environment, 2015[27]). This is supported by the mapping system Nature in Norway (NiN), which provides detailed geo-referenced information on the status of species and ecosystems (Halvorsen et al., 2015[30]). The NiN has the potential to underpin specific, measurable, achievable, realistic and time-bound objectives for ecosystem management. In 2016, the Ministry of Climate and Environment initiated development of a system for assessing ecological conditions in Norwegian ecosystems. As of January 2022, three ecosystems have been assessed: forests, arctic tundra and mountains. The system of integrated ocean management plans has matured and has proven a highly successful mechanism to balance multiple interests in the marine space.

Implementation of the EU Water Framework Directive is well structured, involving all levels of government, as well as multiple sector agencies. Key elements are broad inclusion of stakeholders but with co-ordinating responsibility clearly assigned, measurable objectives with a reporting process attached and strong local anchoring of decision making. This framework could serve as a model for other aspects of ecosystem and land management, especially with regard to cross-sector co-ordination.

Norway has met the Aichi target on protecting land area but needs to develop a more representative network of protected areas

The most important risks to biodiversity and loss of ecosystem services in Norway come from land-use change. Reflecting this, the main policy tool for biodiversity conservation is protection of habitats and landscapes. Protected areas in Norway cover 17% of the mainland (25% including Svalbard) (Figure 5). This is in line with the 2020 Aichi target and above the OECD average. However, protected areas need to include more representative and significant landscape types, especially productive forest land.

Norway has set objectives to preserve significant or representative ecosystem types and those areas needed to protect threatened or endangered species. However, progress to fill gaps in the network of protected areas has been slow. An in-depth evaluation of habitat and landscape types identified 275 sites (totalling 584 km^2) that contain habitat types under-represented in protected areas or with low protection coverage (Miljødirektoratet, 2017[31]). As one reason for the low coverage, areas representing ecosystem types in need of additional protection may be small, scattered, already partially degraded or have high development value. Moreover, about 27% of protected areas are at risk of degradation and require additional action to secure their conservation values.

Figure 5. Protected area in Norway meets its Aichi 2000 target

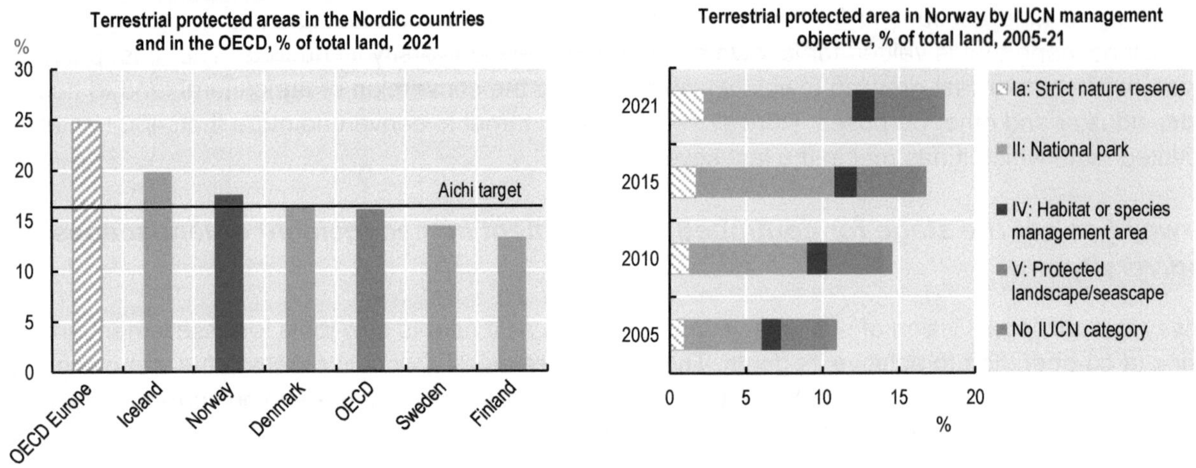

Note: Data exclude protected areas in overseas territories. In Norway, the share of terrestrial area protected, including Jan Mayen and Svalbard, is about 25%. Right panel: Protected areas under management categories of the World Conservation Unit (IUCN) classification. Strict nature reserve and national parks reflect the highest level of protection.
Source: OECD (2021), "Protected areas", *OECD Environmental Indicators* (database), https://doi.org/10.1787/112995ca-en.

StatLink https://stat.link/85rzva

Norway has made progress in wetland conservation. This ecosystem type was the first to have a management system based on clearly defined objectives for ecological status as foreseen in the Nature for Life Biodiversity Action Plan. The aim is to slow conversion of wetlands to other uses, and accelerated restoration of wetlands. A ban on conversion of peatlands to agricultural use to avoid GHG emissions is a rare example in the OECD of agricultural regulations specific to climate change.

Norway uses both soft and hard tools to integrate environmental concerns into land-use management

Every four years, the national government provides input into local decision making. To that end, it expresses expectations for local planners and provides information, support and guidance for the regional and municipal planning process (currently covering 2019-23) (Ministry of Local Government and Modernisation, 2019[32]). County governors and county municipalities provide advice but may also object to local plans if deemed against national or significant regional interests. Management boards with local and regional representation manage protected areas, while county governors mainly handle smaller protected areas. Both operate within the limit of special rules set for each protected area. Sector regulations aim to ensure environmental performance, and sector ministries have significant responsibility for environmental objectives within their domains.

Increased reliance on voluntary protection of forest land, reduced use of the objection process in the Planning and Building Act, and refocusing national guidance on process issues rather than outcomes are all ways to reduce land-use conflicts. In the past, such conflicts have impeded progress on environmental protection. However, eliminating conflicts by increasing local self-determination puts national objectives at risk. A better approach is to find ways to deal with conflict constructively, and the following recommendations are intended to help in this regard.

Municipal land-use planning should better consider national objectives with respect to biodiversity and landscapes

Municipal land-use planning is a primary mechanism affecting the environment, landscape and welfare of citizens. While responsibility for land-use planning is shared among Norway's three levels of government, local municipalities assume most of the environmental management. This division of labour provides important autonomy for decisions whose impacts are often primarily local. However, it is a challenge to ensure that decisions reflect the values and desires of all Norwegians, especially if these effects are small but cumulative over time (Chapter 1, Section 1.4.2).

Local and national priorities for conservation of landscapes and biodiversity may not match. Small municipalities with ageing and shrinking populations, in particular, may prioritise economic and social development over environmental concerns. Differences in competence and local capacity can also be a significant problem.

The central challenge is managing the nationwide effect of local decisions. Closing the gap between local decisions and national objectives requires active engagement by the national government and the public. In the past, the government provided more guidance in its national expectations document regarding desired environmental outcomes of the planning process. However, in recent years it has focused more on ensuring the process is working well (Strand and Næss, 2017[33]). This is perhaps a consequence of the change in responsibility for the Planning and Building Act from the Ministry of Climate and Environment to the Ministry of Local Government and Modernisation. Providing clear national objectives to the different planning actors can improve the probability of achieving them. This is especially important when these objectives are non-local in nature (climate change, biodiversity), and any trade-offs with local, other regional and national objectives may not be appropriately weighted. The Ministry of Climate and Environment is better placed to co-ordinate local planning with respect to national environmental objectives and is already responsible for most related tasks. On the other hand, the Ministry of Local Government and Regional Development has greater expertise in the processes themselves. Sharing responsibility between the ministries can lead to more effective engagement with local planning.

The public has access to local deliberations on land-use plans and can provide comments or raise objections when national issues are at stake. However, more could be done to ensure a broader spectrum of people can participate. In particular, smaller communities may lack capacity to support extensive consultations and the ability to use the existing digital opportunities to facilitate participation.

The costs of participation can be reduced through increased use of digital- and web-based tools to notify citizens of when and how they may provide feedback, share documents and participate in the process. A national nature and environmental appeals board, following the Danish or Swedish model, can help ensure civil society has an effective means to engage in the planning process. This extra venue can help ensure the environment is given more "standing" in government processes. Norway already operates similar types of boards such as for real estate services or consumer complaints.

National governments have sought to reduce the use of objections in the planning process, but objections are not the problem

County governors (who are national entities) and government agencies represent national interests in the planning process. The objection mechanism lets these bodies, regional authorities and the Sami Parliament raise concerns regarding the compatibility of local plans with national priorities. Most of these objections are addressed through mediation and negotiation, but some are referred to the responsible ministry. The government has de-emphasised this objection process in the last decade, preferring increased guidance and negotiation during the planning process (NORUT, 2016[34]; Strand and Næss, 2017[33]). Consequently, the number of objections is expected to continue declining. Between 2008 and 2013, the ministry accepted 112 objections, a figure that dropped to 29 between 2014 and 2019.

The use of objections is a symptom of goal conflicts in the planning process. These will not be eliminated by discouraging the use of objections. Not all such conflicts can be resolved in every planning process at local level. Progress has been made in refocusing the role of the county governors from raising objections to providing more guidance and assistance at earlier stages of the planning process. This helps build capacity in the local municipality and reduces uncertainty. However, county governors must use their discretion in deciding when a local plan may not be compatible with national interests. The Circular T-2/16 provides guidance to county governors regarding issues of national significance but is not definitive. This is because limited tools are available to measure the impact of local decisions on ecosystem health, and to understand how local outcomes contribute to a total effect nationwide. A better solution is more quantification of outcomes to make the process more data-driven.

Better area accounting of ecosystems status and values could provide meaningful guidance in the planning process and reduce the need for objections

Building a link between data on ecosystems and local planning can clarify the effect of local decisions on ecosystem health. It can also give local planners more certainty that they can produce a plan in harmony with national interests. Area accounts, for example, can provide an overview of the total effects of new plan proposals on climate emissions, biodiversity, local nature and soil protection. Such a land-use accounting system can reduce use of objections and align local planning with national objectives. Use of the UN System of Environmental Economic Accounting–Ecosystem Accounting can also help systematically collect and report the needed information.

Good mapping and data for priority species and habitat types make it easier for municipalities to consider threatened biodiversity in development plans. Norway has made great strides in mapping and reporting on the quality of nature types (habitats) through the national nature map initiative (NiN) and in understanding and reporting of the quality of ecosystems through its Nature Index system. An in-depth evaluation of habitat and landscape types that merit supplemental protection and a survey of such sites identified a large number of candidates. This work sets the stage for more concrete input of information into local planning process with respect to national interests.

Compensation methods can help align objectives

The national government can sensitise local governments to important issues surrounding conservation and sustainable use of resources, the value of ecosystem services provided by diverse and healthy landscapes, and the role and importance of local landscapes as part of the larger ecosystem. For example, it could offer funds to help local governments formulate biodiversity plans. Efforts to assist local governments that lack institutional capacity are an important first step and worth continuing, but more can be done to ensure that local action is compatible with national objectives.

Co-financing (or other forms of assistance that put a value on local conservation commensurate with the national benefits that derive from them) can be an economically efficient way to align local and national incentives. Examples include assistance to implement biodiversity plans, increased funding for converting land to protected areas, co-financing of important projects or payments for ecosystem services. Urban Growth Agreements, in place in four major urban areas, are an example of co-financing between local, regional and national governments to achieve the goal of zero increase in vehicle traffic (Chapter 1, Section 1.3.5).

Managing total cumulative environmental impact while preserving the greatest scope for economic growth implies some means by which communities can trade conservation and development opportunities. The idea of "area neutrality" where development in one area is offset by restoration of a similar but degraded landscape elsewhere is worth considering. This approach may also provide a solution where larger cities have ambitious environmental objectives but smaller municipalities view development as essential for their survival. Co-operation between such communities can provide opportunity for both conservation and development where it is most desired.

Voluntary protection schemes reduce conflicts but require additional checks

The budget for forest protection has increased from NOK 231 million (about USD 26.9 million) in 2013 to NOK 435 million (about USD 50.6 million) in 2021. The central government has the right in principle to designate any land for protection and start compensation discussions. However, it may be reluctant to exercise these rights and, indeed, has forsworn doing so for privately owned forest land. Relying on a voluntary approach reduces conflict and reinforces the rights of landowners but may not deliver desired results in a reasonable timeframe.

In 2016, Parliament set the objective to increase protected area from about 5% to 10% of total forest land. This objective aims to protect important habitats and ecosystems and to preserve a representative sample of Norwegian nature for future generations. The government should keep track of progress towards this goal, adjusting the approach if progress is regarded as too slow. For example, it could increase the rate of compensation, particularly for sites most in need of protection.

Co-ordination across sectors is improving, but more can be done

Sector administrations have responsibility to regulate activities and consider environmental concerns within their domains according to their own objectives. This is an important principle in Norway, but the Nature for Life Biodiversity Action Plan also recognises the need to co-ordinate activities to achieve maximum benefit. There are strong signs of improvement in this regard, including river basin management plans, marine management plans, the Trua Natur 2020 plan and the nature strategy for wetlands presented in 2021, among others (Mijødirektoratet, 2020[35]). Identifying which ministry is best placed to co-ordinate action increases the cost effectiveness of interventions and improves the likelihood of success. Co-ordination of the sectors' use of instruments with respect to individual species, habitat types and ecosystems also increases predictability for affected municipalities.

Forestry and agriculture, as land-use sectors affecting biodiversity in Norway, have a particular need to co-ordinate their actions. Both sectors have objectives to preserve activity in all areas of Norway and to support the prosperity of communities and individuals connected to the sector. In practice, they must balance these with objectives for environmental sustainability. Managing the interactions between these sectors, land-use planning and biodiversity objectives requires particular attention.

More is needed to promote climate-smart agriculture

Norway's agriculture sector is small but accounted for about 9% of national GHG emissions in 2020. Agricultural land suitable for arable crops is limited and benefits from many subsidies. In June 2019, the government and farmers' organisations signed a voluntary agreement to reduce GHG emissions by 5 Mt CO_2-eq between 2021 and 2030. Norway is one of few countries with quantified emissions objectives in agriculture. However, the government's climate plan for the agricultural sector is vague and should place a clear focus on cost-effective measures. Moreover, the short timeframe of annual negotiations may prioritise short-term goals at the expense of long-term perspectives.

Norway delivers unevenly across its four agricultural policy objectives (OECD, 2021[36]). Environmental performance and the efficient creation of value added along the food chain are both compromised by support policies linked to production levels. More analytical tools could help analyse the enormous amount of collected data to better understand conflicting goals in the agricultural sector. Supply constraints (e.g. soy imports) also need to be more strongly taken into account to reduce Norway's global carbon footprint. Norway should provide greater flexibility and stronger incentives for farmers to improve agri-environmental outcomes and develop climate-smart agriculture. While producer support in agriculture is among the highest in the OECD, farmers remain exempt from GHG emission taxes. Moreover, agriculture is not part of the EU ETS. A lack of progress could make the sector one of Norway's largest sources of GHG emissions in the future.

Recommendations on land use and biodiversity management

- Continue to develop a management system for ecosystem types as foreseen in the Biodiversity Action Plan and set aggressive timelines for implementation; regularly assess ecological status and set specific, measurable, achievable, realistic and time-bound objectives accordingly.
- Establish quality norms for important threatened ecosystems and species as described in the Nature Diversity Act.
- Set a specific timeline for achieving national objectives regarding protection of representative or significant areas, including with respect to threatened species as part of the supplemental protection process. This includes the goal of 10% forest area protection; set aside a sufficient budget to achieve the desired level of protection in the specified period.
- Be more explicit in national expectations for regional and municipal planning by providing clear objectives to the different actors in the planning system.
- Give the Ministry of Climate and Environment formal responsibility for achieving national biodiversity- and ecosystem-related land-use goals in the context of activities under the Planning and Building Act, with a regular reporting requirement to the government.
- Create a national environmental appeals board to ensure that national objectives are safeguarded.
- Invest in data systems that connect local planning decisions to national environmental outcomes; ensure this information serves a feedback role into municipal strategic planning; develop a model to predict the effect of land-use changes on environmental outcomes.
- Provide funding for ecological compensation to align local and national interests for landscape conservation; assist municipalities with biodiversity action plans to implement them.
- Encourage municipalities to co-operate using the principle of area neutrality to increase opportunities for economic development and conservation simultaneously.
- Set a timeline for updating local plans to minimise the use of the exemption or special dispensation process by municipalities.
- Invest in capacity building for local authorities regarding national environmental priorities and objectives and how they can contribute to achieving them.
- Ensure that multiple objectives of land-using sectors are properly balanced (in both definition and execution) and their actions co-ordinated to achieve national environmental objectives at least cost.
- Phase out output-related support to agriculture, with a view to reducing potentially environmentally harmful incentives; provide greater flexibility and stronger incentives for farmers to improve agri-environmental outcomes and develop climate-smart agriculture.

References

Ahlness, E. (2020), *"Greener Than Them: Environmental Bias and Commitment in Norway", Environmental Bias Experiments, presented to the Center for Environmental Politics/Society for Advancement of Scandinavian Studies, 15 May*, University of Wisconsin. [11]

bedreVANN and Norsk Vann (2020), *Tilstandsvurdering av kommunale vann– og avløpstjenester. Resultater 2020*, bedreVANN and Norsk Vann. [3]

Bruyninckx, H. (2021), "EEA-Eionet Strategy 2021-2030: Delivering data and knowledge to achieve Europe's environment and climate ambitions", Newsletter 04/20, European Environment Agency, Copenhagen. [24]

Ciglič, R. and D. Perko (2013), "Europe's landscape hotspots", *Acta geographica Slovenica*, Vol. 53/1, pp. 117-139, https://doi.org/10.3986/AGS53106. [25]

Circular Norway (2020), *Norway's Circularity Gap Report 2020*, Circular Norway, Oslo. [6]

Environment Norway (2021), "Freshwater", *Environmental Topics*, webpage, https://www.environment.no/topics/freshwater (accessed on 27 December 2021). [2]

EurEau (2021), *Europe's Water in Figures. An Overview of the European Drinking Water and Waste Water Sectors*, EurEau, Brussels. [5]

European City Air Quality Index (2021), *https://airindex.eea.europa.eu/Map/AQI/Viewer*. [37]

Government of Norway (2021), *Norway's Long-term Low-emission Strategy for 2050 Report to the Storting*, Government of Norway, Oslo. [23]

Halvorsen, R. et al. (2015), *Natur i Norge (NiN). versjon 2.0.0.*, Artsdatabanken, Trondheim, http://www.artsdatabanken.no/naturinorge (accessed on 6 December 2021). [30]

Hjorth-Johansen, K. et al. (2021), *Voluntary Subnational Review – Norway: Implementation of the UN's Sustainable Development Goals in Local and Regional Governments in Norway*, Norwegian Association of Local and Regional Authorities, Oslo. [8]

Kattel, R. et al. (2021), "The Green Giant: New Industrial Strategy for Norway", *IIPP Policy Report*, No. PR 21/01, UCL Institute for Innovation and Public Purpose, London. [21]

KPMG (2021), *Net Zero Readiness Index: Norway*, website, https://home.kpmg/xx/en/home/insights/2021/09/nzri-norway.html (accessed on 5 December 2021). [22]

Lier-Hansen, S. et al. (2013), *Naturens goder – om verdier av økosystemtjenester*, Norges offentlige utredninger, Oslo. [29]

Mijødirektoratet (2020), *Trua Natur 2020 - oversendelse til Klima-og miljødepartementet*, Miljødirektoratet, Oslo. [35]

Miljødirektoratet (2017), *Forslag til plan for supplerende vern - Miljødirektoratets anbefalinger*, Miljødirektoratet, Oslo. [31]

Miljoverndepartementet (2011), *Nasjonale forventninger til regional og kommunal planlegging vedtatt ved kongelig resolusjon 24. juni 2011*. [28]

Ministry of Climate and Environment (2015), *Norway's national biodiversity action plan Nature for life*, Norwegian Ministry of Climate and Environment, Oslo. [27]

Ministry of Local Government and Modernisation (2019), *National expectations regarding regional and municipal planning 2019-23.* [32]

Ministry of Petroleum and Energy (2019), *Longship – Carbon Capture and Storage*, Norwegian Ministry of Petroleum and Energy, Oslo. [16]

NORUT (2016), *Samordning av Statlige Innsigelser*, Northern Research Institute. [34]

Norwegian Biodiversity Information Centre (2018), *The Norwegian Red List for Ecosystems and Habitat Types*, https://www.biodiversity.no/Pages/135568/Red_List_for_Ecosystems_and (accessed on 30 January 2022). [26]

OECD (2022), *OECD Economic Surveys: Norway 2022*, OECD Publishing, Paris, https://doi.org/10.1787/df7b87ab-en. [14]

OECD (2021), "Economic Forecast Summary (December 2021)", *Norway Economic Snapshot*, OECD, Paris, https://www.oecd.org/economy/norway-economic-snapshot/. [12]

OECD (2021), "Focus on Green Recovery", *The OECD Green Recovery Database*, webpage, https://www.oecd.org/coronavirus/en/themes/green-recovery (accessed on 20 January 2021). [13]

OECD (2021), "Key findings from the update of the OECD Green Recovery Database", *OECD Policy Responses to Coronavirus (COVID-19)*, 30 September, OECD, Paris, https://www.oecd.org/coronavirus/policy-responses/key-findings-from-the-update-of-the-oecd-green-recovery-database-55b8abba/. [15]

OECD (2021), *Policies for the Future of Farming and Food in Norway*, OECD Agriculture and Food Policy Reviews, OECD Publishing, Paris, https://doi.org/10.1787/20b14991-en. [36]

OECD (2020), "A territorial approach to the Sustainable Development Goals in Viken, Norway", *OECD Regional Development Papers*, No. 3, OECD Publishing, Paris, https://doi.org/10.1787/dc1b182d-en. [9]

OECD (2020), *Sustainable Public Procurement in Norway 2020. MAPS Initiative*, OECD, Paris, https://www.mapsinitiative.org/assessments/MAPS%20Norway%20SPP.pdf. [17]

OECD (2011), *Environmental Performance Reviews: Norway 2011*, OECD Environmental Performance Reviews, OECD Publishing, Paris, https://doi.org/10.1787/9789264098473-en. [4]

OMFIF (2021), "Norway's GPFG should join the Net-Zero Asset Owner Alliance", 3 August, Official Monetary and Financial Institutions Forum, https://www.omfif.org/2021/08/norways-gpfg-should-join-the-net-zero-asset-owner-alliance. [20]

Sachs, J. et al. (2021), *Sustainable Development Report 2021. The Decade of Action for the Sustainable Development Goals*, Cambridge University Press, United Kingdom, https://www.sdgindex.org/reports/sustainable-development-report-2021/#:~:text=Sustainable%20Development%20Report%202021%20The%20Decade%20of%20Action%20for%20the%20Sustainable%20Development%20Goals&text=The%20Sustainable%20Development%20Report%202021,SDGs%. [7]

SDWG (2019), *Good Practices For Environmental Impact Assessment and Meaningful Engagement in the Arctic*, Arctic Council, Sustainable Development Working Group, http://hdl.handle.net/11374/2377. [10]

SEI et al. (2021), *The Production Gap Report 2021*, Stockholm Institute; International Institute for Sustainable Development, Winnipeg; Overseas Development Institute, London; E3G, London; United Nations Environment Programme, Nairobi, http://productiongap.org/2021report. [18]

Statistics Norway (2021), *"Table 08940", StatBank (database).* [1]

Strand, A. and P. Næss (2017), "Local self-determination, process-focus and subordination of environmental concerns", *Journal of Environmental Policy and Planning*, Vol. 19/2, pp. 156-167, https://doi.org/10.1080/1523908X.2016.1175927. [33]

van Dender, K. (2019), "Taxing vehicles, fuels, and road use: Opportunities for improving transport tax practice", *OECD Taxation Working Papers*, No. 44, OECD Publishing, Paris, https://doi.org/10.1787/e7f1d771-en. [19]

Notes

[1] In most OECD member countries, non-compliance detection numbers cover only site inspections. In Norway, the coverage is much broader, which makes comparison with other countries difficult.

[2] Statement by Prime Minister Jonas Gahr Støre at the UN Climate Change Conference in Glasgow, 2 November 2021, www.regjeringen.no/en/aktuelt/statement-at-the-un-climate-change-conference-in-glasgow/id2882242.

[3] In 2021, the petroleum sector represented 41% of total exports, 19% of total investments and 5.8% of employment (Norwegian Ministry of Energy and Petroleum, 2021, https://www.norskpetroleum.no/en/economy/governments-revenues.

Annex 1. Actions taken to implement selected recommendations from the 2011 OECD Environmental Performance Review of Norway

Recommendations	Actions taken
Chapter 1. Environmental management	
Strengthening the implementation of environmental policies	
Strengthen support for regional and local authorities to enable them to fully meet their responsibilities for implementing environmental policies, particularly for environmental impact assessment, enforcement and compliance, and land-use planning.	Every four years, the central government defines "national expectations" regarding regional and municipal planning to promote sustainable development throughout the country. This document typically provides guidance for regional and local authorities. In addition to this guidance, the 2019-23 document includes information on any new or planned revisions of guidelines. Among others, these guidelines define matters of land-use planning. They apply to all municipalities, regardless of their size and competencies. The Norwegian Environment Agency and the Directorate for Cultural Heritage have developed methods and guidance for planning and environmental impact assessments. The circular in 2016 (T-2/16) provides guidance on planning interests of national importance to promote better understanding of the objection process. Drawing on pilot projects in 2016-18 and 2020, the central government has implemented a new subsidy scheme since 2021 to help municipalities develop a municipal sub-plan for biodiversity. This helped increase knowledge of local biodiversity and how to manage it. Norway has worked to improve the mapping of habitat types and make land-use statistics more accessible, including through online platforms with land-use profiles, maps and data visualisation tools. Information intends to inform local planning processes and thereby increase the capacity of local land-use planners.
Reinforce efforts to reduce urban air pollution peaks in winter, including through accelerated renovation or replacement of wood burning stoves and reduction of emissions from road traffic.	Norway is decarbonising its transport sector and has become a world leader in electric mobility. Implementation of the zero growth goal through Urban Growth Agreements (UGAs) has helped reduce car traffic volumes in major cities (Bergen, Oslo, Stavanger and Trondheim). UGAs are implemented through multi-level governance arrangements. Measures include infrastructure investment, increased availability and frequency of public transport, land-use measures, restrictive measures for passenger cars and road tolls. The government plans to adopt five new UGAs (Buskerudbyen, Grenland, Kristiansandsregionen, Nedre Glomma and Tromsø). Meanwhile, it will expand the Oslo UGA to cover Oslo/Akershus. The Oslo area has a congestion charge and road toll rates differentiated according to the environmental performance of vehicles. Fees for studded tyres, an important source of airborne particulates, helped reduce their use in urban areas. The state-owned agency Enova supports measures to retrofit buildings. In addition, some municipalities have provided financial support to households for the replacement of wood burning stoves.
Assess the experience gained from the NO_X tax and associated agreements with the private sector and adjust, as necessary, the policies required to meet the NO_X reduction target.	Norway continued to apply a NO_X tax, which was introduced in 2007. Since 2008, three consecutive NOx agreements have been concluded between business organisations and the Ministry of Climate and Environment. The current agreement covers 2018-25. Norway reduced its NO_X emissions by 29% from 2005 to 2020 and met the 2020 emission reduction target of the Gothenburg Protocol. An evaluation of the NO_X agreements and the associated tax exemption is scheduled for 2022.
Expedite the replacement of ageing water supply and wastewater pipes and the modernisation of sewerage systems to separate waste and storm water, using charges and applying the polluter pays principle.	A 2015 expert group report proposes measures to help municipalities better prevent damage from storm water. Work on legislative amendments to the Act related to Water and Sanitation Plants and the Planning and Building Act is underway. In 2017, Norway revised its national goals for water and health. It introduced a new regulation for operation and maintenance of the drinking water pipe network. As of 2021, the central government has offered co-funding for municipalities and market operators to create stronger incentives for upgrading water pipes. A recent study analyses the potential for rationalisation in the water and wastewater sector, including proposals on how municipalities could renew the pipe networks faster and in a cost-efficient manner. Drawing on key findings, the Ministry of Local Government and Regional Development, the Ministry of Health and Care Services and the Ministry of Climate and Environment work together to identify required action.
Accelerate the development and adoption of river basin management plans and complete institutional arrangements for river management that assure	Norway established river basin management plans (RBMPs) for 2009-15 for selected water bodies and voluntarily applied the EU Water Framework Directive (WFD) for approximately 20% of its water bodies. Each RBD has its own management plan, including environmental

adequate dispute resolution, co-ordination of decision making among water users and appropriate funding of pollution reduction and water management efforts.	objectives and associated action plans. Norway completed – under formal WFD obligations – its first full cycle of RBMPs from 2016-21 and will start a new one from 2022-27.
Climate change	
Agree on clear and realistic domestic mitigation targets for 2020 and 2050, using 1990 as a baseline, that reflect both Norway's wish to serve as a model for other countries and the need to ensure the cost-effectiveness of the climate policy overall.	In 2015, Norway submitted its intended nationally determined contribution (INDC) to reduce greenhouse gas (GHG) emissions by at least 40% in 2030 compared to 1990-levels. Norway ratified the Paris Agreement in June 2016, which entered into force in November 2016. Consequently, Norway's INDC was converted into a nationally determined contribution (NDC). In 2020, Norway submitted an enhanced NDC to the United Nations Framework Convention on Climate Change. The NDC commits Norway to reduce GHG emissions by at least 50% and towards 55% by 2030 compared to 1990 levels. Norway also set a long-term target to become a low-emission society by 2050. It aims to reduce GHG emissions by at least 90-95% by 2050 compared to 1990 levels (enhanced target, initially 80-95%). Norway plans to fulfil its climate commitment in close collaboration with the European Union. The effect of Norway's participation in the EU Emissions Trading System will be considered in assessing fulfilment of its climate targets. The 2017 Climate Change Act established the 2030 and 2050 targets. In 2021, the government presented the comprehensive "Climate Action Plan for the Transformation of Norwegian Society as a Whole by 2030" as a way towards a carbon-neutral future.
Based on the existing monitoring systems, strengthen the mechanism for identifying policy adjustments, if needed, to stay on track to achieve climate targets; use the proposed carbon budget to address the overall impact of the public budget on emissions, and its implications for achieving mitigation targets.	The Climate Change Act entered into force in 2018. It introduced a system of five-year reviews of Norway's climate targets in line with the review cycles of the Paris Agreement. The government reports annually on both mitigation and adaptation efforts to Parliament. It also provides information on the expected effects of every proposed budget on current and projected GHG emissions and removals.
Establish a more consistent price for carbon across the economy, e.g. by removing exemptions from the carbon tax for the sectors that are not covered by the EU ETS; and establish a common carbon shadow price, and a trajectory for future carbon prices, to be used explicitly and consistently in policy assessments.	Since 2011, the government has abolished CO_2-tax exemptions for diesel used in coastal fisheries, antique vessels and machinery, as well as for natural gas and liquefied petroleum gas (LPG) used in coastal fisheries in domestic waters. In 2021, the government presented trajectories for global carbon prices compatible with the Paris Agreement. The government plans a gradual increase of carbon prices and common carbon price guidelines for policy assessments across sectors.
Develop an economy-wide energy efficiency strategy with appropriate incentives; regularly reassess policies to promote energy efficiency and renewable energy generation, taking possible interactions with the "cap" of the EU ETS into account; where interactions occur, these policies should provide co-benefits or effectively address other market failures.	The government published an economy-wide energy strategy (Meld. S 25, 2015-16). The 2021 White Paper "Putting Energy to Work" outlines objectives for a long-term value creation from energy sources. Renewable energy resources for economic growth and job creation is one of its four main goals. The government set a target to reduce energy intensity by 30% by 2030. In 2016, the government tightened threshold standards for new homes and major renovations to "passive house" level. As of 2020, Norway became the first country that formally prohibited use of fossil oil for heating in existing buildings and in new buildings altogether.
Comprehensively review all taxes and exemptions related to motor fuel use, vehicle ownership and use, as well as road pricing with a view to making them more coherent, cost-effective and better targeted to reduce CO_2 and other emissions.	In 2020, the government reviewed all taxes levied on purchase, ownership and use of motor vehicles, including taxes on fuel use, as well as exemptions to specific users or technologies. The 2021 National Budget outlines principles to make these taxes more sustainable, provide more consistent tax income and improve pricing of externalities. These principles provide the framework for annual tax adjustments. The government intends to gradually raise the tax on fuel use to reach NOK 2 000 (about USD 234) by 2030.
Nature and biodiversity	
Focus protection efforts on priority species and selected habitat types, pursuant to the new Nature Diversity Act; integrate the implementation of the Nature Diversity Act into sectoral policies; establish a science-based target for protection of forests, consistent with international obligations and representative of the different forest ecosystems in Norway; build consensus on conservation measures for large carnivores, based on robust research on their population dynamics, natural habitats and impacts on local communities.	The government established 14 priority species and 8 selected habitat types. Norway's national biodiversity action plan, "Nature for Life" (2015), presents a variety of measures for "critically endangered" and "endangered" species and habitats (e.g. protected areas, selected habitat types and priority species, sector-specific regulations and economic incentives). It plans to follow up on priorities set for managing these species and habitat types, along with measures to improve their environmental conditions by 2035. The 2018 Pollinator Strategy and the 2021 action plan aim to protect and help pollinating insects. A regulation for invasive alien species entered into force in 2015. The 2020 action plan outlines measures to combat alien invasive species towards 2025. The central government developed guidance on national planning (Circular T2/16), which can give it ground for objections to municipal plans. This guidance encompasses all environmental interests, including nature, climate, pollution and cultural heritage, and provides some "qualitative valuation" of environmental interests. The government pursued efforts to increase knowledge sharing and develops data visualisation tools to better locate threatened species

	and habitats with a view to raising awareness and improving management. In 2016, Parliament set a goal to protect 10% of Norway's forests, targeting those with important habitats for red listed species and areas. Annual funding for forest protection has nearly doubled over the past decade and reached NOK 435 million (about USD 50.6 million) in 2021. In 2019, the government adopted principles for ecological compensation – as a last resort – if encroachment on especially valuable nature cannot be avoided. It published a guidance document on the general principles in the Nature Diversity Act (2012). This was revised in 2016, with a focus on cross-sectoral provisions.
Strengthen management of protected areas, including by securing necessary financing; assure long-term conservation of particularly valuable and vulnerable areas identified in the sea management plans.	In 2019, the government published an action plan to strengthen management of terrestrial protected areas. The annual budget for the management of protected areas has more than doubled since 2013. More than half of national parks have visitor strategies, and plans for remaining parks are in development. In addition, 16 marine protected areas were adopted by 2021. Marine areas are also included in national parks, nature reserves, etc. Regulation and management of these areas is a priority. The government presented a national plan for the conservation of important areas for marine nature in 2021. This focuses on establishing a more systematic approach to the conservation of areas of importance for marine biodiversity. It is based mainly on the protection of valuable and vulnerable areas identified in the sea management plans.
Strengthen the control of building in coastal zones and along rivers, pursuant to the new Planning and Building Act.	Norway's 2019-23 national expectations document requires that "county and municipal authorities assess land use in the shore line and in and along watercourses in a coherent, long-term perspective, with special regard for natural diversity, cultural heritage environments, outdoor recreation, landscapes and other public interests". National planning guidelines for diversified management of the shore zone were revised in 2021 to clarify national land-use policies and secure national interests in these coastal zones. The guidelines are strictest where pressure for construction is high and where important values need to be protected. This includes coastal areas of the counties of Telemark, Vestfold and Viken, as well as the Oslo area. The government also provides guidance on how to use 3D-modelling in the planning and management of coastal zones.
Pursue efforts to make aquaculture environmentally sustainable, including pest control.	In 2021, the government adopted a new aquaculture strategy, "A Sea of Opportunities", to achieve the goal of sustainable growth in aquaculture. It aims to produce sustainable seafood with a small climate and environmental footprint. For over a decade, Norway has applied a broad range of mitigation measures to stabilise the threats posed to wild salmon from escaped farmed salmon and salmon lice. The country implements a system to adjust production capacity and ensure its environmental sustainability. Norway also considers broader environmental impacts of aquaculture, including strict regulations regarding the management of production sites. Regulations help reduce the environmental impact of pharmaceuticals. Technical requirements for floating fish farms were introduced more than a decade ago. Similar requirements have been applied since 2018 for land-based fish farms. Since 2016, an industry-managed fund has administered mitigating measures in rivers with a high prevalence of escaped fish. In 2017, government adopted a new anti-escaping strategy and increased its budget for surveillance of escapees in rivers. In addition, the government provides incentives (e.g. innovation licences) to develop technology that can reduce the environmental impact of fish farming. Environment surveys through certified agencies are mandatory for all sea-based production sites. If the environmental status of the bottom habitat does not comply with standard acceptance criteria, the aquaculture and/or pollution authorities will impose temporary fallowing of the production site. Norway has adopted a "National Quality Norm for Wild Atlantic Salmon".
Assess the effects on nature and biodiversity of measures for adaptation to climate change.	In 2018, the government adopted national planning guidelines for climate adaptation. These require stakeholders to consider nature-based solutions when planning for actions to adapt society to climate change. Stakeholders must explain why they did not choose nature-based solutions.
Waste management	
Review and adjust, as necessary, the current mix of instruments so as to more effectively and efficiently prevent and reduce waste from the main waste-generating sectors; apply additional measures to reduce waste generation by government agencies, including through public procurement; monitor results and report annually on progress.	Norway revised its waste policy in 2017. Two years later, the Norwegian Environment Agency published a National Waste Management Plan in accordance with the EU WFD. This was supplemented with an annex on hazardous waste in 2021. Norway is revising the regulation on waste electronics, packaging and the system of extended producer responsibility. The Norwegian Environment Agency published a cost-effectiveness analysis on different measures to achieve relevant targets of the EU WFD. The proportion of waste to be recycled is not quantified in the national goal, but the European Union has adopted quantified targets that apply to Norway under the European Economic Area Agreement. Norway notably reduced hazardous chemicals in products. A regulation that prohibits certain products made of single use plastic has been in effect since 2021. Other measures are forthcoming. A voluntary agreement in 2017 between 5 ministries and 12 commercial organisations covers the entire food chain and aims to halve the amount of food waste by 2030. In 2021, the government released its first strategy for developing a green, circular

	economy. It has broad scope and largely applies the new EU Circular Economy Action Plan 2020.
Investigate the effectiveness of volume- or weight-based waste disposal fees to provide further incentives for waste sorting and reduction by households; identify and promote the use of best practice models among municipalities.	Municipalities increasingly differentiate fees by pricing residual waste higher than sorted waste (e.g. different container sizes or less frequent collection of residual waste). Moreover, many municipalities use differentiated fees at designated waste delivery points for the public. Several larger municipal companies use digital tools to register weight.
Encourage the development of municipal and intermunicipal waste management plans to achieve national targets for waste reduction more efficiently, in particular for biodegradable and hazardous waste.	Some municipalities have developed local waste management plans of their own volition. Major changes in the national waste policy will impact municipalities (e.g. increasing recycling rates for municipal waste). Regulations on biowaste, plastic waste and packaging are forthcoming.
Assess the implications of elimination of the incineration tax on emissions of most hazardous substances from incinerators.	Norway reintroduced an incineration tax on GHG emissions effective 1 January 2022. This is part of a general policy to include as much as possible all GHG emissions in a tax scheme or in the EU ETS.
Continue work towards further reduction of hazardous chemicals in products by drawing up proposals for additional substances that would be eliminated by 2020 and encouraging international action in this area; improve data collection on these substances through the product register.	Norway has a national target to phase out use and emissions of substances on the national priority list. This list indicates priority substances for regulations and other measures. Norway works to regulate and limit the use of these substances in line with EU chemicals regulations. It has proposed harmonised classification for a number of substances under the EU CLP (regulation on classification, labelling and packaging of substances and mixtures). It also proposed restrictions of substances under the REACH regulation, and identified several substances to be listed under the Stockholm Convention. The Product Register is the official register of hazardous chemicals in Norway. The register was digitalised in 2015; electronic declaration of chemicals became mandatory as of 2018. Authorities use data in the register to monitor chemicals, analyse risk related to chemical substances and deal with acute situations. The Norwegian Environment Agency will launch a new version of the online platform in early 2022.
Redouble efforts to address problems associated with contaminated sites and contaminated sediments using reduction of negative impacts on human health, cost-effectiveness and public engagement as key guiding principles of the operations.	Norway prioritised actions related to contaminated sites and sediments over the last decades. In the early 2000s, the government prioritised 17 polluted seabed areas for purification. The decision aimed to ensure that environmental toxins are not spread further and do not pollute the surroundings.
Chapter 2. Towards sustainable development	
Continue to improve decision making for implementing the sustainable development strategy, building further on the impressive analytical capacity established for this purpose.	National implementation of the 2030 Agenda for Sustainable Development replaced the National Sustainable Development Strategy. The government has submitted Norway's first national plan to implement the 17 Sustainable Development Goals (SDGs), to be adopted by Parliament in spring 2022. The government ensures annual reporting on the follow-up of the SDGs to Parliament. It is progressively mainstreaming implementation of the 2030 Agenda in sectoral policies and strategies towards 2030. According to the proposed action plan, all strategies, action plans and white papers are screened to ensure SDG-relevance. Meanwhile, the SDGs are systematically integrated into guidance and performance agreements with state agencies and institutions. In 2020, the Ministry of Local Government and Modernisation (renamed the Ministry of Local Government and Regional Development) became the national co-ordinating body for the SDGs. The National Action Plan promotes a whole-of-government approach and establishes measures to ensure better horizontal and vertical co-ordination, as well as stronger co-operation with the private sector, academia and civil society. Norway has already submitted two comprehensive Voluntary National Reviews to the United Nations (2016 and 2021) and another Voluntary Subnational Review.
Further support environmental policy objectives by removing inappropriate exemptions in environmentally related taxes and (other) environmentally harmful subsidies.	In 2011, the government abolished CO_2 tax exemptions for diesel in coastal fisheries, and in antique vessels and machinery, as well as for natural gas and LPG in coastal fisheries and cargo and passenger transport in domestic waters. In 2019, as a follow-up on Aichi target 3, the government began assessing possible negative effects on biodiversity from subsidies, the consequences of possible changes in these subsidies and how they interrelate with other instruments. Within its Climate Action Plan 2021-30, the government proposes to review the effects of a tax on mineral fertilisers to reduce emissions of nitrous oxide. The tax base for biofuels has been expanded.
Consider introducing a broad-based road-charging system, e.g. to address transport-related air pollution, noise and congestion externalities.	Norway raises a significant amount of taxes (road use tax and carbon tax) on the sale of fossil fuel, which internalises externalities to a certain degree. Major cities are surrounded by toll cordons and road tolls are common. The government commissioned a report on a satellite-based road pricing system aimed, initially, at heavy goods vehicles. The report shows such a system would be a significant improvement over the different direct and indirect pricing mechanisms. Implementation will require time; in the interim, the

	government intends to improve the road pricing system.
Consider further greening Norway's agricultural sector, including a shift towards less distorting forms of agricultural support, such as income support and payments targeting specific environmental outcomes.	Agri-environmental measures are implemented as part of the National Environmental Programme, which aims to contribute to sustainable agriculture production with reduced GHG emissions, as well as fulfilling Norway's international commitments on environmental and climate in the agricultural sector. The most important agri-environmental measure in terms of spending is the Acreage Cultural Landscape Support. In June 2019, the government and farmers' organisations signed a voluntary agreement to reduce GHG emissions by 5 million tonnes of CO_2-eq between 2021 and 2030.
Reassess and clarify the objectives of the carbon capture and storage programme (domestic emission reduction, commercialisation, development co-operation); broaden collaboration, particularly targeting partners in countries where coal-fired power plants are under construction or planned	The government's carbon capture and storage (CCS) strategy spans a wide range of activities, from research, development and demonstration (RD&D) to large-scale projects and the promotion of CCS development and deployment on the international stage. Launched in 2020, Longship is Norway's largest ever industrial climate project. It aims to provide CCS technological development in Norway and internationally. The project benefits from long-term funding. The government's investment reached NOK 3.45 billion (USD 0.4 billion) in 2022 out of NOK 17 billion (USD 2 billion) in state aid pledged until 2030. The Technology Centre Mongstad is the world's largest facility for testing and improving CO_2 capture technologies on an industrial scale. CLIMIT – Norway's national RD&D programme of CCS technology – also yielded results for CCS development.

Source: OECD Secretariat based on country submission.

Chapter 1. Towards sustainable development

This chapter provides an overview of economic and social development, and major policy developments in the environmental sectors, including climate, air, freshwater, waste and materials (biodiversity is covered in Chapter 2). Drawing on indicators from national and international sources, the chapter tracks progress towards achieving national goals and international commitments and targets, and looks at the environmental governance and management system. It also assesses the environmental effectiveness and economic efficiency of the environmental policy mix, including fiscal and economic instruments, regulatory and voluntary instruments, and investment in environment-related infrastructure. The chapter concludes with a reflection on opportunities for fostering a just and equitable transition to a green, low-carbon society.

1.1. People, economy and sustainable development

1.1.1. Life in Norway

Norway is a northern European country with a small population of 5.4 million people and a large coastline of nearly 29 000 km, including fjords and bays. About 80% of Norway's population lives less than 10 km from the sea. Due to harsh climatic conditions, a large part of the country is unsuitable for settlement. Norway's northern areas are sparsely populated, and are notably the traditional home of the Sami minority (about 20 500 registered Sami voters[1]). After Iceland, Norway has the second lowest population density in Europe. However, the large majority of its population lives in urban areas, with a dense population reaching nearly 2 000 people per square kilometre in the Oslo area. Norway's population is growing slowly but steadily. It is expected to reach close to 6 million people by 2050 (Statistics Norway, 2021[1]). On average, the country also welcomes some 6 million tourists per year (2016-19, pre-COVID-19).

Figure 1.1. Norwegians are more satisfied with their lives than the OECD average

Norway's current well-being

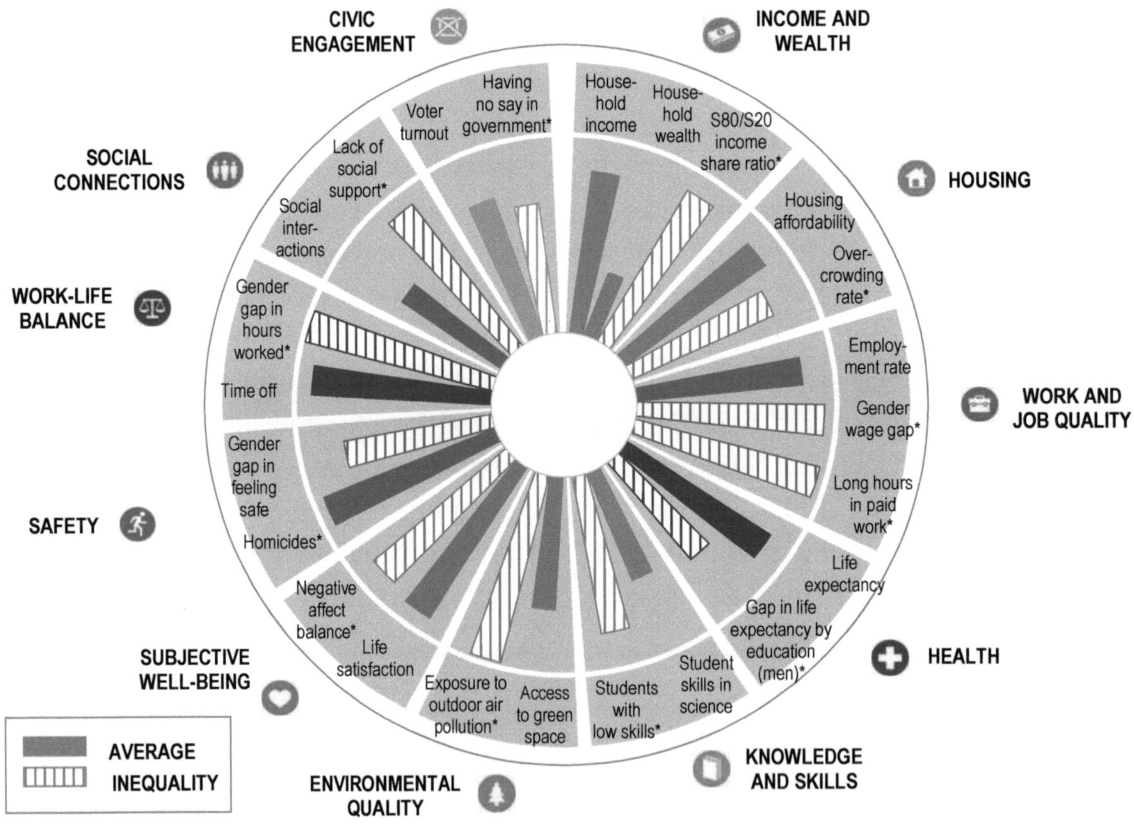

Note: This chart shows Norway's relative strengths and weaknesses in well-being compared to other OECD countries. Longer bars always indicate better outcomes (i.e. higher well-being), whereas shorter bars always indicate worse outcomes (lower well-being) – including for negative indicators, marked with an *, which have been reverse-scored. Inequalities (gaps between top and bottom, differences between groups, people falling under a deprivation threshold) are shaded with stripes. Data for negative affect balance, the gender gap in feeling safe and lack of social support refer to 2021 or 2020. All other data refer to 2019 or the latest available year.
Source: OECD calculations based on OECD (2022), "How's Life? Well-Being", *OECD Social and Welfare Statistics* (database).

Life expectancy at birth is estimated at 83.2 years, higher than the OECD average. It is expected to rise another five to six years by 2050, increasing the share of people of retirement age. Norwegians have a generally good level of education and skills. Pupils in Norway scored above the OECD average in reading literacy, maths and science in the OECD Programme for International Student Assessment. Girls largely outperformed boys. Norway is also among the most advanced countries in terms of gender equality. Nearly half of representatives elected to the Norwegian Parliament are women.

Norway's population enjoys good health in general. The country has a well-developed health system with universal coverage and quality health services that are financially accessible to nearly all. Health spending per capita in Norway (about NOK 70 000 or USD 7 400) is about two-thirds higher than the EU average. Non-communicable diseases and social inequities are among the key public health challenges. The health impact of the COVID-19 pandemic was significantly lower in Norway compared to other European countries. By November 2021, more than 70% of adults were fully vaccinated. However, another wave of infections hit Norway at the end of 2021, prompting the government to re-introduce containment measures.

Life satisfaction in Norway is high. The country regularly ranks among the top ten countries in terms of happiness, along with other Nordic countries. It also performs well in nearly all dimensions of well-being (Figure 1.1). Norwegians enjoy a good work-life balance and are comparatively "less stressed". Only 3% of Norwegian employees work long hours, far below the OECD average of 11%. Norwegians also have a green lifestyle. In all, 91% of Norway's people declared they enjoy outdoor activities (Statistics Norway, 2020[2]).

1.1.2. Economic performance

Norway has a small and open economy with a substantial petroleum sector. With USD 62 800 per capita in 2020, Norway is among the richest OECD countries. Income inequality in Norway is lower than in most advanced economies (OECD, 2021[3]). Like other Nordic countries, the country has an extensive system for social protection. While labour force participation has weakened somewhat over the past two decades, Norway's employment rate is still largely above the OECD average.

Mainland gross domestic product (GDP) annual growth contracted by 2.3% in 2020. The tourism and transport sectors were hardest hit. The government provided substantial support to people and businesses via several emergency and recovery packages (Section 1.7.1). However, Norway has been recovering comparatively quickly from the economic impacts of the global pandemic (Figure 1.2). Prior to the slowdown brought about by the Omicron variant, Mainland real GDP of Norway was projected to increase by 4.2% in 2022 (OECD, 2021[3]) (Figure 1.2). Provision estimates incorporating the slowdown suggest growth will be around 3.7%. The unemployment rate is set to fall further once the impact of the Omicron wave has passed.

Norway's economy has increasingly diversified. The service sector accounts for close to 66% of the economy, the industry sector represents 33% (including mining and construction) and the primary sector about 2%. The oil and gas sector accounts for a substantial share of economic activity. However, its share within national GDP is shrinking, from a peak of 25% in 2012 to 14% in 2021. To date, the petroleum sector represents 41% of total exports, 20% of total investments and 5.8% of employment (Ministry of Energy and Petroleum, 2022[4]). While a comparatively small player at the global scale (0.7% of world oil reserves and 1.7% of gas reserves), Norway is one of the world's largest energy exporters. The vast majority of Norway's crude oil exports is exported to other European countries. In 2020, Norway was the second largest exporter of gas within OECD member countries, following the United States. A network of subsea pipelines connects Norway to other European countries.

Figure 1.2. Norway's economic output is projected to reach above pre-pandemic levels in 2022

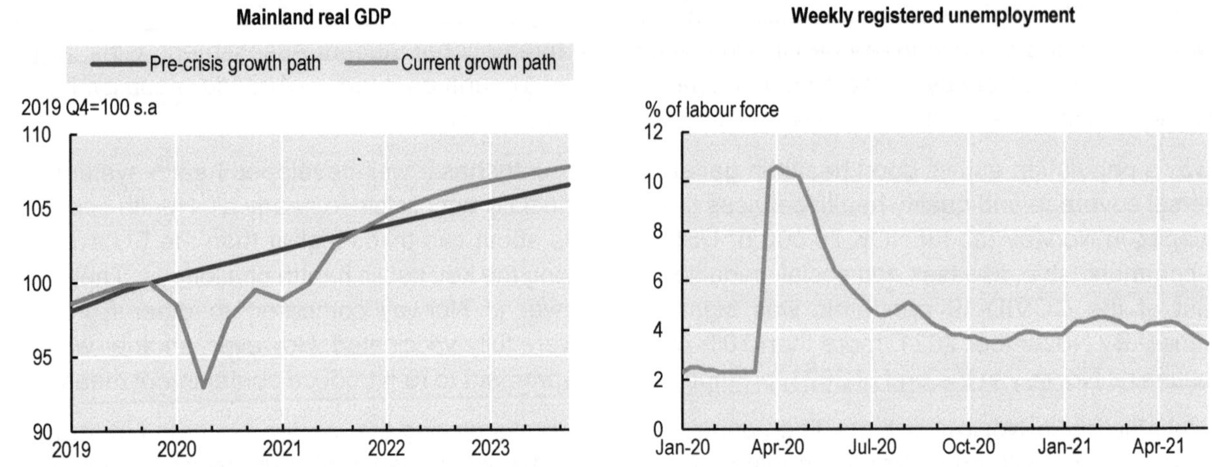

Note: The pre-crisis growth path is based on the November 2019 *OECD Economic Outlook* projection, with linear extrapolation for 2022 and 2023 based on trend growth in 2021 (left panel). The registered unemployment data include temporary layoffs (right panel).
Source: OECD (2021), *OECD Economic Outlook*, Volume 2021 Issue 2 based on *OECD Economic Outlook*, No.106 and 109 (databases) and Norwegian Labour and Welfare Administration.

StatLink https://stat.link/zw6k9o

The European Green Deal and its climate framework will heavily impact Norway, notably in the medium and long term (2030-50) (European Commission, 2019[5]). According to EU projections, fossil fuels will still provide about half of the EU's energy requirements by 2030. Natural gas is set to be phased out later and might still represent about 10% of Europe's energy mix by 2050. Norway currently covers about a quarter of EU gas demand and is usually considered as an attractive and reliable business partner.

The government's total net cash flow from the petroleum industry is estimated at NOK 272 billion in 2021 (about USD 31.6 billion). This is about NOK 90 billion (USD 10.5 billion) higher than the estimates of the National Budget 2022 thanks to high oil and gas prices (Ministry of Energy and Petroleum, 2022[4]). Despite the global recession, Norway's main sovereign wealth fund grew by 8% in 2020. Created in 1990 to ensure sustainable, long-term management of Norway's oil resources for current and future generations, the Government Pension Fund Global counted about NOK 12.3 trillion (USD 1.4 trillion) or close to NOK 2.3 million (USD 267 500) per inhabitant at the end of 2021. It is the world's largest sovereign wealth fund.

Considering its large coastline of nearly 29 000 km and some 7 000 ships in Norwegian waters, Norway has a strong interest in developing a sustainable maritime sector (Section 2.5.2). Norway's Climate Action Plan 2021-30, presented in a white paper to Parliament in 2021, includes a focus on green public procurement, green innovation and infrastructure. It aims at halving emissions from domestic shipping and fisheries by 2030, compared to 2005 levels. With a production of about 4 million tonnes per year, Norway is a net exporter of fish and fish products with a value of USD 10.8 billion (77% from aquaculture and 23% from fisheries) (OECD, 2021[6]). Over 30 000 people are employed in the seafood sector.

1.1.3. Progress towards the Sustainable Development Goals

For more than a decade, Norway maintained the top position on the Human Development Index. The country ranked seventh on the 2021 index of countries' progress towards achieving the Sustainable

Development Goals (SDGs), which was topped by three Nordic countries (Finland, Sweden and Denmark). Norway has already fully achieved six goals and is making good progress towards achieving four more (Figure 1.3). However, like many other OECD countries, the country still faces “significant or major challenges” for several goals, including climate action, sustainable consumption patterns and biodiversity protection. Most of the remaining challenges are related to the increase of environmental pressures.

In 2015, Norway adopted a national plan to implement the 17 SDGs. The government ensures annual reporting on the follow-up of the SDGs to Parliament (*Storting).* It is progressively mainstreaming implementation of the 2030 Agenda in sectoral policies and strategies towards 2030. According to the plan, all strategies, action plans and white papers are screened to ensure SDG-relevance, while the SDGs are systematically integrated into guidance and performance agreements with state agencies and institutions. Statistics Norway maintains a dedicated platform with facts and figures on Norway’s progress towards achieving the SDGs.

In 2020, the Ministry of Local Government and Modernisation, which is also in charge of regional development, became the national co-ordinating body for implementing the SDGs. It aims to promote local ownership and increase cross-sectoral co-operation. Municipalities, regional authorities and, more broadly, civil society now play a stronger role in the implementation of the SDGs. The 2021 National Action Plan promotes a whole-of-government approach and establishes measures to ensure better horizontal and vertical co-ordination, as well as stronger co-operation with the private sector, academia and civil society. Norway already submitted two comprehensive Voluntary National Reviews to the United Nations (2016 and 2021) (Ministry of Local Government and Modernisation, 2021[7]) and another Voluntary Subnational Review (Hjorth-Johansen et al., 2021[8]).

Figure 1.3. Norway is on track to achieve many but not all sustainable development goals

Note: The full title of each SDG is available here: https://sustainabledevelopment.un.org/topics/sustainabledevelopmentgoals.
Source: Sachs, J.D. et al. (2021), *The Decade of Action for the Sustainable Development Goals, Sustainable Development Report 2021*, https://dashboards.sdgindex.org.

At the regional level, the newly created county of Viken endorsed the SDGs as a holistic framework for the Regional Planning Strategy for a Sustainable Viken 2020-24 (OECD, 2020[9]). At the local level, 95% of municipalities have started working with the SDGs (Hjorth-Johansen et al., 2021[8]). Thirty municipalities monitored key performance indicators of the United for Smart Sustainable Cities. The Oslo SDG Initiative analyses transformations required for implementation of the 2030 Agenda. However, progress towards implementing the SDGs is uneven (OECD, 2021[10]). Some more advanced municipalities operationalised and integrated the SDGs into strategic plans and management processes. Others remain at the inception phase. Speed and progress in local implementation and ownership largely depend on three factors: the size of municipalities (larger ones are doing better), political commitment (higher in centrally located municipalities) and, to a less extent, budgetary constraints or capacity issues (Hjorth-Johansen et al., 2021[8]).

The role of local authorities in the implementation of the SDGs needs to be further strengthened. Counties and municipalities need to be fully involved in national decision making from early planning to monitoring and evaluation. At the same time, they must strengthen their capacity to work with the SDGs "strategically and systematically" (OECD, 2020[9]). The national government needs to further promote policy coherence, multi-level governance and multi-stakeholder partnerships to move beyond a goal-by-goal approach rooted in specific sectors. Inter-ministerial co-ordination between different policy areas could be improved. Specifically, ministerial departments should invest more in interdisciplinary expertise (e.g. internal mobility) and pay more attention to cross-sectoral spillovers to better integrate policies across sectors.

1.2. Selected environmental trends and performance

1.2.1. Key energy trends

Energy structure, intensity and use

Thanks to the widespread use of clean electricity – primarily hydropower – Norway has one of the most decarbonised power sectors of Europe and of the OECD area (Figure 1.5). Primary energy supply decreased by 16.5% from a peak of 32.8 million tonnes of oil equivalent (Mtoe) in 2013 to 27.4 Mtoe in 2019 (IEA, 2021[11]). Norway is energy self-sufficient with a surplus of renewable electricity in normal years. It has become Europe's largest energy exporter (Figure 1.4).

Figure 1.4. Norway is energy self-sufficient and has become Europe's largest energy exporter

Energy production, supply and consumption, 2019

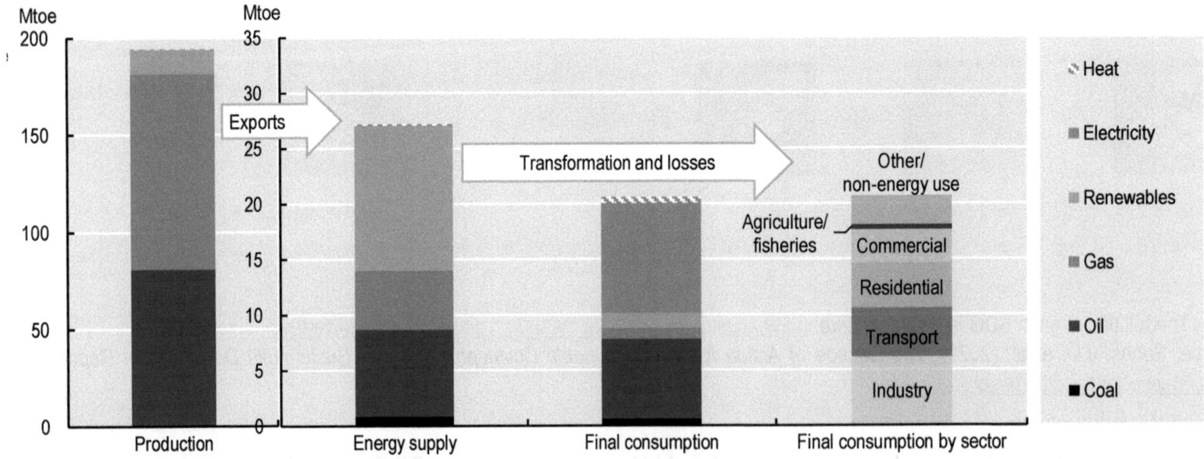

Note: Data presented in the chart exclude negligible quantities of non-renewable waste.
Source: IEA (2021), *IEA World Energy Statistics and Balances* (database).

StatLink https://stat.link/li5wkg

Following recent increases,[2] Norway's oil production is set to increase until 2024 and then expected to decline by around 2% each year on average between 2025 and 2040 (IEA, 2019[12]). Gas production will peak slightly later around 2030. Production will first and foremost decline due to resource depletion rates rather than a planned transition (Sanner and Bru, 2021[13]).

Oil, natural gas and coal together represented only about 50% of Norway's total energy supply (TES) in 2020, compared to 78% in the OECD as a whole (Figure 1.5). Norway has reduced the share of fossil fuels since 2013 with a view to cutting greenhouse gas (GHG) emissions. Coal made up about 3% of TES for the past few decades. In 2021, the government announced the closure of its only coal-fired power plant in Svalbard. At the same time, it released a new energy plan for Longyearbyen as part of its 2022 budget to increase the share of renewables in Svalbard. A remaining Russian coal mine is also set to close down. This is a highly symbolic, positive development with a view to protecting the Arctic area. Norway does not use any nuclear power in its energy supply.

The government's 2021 White Paper "Putting Energy to Work" outlines objectives for a long-term value creation from Norwegian energy sources. The strategy aims at setting predictable framework conditions to help the country advance towards a low-carbon society. It defines four main goals: renewable energy resources for economic growth and job creation; electrification; establishment of new, profitable industries; and maintenance of a "future-oriented Norwegian oil and gas industry" (Ministry of Petroleum and Energy, 2021[14]). The paper outlines a series of pilot projects to develop new, cost-efficient, climate-friendly solutions and technologies in line with the objectives of its Climate Action Plan 2021-30 (Ministry of Climate and Environment, 2021[15]). The government invests heavily in technological developments offered by offshore wind, renewable hydrogen, and carbon capture and storage (CCS).

Figure 1.5. Norway's energy mix is much more decarbonised than the OECD average

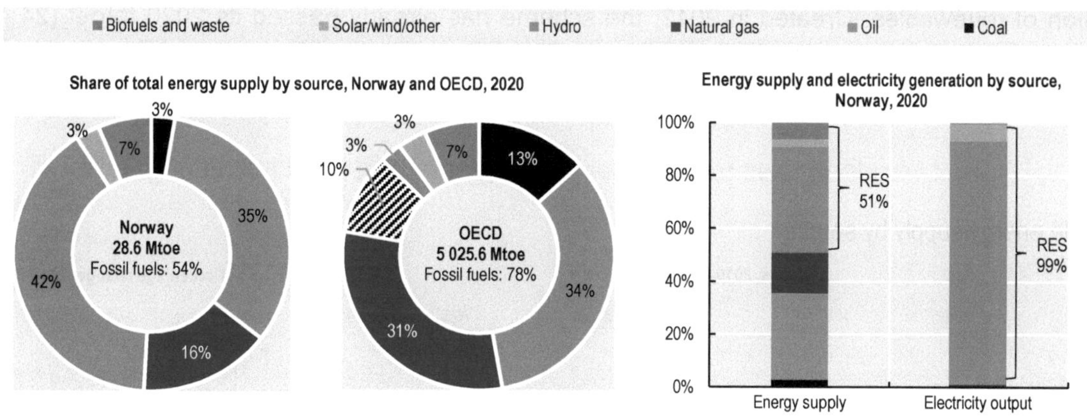

Note: The breakdown of energy supply excludes heat and electricity trade, but percentages shown reflect ratios calculated on total energy supply. Biofuel and waste include negligible quantities of non-renewable waste.
Source: IEA (2021), *IEA World Energy Statistics and Balances* (database).

StatLink https://stat.link/vonsc1

However, the plan also foresees continued support for Norway's petroleum exploration policy. This includes "regular concession rounds to ensure that new areas for exploration are made available to the industry" (Ministry of Petroleum and Energy, 2021[14]). This approach may exacerbate Norway's petroleum lock-in and industrial path dependency (Kattel et al., 2021[16]). While the plan indicates that emissions from oil and gas production shall be cut by 50% by 2030 and reach net zero by 2050, continued oil exploration poses a risk of stranded assets given the global and, especially European, ambition of reducing fossil fuel use to reach net zero by 2050. There are concerns that it could slow down the shift from a fossil-driven to a fully green industry strategy (SEI et al., 2021[17]). On the other hand, Norway could play a crucial role as provider of transitional energy sources, notably gas, with a view to ensuring energy security in Europe and facilitating its clean energy transition. It is too early to assess the impact of the new energy strategy. The recent government change may also impact strategic orientations. The government is preparing a supplementary document. Both strategic documents were scheduled to be discussed in Parliament by mid-2022.

Renewables

Following Iceland, Norway has the second largest share of renewables, representing more than half of its energy mix and 99% of its electricity output (Figure 1.6). It overachieved its national target of a 67.5% share of renewable energy in gross final energy consumption in 2020, in line with the EU Directive on renewable energy. Renewables represented a share of 26% in the transport sector, largely outperforming the 10% target set in 2012.

Norway is the largest hydropower producer in Europe and is among the largest worldwide. Hydropower represents the large bulk (90.2%) of Norway's electricity production (Statistics Norway, 2021[18]). The country has significant hydropower reservoir capacity. The share of wind power has increased ten-fold from 2005 to 2019, representing about 4% of renewables (Figure 1.6). Norway installed about 1.5 GW of wind capacity in 2020. The government's energy white paper outlines steps to facilitate offshore wind power, both floating and bottom-fixed installations (Ministry of Petroleum and Energy, 2021[14]).

Norway's renewables sector is rapidly growing. The creation of new power lines to Germany and the United Kingdom will allow Norway to better integrate with the European electricity market. The joint Norway-Sweden green power support scheme has been the main policy instrument for increasing production of renewables. Created in 2012, the scheme has already passed its 2020 target (24.4 TWh) thanks to technological and market advancements. The governments of Norway and Sweden decided to end the support scheme by 2035, ten years earlier than planned.

Figure 1.6. Hydropower dominates the renewable energy mix, but wind power is growing rapidly

Renewable energy supply by source

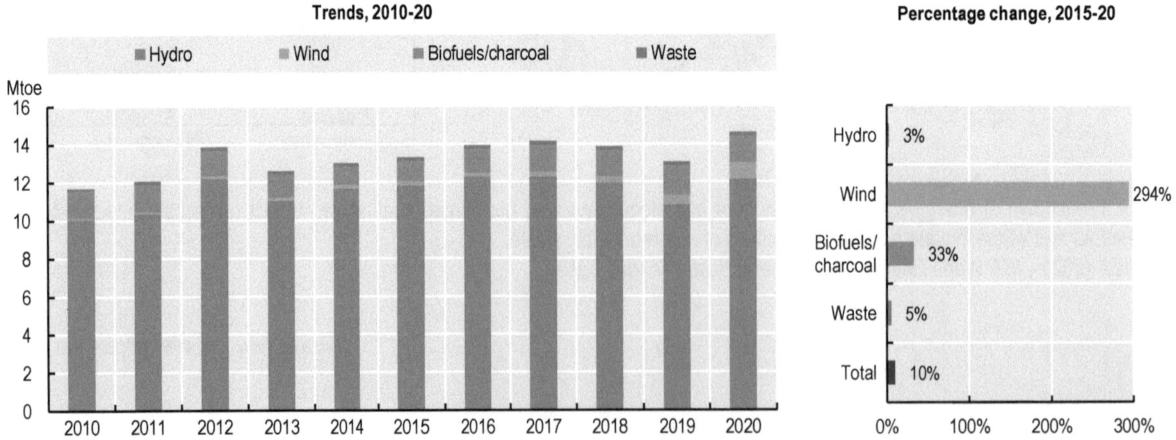

Source: IEA (2021), *IEA World Energy Statistics and Balances* (database).

StatLink https://stat.link/1mhur8

Energy intensity and efficiency

Norway has increasingly decoupled energy demand and related environmental effects from growth. Over the past decade, it has accelerated deployment of renewables and improved energy efficiency thanks to enhanced technology and electrification of the transport and residential sectors. Nevertheless, Norway's energy consumption per capita, which historically has been among the highest in the OECD, is still slightly above the average. This is due notably to high energy consumption in the industry sector, as well as household heating needs due to the cold Scandinavian climate. Improving energy efficiency thus needs to remain a priority for such an energy-intense economy.

Norway's total final energy consumption curve has been relatively flat over the years (Figure 1.7). The country is close to reaching the level of 2005. Further efficiency gains will allow Norway to pursue this downward trend despite increasing economic activity. Industry remains the largest energy-consuming sector but already consumes less than in 2005, primarily due to the continuing shift to services. The biggest reduction in fossil fuel energy consumption will come from the transport sector (Section 1.3.5). This is due in large part to Norway's large-scale rollout of electric vehicles (EVs), which are about three times as energy efficient as internal combustion engine vehicles (IEA, 2021[19]).

Figure 1.7. Norway has decoupled energy demand and related environmental effects

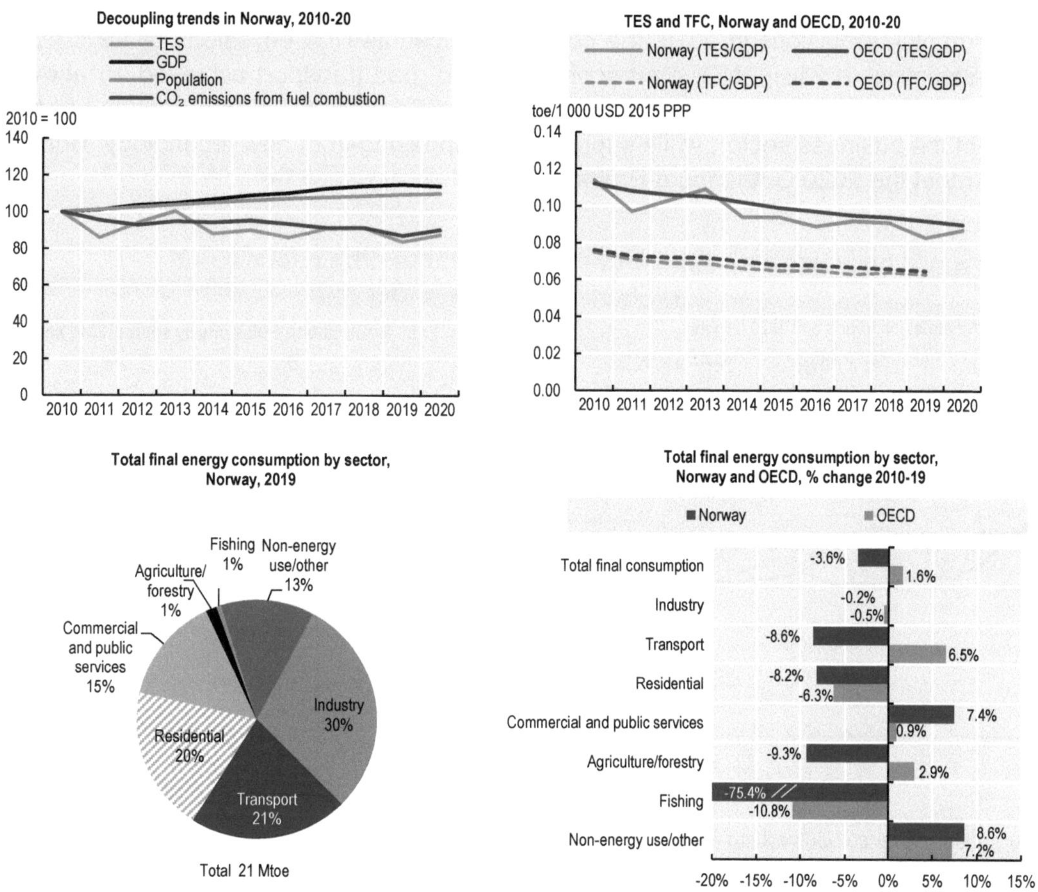

Note: TES = total energy supply; TFC = total final consumption. Gross Domestic Product (GDP) is expressed at 2015 prices and purchasing power parities.
Source: IEA (2021), *IEA World Energy Statistics and Balances* (database); IEA (2021), *IEA World Greenhouse Gas Emissions from Energy* (database).

StatLink https://stat.link/9gjonr

The country has high energy-efficiency standards for building performance that were effective at reducing energy consumption and CO_2 emissions from using energy, and in particular from heating dwellings. According to government calculations, Norwegian energy efficiency policies led to a reduction of 16 TWh between 2014 and 2020, largely exceeding the 2016 target of 10 TWh by 2030. In 2016, the government tightened threshold standards for new homes and major renovations to "passive house" level. As of 2020, it became the first country that formally prohibited use of fossil oil for heating in existing buildings and in new buildings altogether. Energy consumed by the residential sector is thus increasingly carbon-free. Moreover, there is scope for greener housing construction and building materials (OECD, 2022[20]). Building homes, and associated production and disposal of building materials, has significant environmental costs. A stronger focus on the life cycle of buildings could help Norway further decarbonise the building sector (e.g. reduced use of materials, use of low-carbon materials, re-use of materials).

1.2.2. Atmospheric emissions and air quality

Norway's pollutant emissions and intensities of fine particulate matter ($PM_{2.5}$), nitrogen oxide (NO_x), sulphur oxide (SO_x) and black carbon have all decreased over the past decade. Norway reached its air emission targets for 2020 (Figure 1.8) except for ammonia (NH_3) and a recent increase in emissions of non-methane volatile organic compounds due to increased use of disinfectants during the pandemic. The largest emissions of black carbon originate from the transport sector and wood combustion in residential heating; both emission sources have been considerably reduced. While Norway had failed to meet the Gothenburg Protocol target on NO_x emissions in 2010, the country reduced its NO_x emissions by 29% from 2005 to 2020 (Norway Statistics, 2021[21]). NO_x emissions related to road transport achieved an above-average reduction of 40%. Moreover, the NO_x tax and the Business Sector's NO_x Fund contributed to reducing NO_x emissions in the business sector, while supporting the phasing-in of new technology. Both measures helped Norway meet the 2020 Gothenburg Protocol target.

Figure 1.8. Norway's pollutant emissions have decreased over the past decade

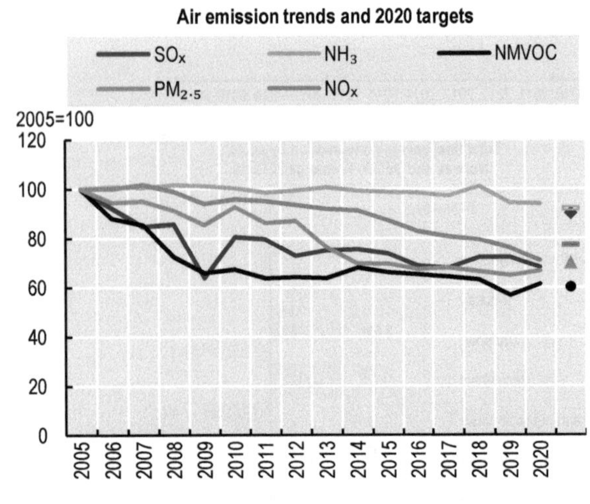

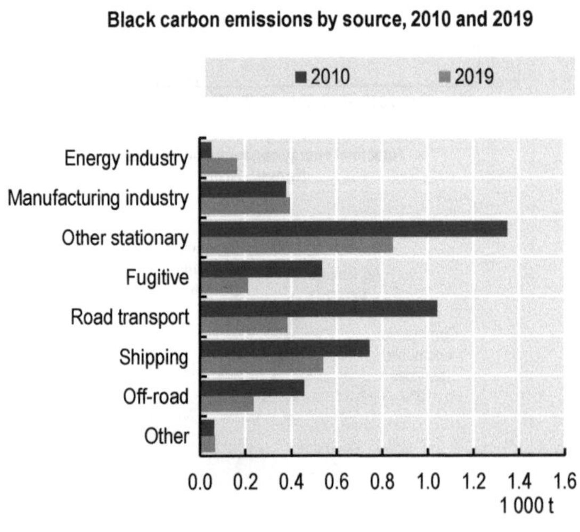

Note: 2020 targets under the revised Gothenburg Protocol to the Convention on Long-range Transboundary Air Pollution.
Source: EMEP (2022), *WebDab* (database); Statistics Norway (2021), *StatBank* (database).

StatLink https://stat.link/6nxtyk

Norwegians enjoy good overall air quality (Figure 1.9). Premature death attributed to $PM_{2.5}$ exposure in Norway is less than one-third the OECD average. Norway complies with EU directives on air quality standards and will continue to follow the EU zero pollution agenda closely. In addition, the country has set more ambitious local and national targets, supported by excellent nationwide air quality monitoring services. Norway's four major cities rank in the top 20 of the European City Air Quality Index.

Nevertheless, nearly all larger cities in Norway face localised air pollution problems and periodic worsening of air quality with high peak PM_{10} concentrations during winter and into spring. Thanks to measures such as the zero-growth goal, EVs and replacement of wood stoves, local air quality in urban areas is expected to further improve in the coming years. Fees for studded tyres, an important source of airborne particulates, helped reduce their use in urban areas. Beyond health impacts and noise, air pollution also threatens biodiversity, which requires targeted solutions for protected areas. For example, Parliament adopted a resolution in 2018 to stop emissions from cruise ships and ferries in world heritage fjords by 2026 at the latest. This would transform these fjords into the world's first zero-emission zones at sea.

Figure 1.9. Norway's cities enjoy good air quality

Annual average concentration of $PM_{2.5}$

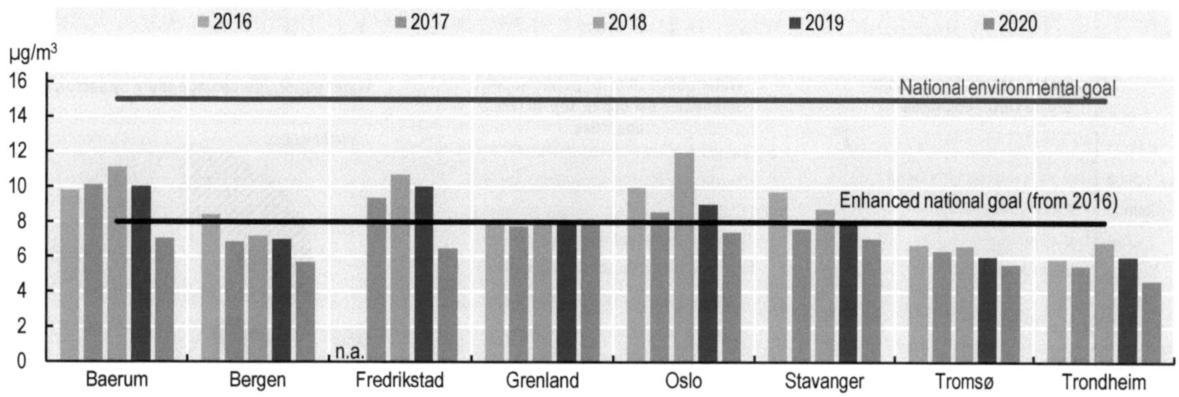

Source: Country submission.

StatLink https://stat.link/1eb4ax

1.2.3. Water resources management

Water quantity and quality

Norway has abundant water resources and is endowed with a large number of lakes and river habitats. This is why the intensity of water use (withdrawal as a percentage of available resources) continues to be low. At the same time, water abstraction for public supply (intensities per capita), is among the highest within the OECD area, due to high water consumption and significant water losses (Figure 1.10).

Freshwater ecosystems are threatened by human activities (e.g. pollution and hydropower production) and other pressures such as acid rain, the spread of alien species and high numbers of salmon lice. Fish farming and lice are identified as the main threats to wild salmon in the 2021 Red List for Species. More than two-thirds of Norway's largest rivers are zoned for hydropower production, which was partly responsible for reducing the salmon population in affected streams. According to the Norwegian Environment Agency, river regulation schemes have negatively affected 23% of Norway's salmon rivers. However, several initiatives aim to reduce these negative impacts. Agriculture, municipal sewage and fish farming are the main sources of water contamination in Norway. Norway has one of the highest nitrogen balances per hectare among OECD countries due to widespread application of fertilisers (OECD, 2021[22]).

Norway has implemented the EU Water Framework Directive (WFD) since 2007 with a view to achieving good ecological and chemical status for all inland, transitional and coastal waters and groundwater bodies. Norway counts 15 river basin districts (RBDs), including cross-border basins that share water courses with Finland and Sweden. Each RBD has its own management plan, including environmental objectives for water bodies and associated action plans. Norway completed – under formal WFD obligations – its first full cycle of river basin management plans from 2016-21 and will start a new one from 2022-27.[3]

According to national assessments, about one-third of Norway's freshwater bodies do not meet the WFD criteria for good ecological status, including 12% categorised as "heavily modified" (Environment Norway, 2021[23]). Norway is doing overall better than most European countries, but the ecological status of water bodies has deteriorated over the past decade (Table 2.1). Ecological conditions are generally better in central and northern parts of Norway, and poorer in more densely populated areas of the south. Norway needs to redouble efforts to reach its target of restoring 15% of degraded ecosystems by 2025, including water-related ecosystems. While Norway has made progress towards integrated water resource management, it still has a way to go to fully meet its obligations under the WFD.

Figure 1.10. Norway has abundant water resources but needs to tackle significant water losses

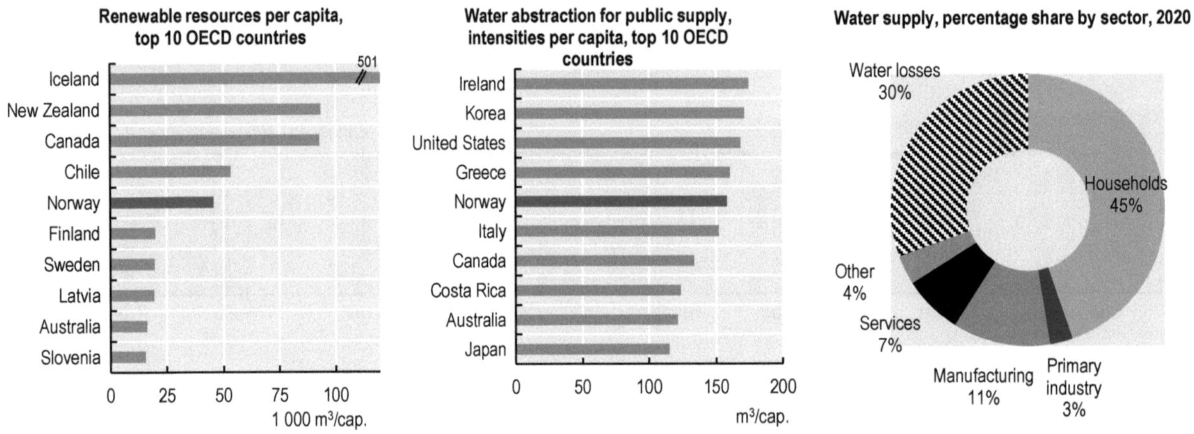

Note: Data refer to freshwater resources availability and abstraction for 2019 or latest available year, data earlier than 2015 have not been taken into account.
Source: OECD (2021), *OECD Environmental Statistics* (database); Statistics Norway (2021), "Water supply and safety and preparedness plans", *StatBank* (database).

StatLink https://stat.link/goy1rz

Drinking water supply

The supply of drinking water is good: nearly 90% of Norwegians have access to treated drinking water from waterworks with high quality standards. Surface water provides 90% of drinking water. About half a million people (or 10%) get water from private wells or other small water plants for which the quality is largely unknown. Leakage from the drinking water supply system is estimated at 30% (Environment Norway, 2021[23]). This represents not only a significant loss of water resources but also a potential risk for microbiological contamination in drinking water. Water supply systems are often more vulnerable in small municipalities, notably in terms of water supply stability and the ability of drinking water utilities to prepare and respond to emergencies (bedreVANN and Norsk Vann, 2020[24]). Information on drinking water quality could be made accessible directly on websites of municipalities. This would enable consumers to easily consult relevant information on their drinking water sources as well as inspection reports.

Wastewater treatment

Most people are connected to municipal wastewater systems. However, only 60% of Norway's population is connected to advanced wastewater treatment plants with biological or chemical treatment methods. This is one of the lowest shares in the OECD area (Figure 1.11). The share of primary wastewater treatment is particularly high in remote areas.

Norway counts about 2 700 municipal wastewater treatment plants (Norwegian Environment Agency, 2021[25]). The county governor is the pollution control authority for about 330 larger plants that treat wastewater from the vast majority of the population (3.9 million people). Meanwhile, municipalities manage most of the small wastewater treatment plants, which serve a small percentage of the population. In addition, some 350 000 treatment plants deal with wastewater from about 800 000 people who live in sparsely populated areas. New treatment systems are also being built for individual houses and cabins, while other buildings are connected to the public sewerage system.

Many municipalities have sewage systems that do not comply with pollution regulations and permits. According to national statistics from 2020, more than half of the population was connected to wastewater facilities that do not comply with pollution permits (Onstad, 2021[26]). This calls for regular inspections and the use of coercive fines.

Figure 1.11. Most Norwegians are connected to municipal wastewater treatment systems, but the share of primary treatment is high

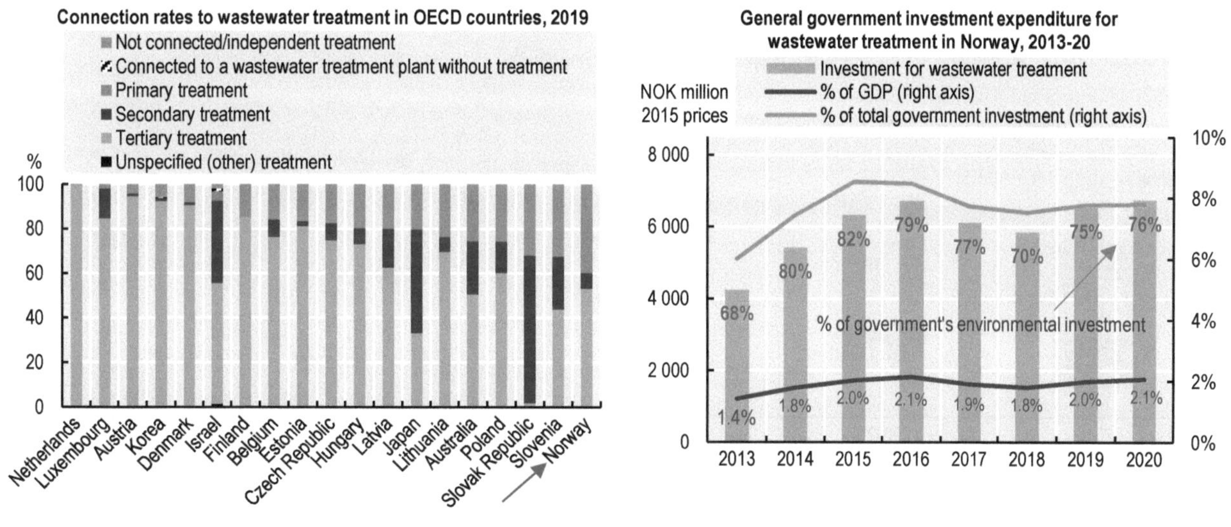

Note: Left panel: 2019 or latest available year. Data for Norway refer to 2020.

Source: Berge G. and M.E. Onstads (2021), *Kommunale avløp 2020* [Municipal Sewers 2020], Report 2021/39, Statistics Norway; OECD (2022), "Water: Wastewater treatment", *OECD Environment Statistics* (database).

StatLink https://stat.link/hb4ivj

As noted in the previous OECD EPR of Norway (OECD, 2011[27]), the country's ageing water infrastructure requires urgent upgrades. It also needs to adjust to new climate challenges, such as increased precipitation, floods and rising sea levels. The rate of infrastructure improvement has been slow despite quite substantial investment (Section 1.6). There is scope for improving operational efficiency of water services and co-ordination between different administrative levels.

1.2.4. Transition to a resource-efficient economy

Waste management

Norway is not on track to meet its objective of decoupling waste generation from economic growth. Waste generation in Norway reached a record high in 2019. According to national statistics, Norway generated 12.2 million tonnes of waste in 2019 (+3% compared to 2018). At the same time, it recovered 71% of waste and recycled about 41% of collected municipal waste; recycling remained fairly stable overall. The construction sector bypassed the industry sector for the largest waste volume (26%). While the industry managed to considerably reduce waste generation, the shares of private households and service industries have been steadily increasing, representing 20% and 18%, respectively (Figure 1.12).

The average Norwegian produced 772 kg of municipal waste, among the highest amounts in Europe (OECD Europe average = 499 kg per capita). However, the definition of municipal waste has been changing over the years, which makes it difficult to compare data. The Waste Management Plan for 2020-25 includes a waste prevention programme and proposals for changes in waste infrastructure to prepare for tightened directives within the EU Zero Waste Strategy. The government reiterates its national goal that growth in waste generation should be significantly lower than economic growth. Some municipalities also prepared local waste management plans.

Figure 1.12. Norway is not on track to decouple waste generation from economic growth

Total waste by source, trends and projections

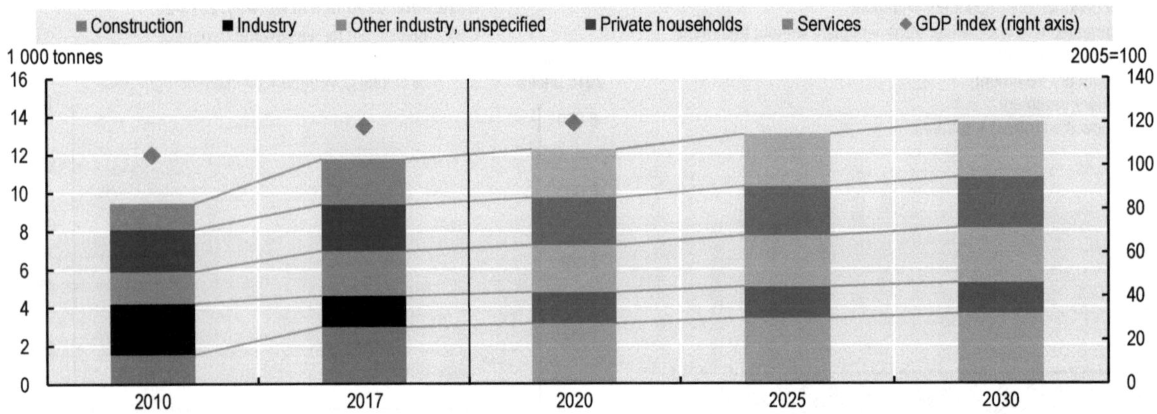

Note: Change in classification implemented in 2012 concerning mainly the breakdown for industrial and construction waste. Estimates for 2020, 2025 and 2030.
Source: Statistics Norway (2021), "Waste accounts", *StatBank* (database).

StatLink https://stat.link/iqf264

Norway's waste treatment profile is similar to its Scandinavian neighbours, Finland and Sweden; nearly half of Norway's municipal waste is treated by incineration with energy recovery, while landfilling has almost disappeared following a landfill ban in 2009 (Figure 1.13). The country will need to significantly increase its recycling capacity. Norway transposed the EU directive of 2018 and still has a way to go to prepare at least 55% of municipal waste for re-use or recycling by 2025; 60% by 2030 and 65% by 2035.

The country has excellent waste treatment facilities, with cutting edge technology for waste sorting. While more flexible regulations are needed, extended producer responsibility schemes and better incentives are key to creating demand for secondary raw materials, notably in the construction sector. Technical building standards need to be adjusted to enable increased use of recycled building materials.

Bio-waste collection in Norway was introduced in the 1990s. Today, about 70% of Norwegians live in municipalities with source separation of bio-waste and door-to-door collection of food waste. The collection rate from households is estimated at 69%. To fill the gap, collection of "household-like" food waste could be made mandatory as suggested by the Environment Protection Agency in 2017. Collected food waste is increasingly used for biogas production. For example, a biogas plant has been producing green fuel for Oslo's city buses since 2014.

Figure 1.13. Norway uses incineration with energy recovery but needs to further boost recycling

Municipal waste management, by type of treatment, 2019

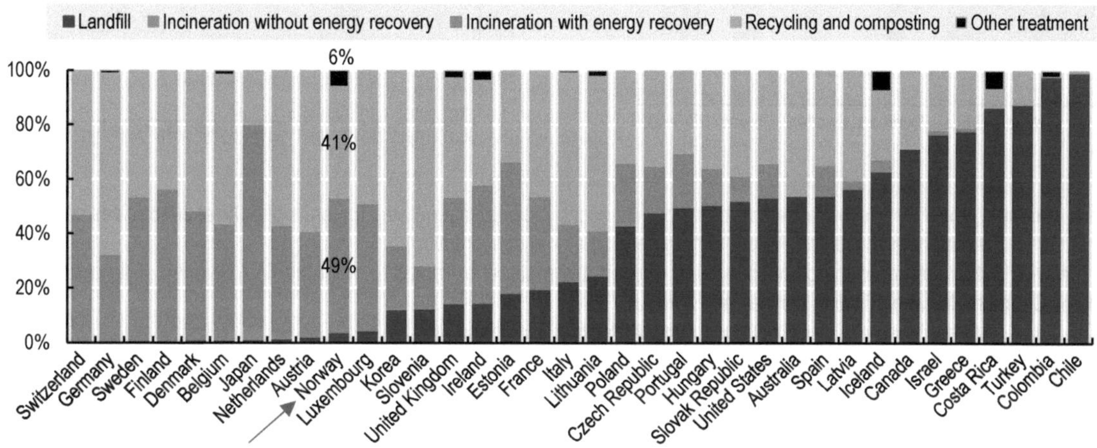

Note: Household and similar waste collected by or for municipalities. Includes bulky waste and separate collection. Canada: data include construction and demolition waste. Latvia: data for "other treatment" refer to biodegradable waste recovery for biogas production.
Source: OECD (2021), "Waste: Municipal waste", *OECD Environment Statistics* (database).

StatLink https://stat.link/kfo63t

Circular economy and global material footprint

Promoting sustainable consumption patterns is a key challenge for Norway. The country has one of the world's highest material consumption rates, a high material footprint per capita and low material productivity (Figure 1.14). The government released its first strategy for developing a green, circular economy in July 2021. The strategy sees the transition to a circular economy as an opportunity to foster value creation and sustainability (Ministry of Climate and Environment, 2021[28]). It has broad scope and largely applies the new EU Circular Economy Action Plan 2020 (European Commission, 2020[29]). The linear pattern of "take-make-use-dispose" does not provide producers with sufficient incentives to make their products more circular. Only a small share of products is cycled back into the Norwegian economy (Circular Norway, 2020[30]).

As the European Union sets global standards in product sustainability, Norway could benefit from a stronger focus on life cycle thinking, eco-design, the right to repair, etc. Policy makers need to create an enabling environment to facilitate the transition towards a circular economy. Typically for many developed economies, material footprint originates in part from outside Norway. A more holistic strategy would allow

Norway to better understand and consider global environmental impacts. Actions should tackle all economic areas to reduce Norway's material footprint (e.g. construction, forestry and wood products, energy transition, circular food systems). They should focus on reducing absolute levels of resource consumption. This involves further educating and empowering consumers to make informed decisions (e.g. use of sustainability labels).

Figure 1.14. Norway has low material productivity and a high material footprint per capita

Material productivity and material footprint, Nordic countries and OECD averages

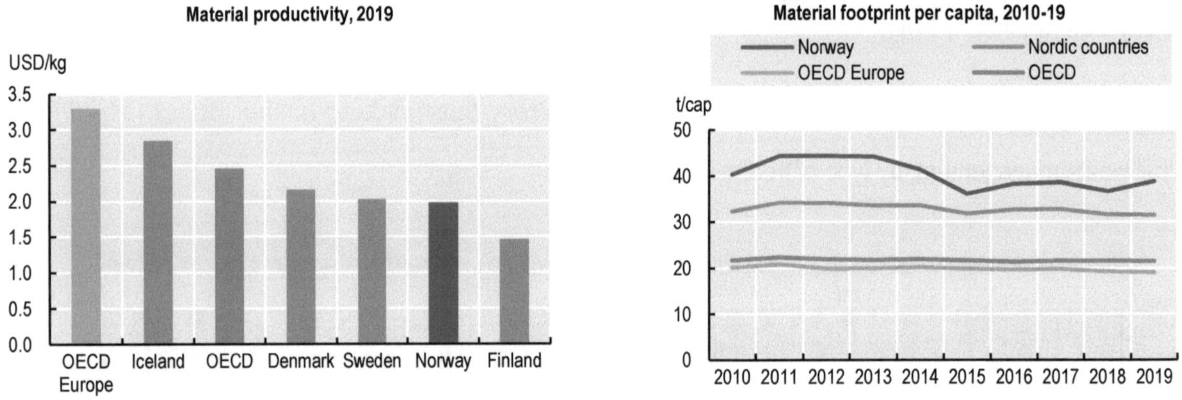

Note: Left panel: Material productivity is expressed as the amount of economic output generated (in terms of GDP at 2015 prices and purchasing power parities) per unit of materials consumed (in terms of domestic material consumption).
Right panel: Material footprint refers to the global allocation of used raw material extracted to meet the final demand of an economy. Nordic countries include Denmark, Iceland, Finland, Norway and Sweden.
Source: OECD (2022), "Material resources", *OECD Environment Statistics* (database).

StatLink https://stat.link/ehqft6

1.3. Progress towards climate targets

1.3.1. Main policies and measures

Norway is a frontrunner in advancing climate action. Already in 2007, Norway pledged to be the first country to become carbon-neutral by 2050. Parliament approved a proposal in 2016 to accelerate carbon emission cuts and carbon offsetting to reach this ambitious goal by 2030. In parallel, Norway also committed to zero deforestation, making it the first nation to ban public procurements that contribute to rainforest destruction. In 2021, Norway's government presented the comprehensive "Climate Action Plan for the Transformation of Norwegian Society as a Whole by 2030" as a way towards a carbon-neutral future (Ministry of Climate and Environment, 2021[15]).

Norway's climate policy builds on the objectives of the global climate agenda. The country participates in the implementation of the UN Framework Convention on Climate Change (UNFCCC), the Kyoto Protocol and the Paris Agreement. Participation in the EU Emissions Trading System (ETS) was a major factor in achieving Norway's commitments under the Kyoto Protocol (2008-12 and 2013-20), along with carbon credits under the Clean Development Mechanism and domestic measures. The 2017 Climate Change Act, the 2020 Nationally Determined Contribution under the Paris Agreement and the Climate Action Plan 2021-30 lay out the framework of Norway's climate action. The government provides annual reporting on both mitigation and adaptation efforts to Parliament.

Norway defined the following climate goals:

- **Climate target for 2030**: reduce GHG emissions by at least 50% and towards 55% by 2030 compared to 1990 levels (enhanced target, initially: 40%).
- **Climate neutrality by 2030**: emissions must be offset by climate action through emissions trading systems or other international co-operation.
- **A low-emission society by 2050:** reduce GHG emissions by at least 90-95% by 2050 compared to 1990 levels (enhanced target, initially 80-95%).

These national targets are among the most ambitious worldwide, going beyond the commitments of many other OECD countries. They are closely aligned with the enhanced ambition of the EU-wide 2030 Climate and Energy Framework under the EU Green Deal (European Commission, 2019[5]) (Table 1.1). Moreover, many counties, cities and municipalities have set net zero goals and contribute to fulfilling Norway's national ambitions. The city of Oslo has an ambitious climate action plan and climate budget covering all relevant sectors. Norway benefits from broad political consensus and popular support for climate action. According to one report, 61% of Norwegians believe that on a global scale their country will succeed in reducing climate gas emissions, while 39% believe that climate change is the greatest challenge of our time (Kantar, 2020[31]).

Box 1.1. Norway's main climate policy initiatives 2016-21

June 2016: Government ratifies the Paris Agreement on Climate Change.

June 2016: Parliament adopts climate neutrality target for 2030.

June 2017: Climate Change Act sets legally binding long-term goal of a low-carbon society by 2050.

October 2019: Government adopts EU agreement to expand co-operation for 2021-30, notably covering non-ETS sectors.

February 2020: Government submits enhanced Nationally Determined Contribution to the UNFCCC.

September 2020: Government launches Longship project on CCS (Box 1.6).

January 2021: Government presents Climate Action Plan 2021-30.

April 2021: Government launches Strategy for Climate Adaptation, Prevention of Climate-related Disasters, Fight against Hunger.

1.3.2. Close co-operation between Norway and the European Union

Norway plans to fulfil its climate commitment in close collaboration with the European Union, drawing on its long-standing climate partnership within the European Economic Area (EEA) Agreement (Table 1.1). Norway has participated in the EU ETS since 2008, which covers about half of Norwegian emissions. Moreover, the European Union, Norway and Iceland adopted a new co-operation agreement in 2019, covering 2021-30 and expanding the scope of the climate partnership. Under the EU Effort Sharing Regulation, Norway commits to reduce GHG emissions in sectors outside the scope of EU ETS (agriculture, transport, waste, building sectors and small industrial/commercial facilities) by 40% compared to 2005 levels. Norway also committed to applying the no-debit rule under the EU regulation on land use, land-use change and forestry (LULUCF). By participating in all three pillars of EU climate policies, Norway contributes to achieving the EU's ambition to become the first climate-neutral continent.

Table 1.1. Norway and EU commitments to reduce GHG emissions, compared to 1990 levels

Goals	Norway's Climate Change Act 2017	Norway's Nationally Determined Contribution 2020	EU Climate and Energy Framework 2030 (released in 2020)
2030 target	at least 40% emission cuts	at least 50% and up towards 55% emission cuts	at least 55% net emission cuts
2050 target	at least 80-95% emission cuts	at least 90-95% emission cuts	remaining emissions need to be balanced off
Climate neutrality	no mention	by 2030, parliamentary decision of 2016	by 2050, legally binding law (approved by EU Parliament and the European Council in June 2021)

Source: Ministry of Environment and Climate (2021); EU Climate and Energy Framework 2030 (2020).

1.3.3. Greenhouse gas emissions trends and projections

Norway is a small GHG emitter with absolute emission levels similar to other Nordic countries. Despite its small population size and significant oil and gas production, Norway's emission level per capita (9.4 tonnes of CO_2-eq) remained below the OECD average of 11.3 tonnes in 2019. In terms of emission intensity, Norway recorded one of the lowest levels in the OECD area (OECD, 2022[32]). Similar to other OECD countries, energy industries, dominated by oil and gas production, are the largest emitting sector (Figure 1.15). They contribute to nearly a third of the country's GHG emissions. Despite targeted climate action, the transport sector still contributes about a quarter of Norway's emissions. It is followed by industrial processes and product use, agriculture, residential and other sectors and fugitive emissions from fuel. The structure of emissions is expected to remain substantially unaltered by 2030 (Figure 1.16).

Norway has decoupled emissions from GDP growth. Since 1990, Norway's emission levels varied between 47.5 million (1992) and 56.9 million tonnes of CO_2-eq (2007) (Figure 1.15). After peaking in 2007, domestic GHG emissions have declined, albeit more consistently in the second half of the 2010s. In 2020, they were about 10% lower than in 2010 but only about 4% lower than in 1990 (Statistics Norway, 2021[33]).

Figure 1.15. Norway's GHG emissions are close to 1990 levels

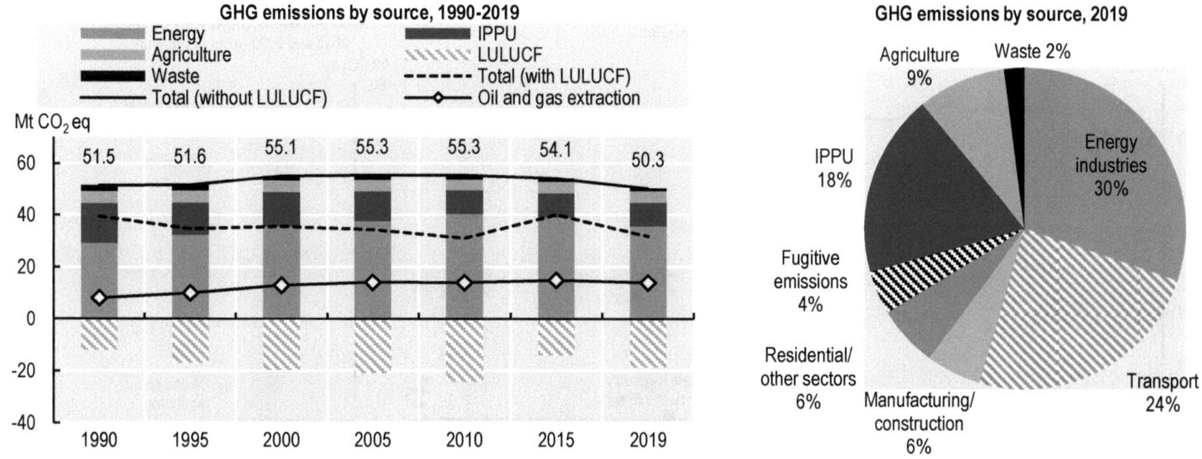

Note: IPPU = industrial processes and product use. LULUCF = land use, land-use change and forestry.
Source: UNFCCC (2021), *Greenhouse Gas Inventory* (database).

StatLink https://stat.link/apt8h9

The starting point for emissions reductions in Norway was low because its energy mix was already largely decarbonised, leaving few remaining quick wins. The expansion of offshore oil and gas resources over the past decades also contributed to increasing GHG emissions (Figure 1.15). These emissions have been relatively decoupled from production since 2016. The Norwegian petroleum industry has comparatively high environmental and climate standards. Many oil and gas companies committed to reach net zero emissions by 2050.

Despite the economy-wide decarbonisation efforts, Norway is far from reaching its initial goal of cutting 40% of emissions by 2030, and even more so from its enhanced goal of 50% and towards 55%. According to projections of the 2022 National Budget (Ministry of Finance, 2021[34]), Norway will emit around 41.2 million tonnes of CO_2-eq by 2030 (Figure 1.16). This represents a reduction of 20% of emissions compared to the 1990 level. These estimates do not yet include measures of the Climate Action Plan 2021-30 or the effects of Norway's participation in the EU ETS. There is also some uncertainty regarding calculation methods of the effects of Norway's EU ETS participation. However, Norway will likely face a gap to achieve the 2030 emissions reduction target.

The government intends to accelerate domestic emission cuts. The Climate Action Plan 2021-30 sets out detailed targets and policy measures for each sector with a view to reaching a 45% reduction in the non-ETS sector (exceeding the EU target of 40%). However, promoting low-carbon technologies is costly in the short term. Norway needs to further analyse impacts of policies to improve the cost effectiveness of existing measures (Section 1.5.3). With high marginal costs of reducing domestic GHG emissions, the purchase of foreign emission credits often makes economic sense. Moreover, Norway's large forest areas – about a third of total land area – provide a substantial carbon sink, representing nearly half of annual GHG emissions. Natural carbon stocks of mainland Norway are more than twice as large as the average for the world's land areas. Norway is on track to increase forest cover and enhance carbon sinks (Climate Action Tracker, 2021[35]). Ongoing efforts are needed.

Figure 1.16. Norway has a way to go to reach its 2030 climate targets

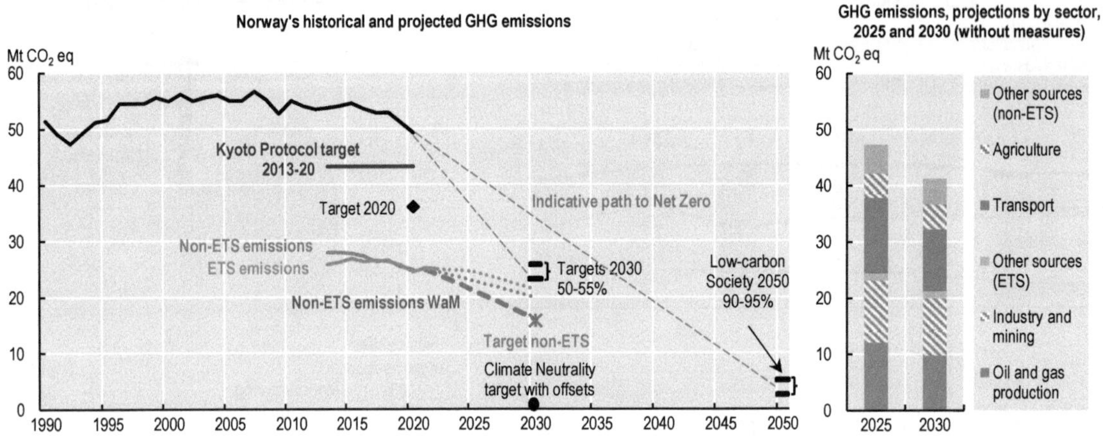

Note: IPCC = Intergovernmental Panel on Climate Change; LULUCF = land use, land-use change and forestry. The projections and effort sharing target apply different metrics (Global Warming Potential of IPCC's fourth and fifth Assessment Reports, respectively). The dotted line shows GHG emissions projections with existing measures. The dashed line (with additional measures - WaM) shows projections for the non-ETS sector, including the measures of the Climate Action Plan 2021-30. Data exclude emissions trading. Norway co-operates with the European Union to fulfil the 2030 climate target. The impact of this co-operation, especially Norway's participation in the EU Emissions Trading System, must be considered in assessing progress towards this target. Thus, reduction in domestic emissions cannot be used as the sole indicator to assess Norway's progress.
Source: EEA (2021), Member States' greenhouse gas emission projections (database); ESA (2021), Climate Progress Report 2021; Statistics Norway (2021), "Table 08940", StatBank (database).

StatLink https://stat.link/erd0y3

1.3.4. Norway's global carbon footprint

As Norway is a small and open economy, the focus on national GHG emissions alone provides only a partial picture of Norway's global carbon footprint. While the country is not legally responsible for GHG emissions outside Norway, implicit emissions from its oil and gas used abroad are significant. However, as most Norwegian oil and gas are exported to Europe, embodied emissions are largely covered by ETS or non-ETS European carbon-pricing mechanisms (OECD, 2022[20]).

In today's interconnected world, as do other OECD countries, Norway needs to look for a more coherent approach to climate and environmental policies. Such policies should better reflect the country's global carbon footprint and spillover environmental impacts. These impacts include transboundary pollution flows; environmental impacts embedded in traded goods and services; and exploitation of international common pool resources.

International institutions are developing indicators and new metrics to better capture international spillover effects. Norway could usefully develop national indicators using environmentally extended multi-regional input-output, material flow analysis and life cycle assessment to better understand its economy-wide global footprints. This could help better track the environmental impact of trade. Such results could inform environmental impact assessments (EIAs) during the permitting and licensing process.

1.3.5. Decarbonising transport

Transport demand is growing, and emission cuts in the transport sector thus play a key role in achieving Norway's climate and environmental goals. It is difficult to make robust projections on future transport demand. This is especially the case given uncertainty related to long-term impacts of the COVID-19 pandemic (e.g. teleworking, demand for air travel, reduction of unnecessary travel, challenges related to social distancing in public transport, etc.).

Norway has set ambitious transport decarbonisation policies. Its Climate Action Plan 2021-30 sets out key objectives for the transport sector, which aims at halving emissions in 2030 compared with 2005 levels, beyond the EU target of 40%. The government's transport goals, strategies and priorities are detailed in the National Transport Plan 2022-33 (Ministry of Transport, 2021[36]). A broad range of economic instruments and regulatory instruments is used to decarbonise all transport sectors (Section 1.5).

Norway has comparatively high levels of short-distance, infra-national air traffic due to the large number of fjords, offshore islands and sparsely populated mountainous areas. Domestic aviation contributed to 9% of GHG emissions in the transport sector (Figure 1.17). The EU ETS has so far been the main policy instrument for the aviation industry.

For a long time, the rapidly growing demand for mobility has outpaced progress in decarbonising the transport sector. Transport emissions peaked in 2012 (15 million tonnes of CO_2-eq) and decreased by 8.9% from 2005 to 2019. The impacts of Norway's EV rollout and related emission cuts became strongly visible as of 2016 (Figure 1.17). According to national projections, transport emissions are projected to decrease by nearly one-third from 2019 to 2030. Nevertheless, Norway needs to further accelerate electrification of the transport sector to halve transport GHG emissions by 2030.

Figure 1.17. Emissions from road transport and domestic navigation are shrinking

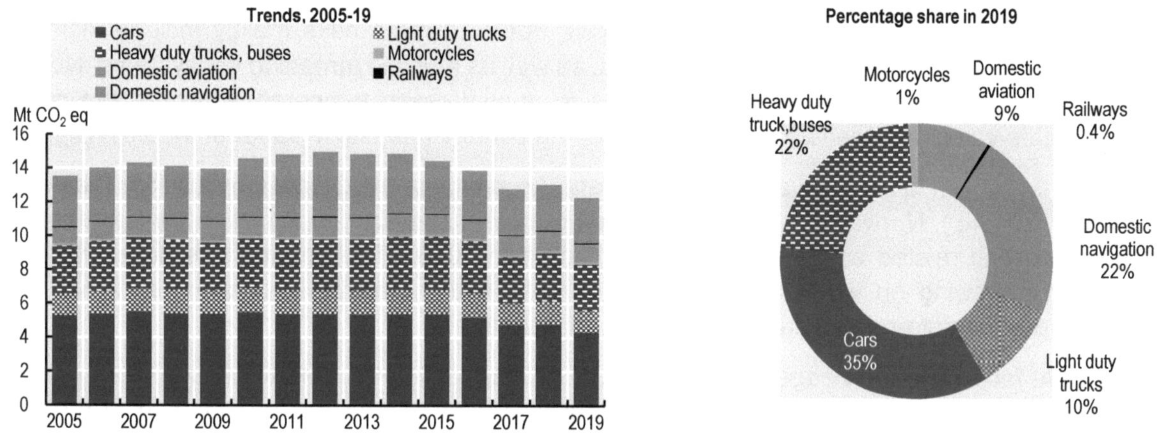

Source: UNFCCC (2021), *Greenhouse Gas Inventory* (database).

StatLink https://stat.link/5nre3z

1.3.6. Towards sustainable transport systems

Road transportation remains the privileged mode in Norway. In 2020, of 5.7 million registered vehicles, some 2.8 million were passenger cars (Statistics Norway, 2021[37]). Norway has more vehicles than people. It will be important to take a broader approach to electric mobility and promote structural changes towards shared mobility and integrated sustainable services.

The implementation of the zero-growth goal through Urban Growth Agreements has helped reduce car traffic volumes, cut emissions and improve the quality of life in Norway's major cities. Such agreements should be rapidly extended to medium-sized cities and smaller urban areas.

The National Transport Plan sets a long-term goal of a 20% share of cycling in urban areas and 8% nationwide. Some 173 km and 322 km of cycle-friendly infrastructure was created in 2019 and 2020, respectively. However, Norway does not have a targeted strategy to translate its national commitment into practice; investment priorities remain mostly focused on the road sector. While acknowledging specific needs of its sparsely populated areas,[4] Norway could make it a stronger priority to develop more and cheaper alternatives to private vehicle use. The government could further re-orient investments in more sustainable transport systems and public transport. This would also bring broader societal benefits for people's health while improving accessibility.

Despite its great achievements in the EV sector, Norway needs to redouble efforts and make more structural changes to establish sustainable transport systems to meet its 2030 target. This involves promoting behavioural changes, placing a stronger focus on shared mobility services and shifting from increased mobility towards improved accessibility. The rail system needs to be further modernised and become a cheaper alternative to road and air transport. Airport expansion is counterproductive to reducing GHG emissions and environmental concerns need to be better reflected in any new plans. This is an opportune moment to rethink mobility and develop a socially fair and spatially balanced transport system.

1.3.7. Climate change adaptation

Annual mean temperature for mainland Norway has increased by about 0.8°C and annual precipitation by nearly 20% over the past 100 years (OECD, 2013[38]). Future climate risks mainly include increasing exposure to extreme weather events and related risks, as well as multiple threats to ecosystems. Northern Norway is likely to experience the greatest changes in annual mean temperature, where the median warming estimates varies between 2-6°C by the end of the century (Hanssen-Bauer et al., 2017[39]).

Norway has so far proven to be relatively climate resilient. According to the Global Climate Risk Index 2020 (Eckstein et al., 2019[40]), Norway was among the least climate-vulnerable countries in terms of fatalities, material damage and related economic losses (ranked 94 in 2018). The country has developed early warning systems drawing on various specialised agencies and monitoring programmes. It has good capacity to adapt to climate-related hazards and natural disasters.

The government facilitates knowledge sharing to make society less vulnerable to climate change via an online platform (Klimatilpasning.no) targeting municipalities. Adaptation is an integral part of municipal responsibilities. Local authorities can draw on planning guidelines aimed at improving coherence in the application of instruments in local adaptation work. KLIMAFORSK, a ten-year climate programme of the Research Council of Norway, aims to raise knowledge and awareness of climate change. Norway also contributes to the EU-wide knowledge-sharing platform Climate-ADAPT and to the implementation of the EU Strategy on Adaptation to Climate Change.

1.4. Institutions, regulation and compliance

1.4.1. Institutional framework

Norway is a unitary state with an administrative structure composed of three levels: national (central government), regional (counties) and local (municipalities) (Figure 1.18). Municipalities and county authorities have the same administrative status. The central government supervises municipal and county administrations. The county governor is the main representative of the central government in charge of supervising local authorities. Governors can also receive appeals against many municipal decisions. This makes governors an important link between local and national levels.

All decisions on environment-related legislation and taxation are made by the 169-seat unicameral Parliament (*Storting*), which is elected every four years. The Norwegian government is responsible to Parliament. Reports on the state of the environment are included in the annual state budget for the Ministry of Climate and Environment. The Sami Parliament (*Sametinget*) promotes the language and the interests of the Sami population.

Local authorities are responsible for most aspects of environmental management. Municipalities manage local pollution control, while county governors and the Norwegian Environment Agency control pollution at the regional and national levels, under the guidance of the Ministry of Climate and Environment. Academics and advisory bodies are closely involved in policy formulation. The short distance between research and policy-making bodies is a clear asset of the Norwegian system. Policy making is transparent and public consultations are conducted for all draft laws. Norwegian citizens place a high level of trust in public institutions and the judiciary system in particular. Norway reported the second highest confidence in national government among OECD members in 2020 (83%, compared to 68% in 2006) (OECD, 2021[41]).

With about 700 000 inhabitants, the capital city of Oslo is the largest municipality and also has the status of a county. Oslo has a dedicated climate strategy along with comprehensive plans for land use, housing and transportation for the whole Oslo area (City of Oslo, 2020[42]). However, only ten municipalities have more than 50 000 inhabitants and most have fewer than 5 000.

The government initiated a major reform in 2014 to strengthen local democracy by transferring power and responsibility to larger, more robust municipalities and regions. The reforms aim to secure professional welfare services throughout the country, develop sustainable entities and advance local planning. In 2017, the government decided to reduce the number of counties from 19 to 11 and encouraged municipalities to merge voluntarily. In line with the European trend of municipal amalgamation, the number of Norwegian municipalities has progressively decreased since the early 1960s. As of 2020, Norway is divided into 11 counties and 356 municipalities (down from 428). The mergers created six new counties. With more than 1.2 million inhabitants, the new county of Viken is the most populous, accounting for nearly a quarter of total population. Some county mergers have been controversial, but counties may be able to undo them.

Norway needs to capitalise on existing spatial development dynamics. This can help improve the quality of public services and promote balanced regional development. While mergers provide opportunities for efficiency gains, they also need to make sense for people and maximise societal well-being. Building trust and improving well-being are both critical prerequisites to gain social acceptance for territorial reforms. Cost-benefit analysis and *ex post* evaluations of recent mergers could help better understand short- and long-term impacts and inform a healthy public debate about the future.

National government and horizontal co-ordination

Norway was among the first countries to establish a Ministry of Environment in 1972 (renamed the Ministry of Climate and Environment in 2014). Over time, it has developed an extensive framework for environmental policy. The ministry initiates, develops, implements and monitors measures to protect the environment. It also seeks to mainstream green policies and influence sectoral ministries. In addition, it co-ordinates the government's environmental policy objectives. Its core tasks include formulating government policies; preparing white papers, national plans and guidelines; and issuing regulations. A large number of decentralised advisory bodies and implementation agencies support its work (Box 1.2).

Many sectors contribute to achieving Norway's environmental objectives by incorporating environmental concerns and measures. The Ministry of Petroleum and Energy manages energy resources (oil, gas, hydropower and renewables), while the Ministry of Transport implements sustainable mobility policies. For its part, the Ministry of Agriculture and Food is responsible for sustainable agriculture and forest management. The Ministry of Local Government and Regional Development oversees many management tasks under the Planning and Building Act and has shared responsibility for EIAs. It also co-ordinates the government's work on sustainable development.

Decision making in Norway is strongly consensus-oriented, benefiting from close ministerial co-operation. The country also uses extensive informal co-ordination between cabinet and parliamentary committees and party organisations, which further smooths the decision-making process. A line ministry usually leads on a specific process and co-ordinates with other relevant ministries and stakeholders. If other ministries agree, the government can move forward with a new law, white paper or guidelines. In case of disagreement, a consensus is built in cabinet meetings. The recent transfer of some agencies to the Ministry of Climate and Environment reflects Norway's commitment to bring stronger attention to climate and environmental issues (Box 1.2).

Box 1.2. Norway's specialised environmental-focused bodies

Enova

The Trondheim-based state-owned enterprise helps reduce GHG emissions and develop new energy and climate technology. In 2018, the responsibility for Enova was transferred from the Ministry of Petroleum and Energy to the Ministry of Climate and Environment. This reflects Enova's growing importance as a climate instrument and favours a more holistic approach to climate policy development.

Norwegian Environment Agency

The Norwegian Environment Agency plays a key role in ensuring implementation of environmental policies, managing nature and preventing pollution. It serves as Norway's regulatory authority, conducts inspections, monitors the state of the environment and advises the ministry on key environmental challenges. It was created in 2013, following a merger of the former Climate and Pollution Agency and the Norwegian Directorate for Nature Management, and is professionally independent. The Norwegian Nature Inspectorate (SNO) is part of the agency.

Norwegian Biodiversity Information Centre

The Norwegian Biodiversity Information Centre develops and spreads knowledge on biodiversity. Work draws on close co-operation with the scientific community, as well as with policy makers, managers and other data users.

The Norwegian Meteorological Institute (MET Norway)

Created in 1866, MET Norway is Norway's oldest environmental institute. It provides weather forecasts, climate monitoring, emergency preparedness and research in meteorology, oceanography and climatology. In 2018, MET Norway was transferred from the Ministry of Education and Research to the Ministry of Climate and Environment.

Norwegian Polar Institute (NPI)

Established in 1948, the Norwegian Polar Research Institute is a directorate under the Ministry of Climate and Environment that focuses on environmental management needs in the Arctic and Antarctic. It is in charge of scientific research, mapping and environmental monitoring of the polar regions, and operates research stations in Svalbard and in the Antarctic.

Directorate for Cultural Heritage and Norwegian Cultural Heritage Fund

The directorate acts as the advisory and executive body of the Ministry of Climate and Environment for the management of the cultural environment. As of 2020, counties are in charge of most management tasks in the cultural environment area. The Norwegian Cultural Heritage Fund is a subordinate agency of the Department of Cultural Heritage.

Svalbard Environmental Protection Fund

The fund's resources initiate promising projects to conserve and protect the rich natural environment and cultural heritage on the Svalbard islands in line with the Act on Protection of the Environment in Svalbard.

Norwegian Centre against Marine Litter

The centre was established in 2018 as a subordinate agency of the Ministry of Transport, known as Norwegian Centre for Oil Spill Preparedness and Marine Environment. From January 2022, it became a government agency under the Ministry of Climate and Environment. It is located in northern Norway on Lofoten Island. As of 2022, it will provide, among others, expertise on marine litter prevention and management, and will co-ordinate and provide financial support for clean-up activities.

Source: Country submission.

Local government and vertical co-ordination

Norway applies the subsidiary principle to perform tasks at the lowest effective level. A general trend towards decentralisation has been observed over the past decades. Norway has emphasised local democracy, acknowledging that challenges and opportunities vary from place to place. It has highlighted the value of locally tailored solutions in the context of great geographic dispersion.

Every four years, the central government sets national expectations regarding regional and municipal planning with a view to promoting sustainable development throughout the country. The 2019-23 national expectations document (Ministry of Local Government and Modernisation, 2019[43]) provides an overview of the relevant central government planning guidelines to support county and municipal planning (Section 2.5).

Counties are mainly responsible for regional development policies, secondary education, regional roads and environmental issues, including those related to the cultural environment. The county municipality, governed by a council, is the democratically elected body for the region. Responsibilities of county municipalities are largely defined by government rules and regulations. Recently, they took over all tasks related to secured outdoor recreation areas in order to pool resources and promote more efficient and predictable management. The new government intends to further strengthen their role as a community developer.

Municipalities provide a large number of welfare services and are responsible for most aspects of environmental management. They also increasingly participate in the management of protected areas and play an important role in reaching Norway's ambitious climate goals. Some municipalities have a dedicated environment officer.

Despite large differences in geography, area and population size, municipalities have the same rights and responsibilities. Smaller municipalities often have limited capacity and face many challenges to fulfil all required functions. Differences in implementation capacity, the influence of local interests and greater institutional autonomy have led to uneven application of environmental regulations and national guidelines. Limited local capacity has also contributed to developing increased inter-municipality co-operation, particularly on waste management. However, it is crucial to further strengthen the capacity of small municipalities, especially in remote areas. They often face trade-offs between economic, social and environmental objectives. Norway could benefit from stronger inter-municipal learning to share expertise and good practices.

Figure 1.18. Local authorities are responsible for most aspects of environmental management

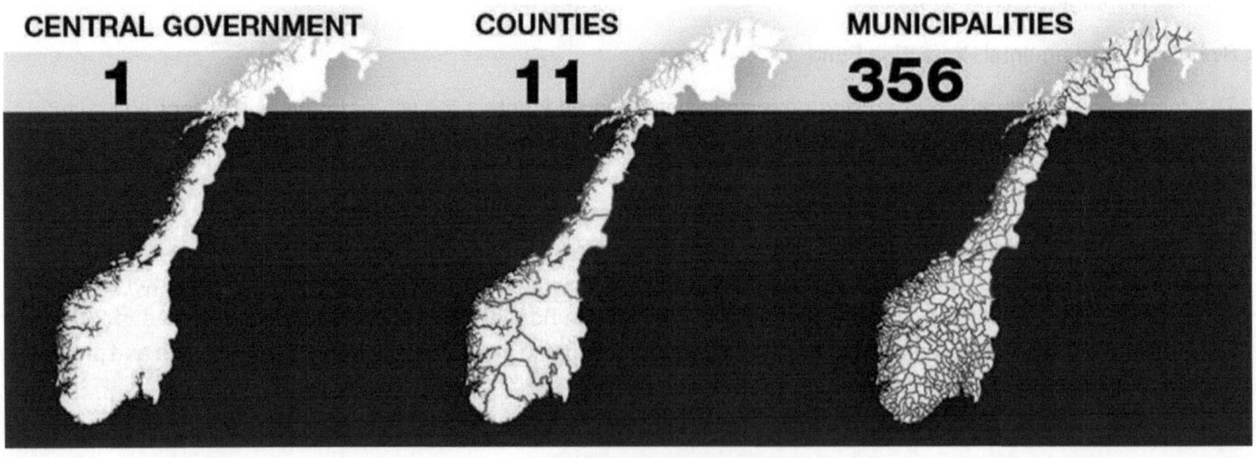

Note: Image adjusted from the Norwegian Agency for Local Governments (KBN).
Source: Country submission.

1.4.2. Regulatory framework for environmental management

As a member of the EEA, Norway applies many environment-relevant EU directives (e.g. the WFD, EU Waste Framework, EU air quality directives, chemicals regulations). On climate action, Norway has been part of the EU ETS since 2008. In 2019, Norway, Iceland and the European Union agreed to strengthen their co-operation to fulfil the 2030 climate target. Norway committed to applying the Effort Sharing Regulation and the LULUCF Regulation in 2021-30. Substantial parts of legislative proposals related to the European Green Deal will fall within the scope of the EEA Agreement. Norway has also developed its own national regulatory frameworks in areas outside the scope of the EEA (e.g. for agriculture, fisheries, biodiversity).

Environmental assessment

Norway has more than 30 years of experience with environmental assessments. EIAs – a vital tool for integrating environmental concerns into project approval – have contributed to an orderly planning process and strengthened public engagement in Norway. Planning is further supported by strategic environmental assessment (SEA), which focuses on potentially significant environmental impact of proposed plans, programmes or policies.

Norway incorporated EU directives of 2014 on EIA and SEA into its legal system in 2017. The country's environmental assessment system has three separate processes: one for land-based projects, one for maritime projects and a dedicated process for projects on Svalbard.[5] An EIA decision is mandatory for all category 1 operations (major industrial and infrastructure projects); without a validated EIA, no permit can be issued. For facilities with lower environmental impacts, permits are sometimes granted without an EIA. The Norwegian Environment Agency maintains a dedicated web portal that offers guidance and examples of good practices on EIA and SEA.

Since 2013, the Ministry of Climate and Environment and the Ministry of Local Government and Modernisation have shared responsibility for environmental assessments. These processes are primarily integrated into the ordinary procedure for land-use planning and applications for licences and permits. The Norwegian system applies an integrated approach involving "competent authorities" – either the relevant municipality or a sectoral authority. For example, road authorities take decisions on major road transport infrastructure; energy authorities examine energy-related projects. The competent local, regional or sectoral authority makes the final decision, which interested parties can challenge in court.

While environmental assessments are conducted at national level for major projects (e.g. national infrastructure, renewable energy projects), local municipalities are responsible for EIA in most cases. The local authority may be both the applicant and the competent authority. This double role creates a potential conflict of interest, particularly in smaller municipalities, as there is no independent authority in the approval process. The local authority is required to act objectively and the "two roles shall as far as possible be kept administratively separate" (Ministry of Climate and Environment, 2017[44]). In practice, however, local interests may sometimes lead to sub-optimal decisions as regards environmental outcomes: EIAs may address only direct and immediate on-site effects. Limited local capacity can also undermine the quality of the EIA process. Every municipality should benefit from the expertise of a dedicated environmental officer. More room should be given to independent, critical, interdisciplinary voices in local decision-making processes.

Box 1.3. Improving environmental impact assessment in the Arctic region

The Arctic region is characterised by sparse population, unique biodiversity, fragile ecosystems and slow flora and fauna recovery rates from disturbance. The Norwegian Arctic is home to close to half a million people. On average, about 10% of the population is indigenous. The Arctic EIA project – involving members of the Arctic Council* – gathered examples of good practices from across the Arctic. Findings are presented in a report that identified three broad areas for improvement: i) meaningful engagement; ii) use of different types of knowledge – indigenous, local and scientific; and iii) transboundary environmental impacts. Public participation in the early planning phase is a key feature of the EIA process. It is especially relevant for the fragile Arctic areas where impact assessments must be better informed by people with knowledge and expertise of local livelihoods. This can be a lengthy process and requires a lot of flexibility. The report recommends building a relationship and trust among the affected communities at the earliest possible stage. Competent authorities "need to talk to scientists and locals at the same time – not scientists first and locals after" (SDWG, 2019[45]). Some members of the Sami Reindeer Herders' Association of Norway suspect consultation processes are undermined by asymmetric information, unequal negotiation power and lack of transparency. Investors might be tempted to strike a deal with locals that may neither benefit all members of affected communities nor allow protection of biodiversity and fragile ecosystems. Promoting effective and meaningful engagement and incorporating indigenous knowledge remains a common challenge in the Arctic region. The report stresses that dialogue has to be seen to help find better solutions and more strongly influence project design at an early stage. This requires continuous dialogue, beyond one-off consultations. As in other countries, EIAs need to better inform the project design and decision-making process; the engagement needs to be pursued throughout the mitigation and monitoring phases. The follow-up component is nearly always missing.

Note: *Canada, Denmark, Finland, Iceland, Norway, the Russian Federation, Sweden and the United States.
Source: (Arctic Council, Sustainable Development Working Group, 2019[46]).

Environmental permitting and licensing

Environmental permitting is a key instrument for reducing industry's environmental impacts while also promoting technological innovation. Norway has integrated environmental permits. Applications for pollution control permits for businesses must be submitted to the Norwegian Environment Agency or to the environmental department of the pertinent county governor, depending on risk and the scale of projected environmental impacts. The Norwegian pollution control system has a high degree of transparency. Within the Pollution Release and Transfer Register (Norwegian Environment Agency, 2021[47]), all permits, inspection and annual compliance reports are available on line. The website provides access to permitting and inspection information accompanied with data visualisation tools on reported emission and plant-specific information such as production outputs. This helps users visualise the plant's impact on the environment. The European Environmental Bureau commended Norway for "offering citizens industrial pollution permitting information of a high standard and in a user-friendly manner" (EEB, 2017[48]). Norway's information sharing system on industrial pollution ranked the best in Europe (EEB, 2017[48]).

1.4.3. Compliance assurance

Norway has a solid compliance assurance system using a combination of compliance promotion, monitoring and enforcement. The Norwegian Environment Agency and the respective county governors, who conduct inspections, have a joint compliance monitoring strategy for 2016-20 and share a corporate database of inspection results across all sectors. The strategy aims to ensure quick and strict follow-up on serious breaches of regulations; uniform practices through good routines, tools and clear job descriptions; and better and faster communication on inspection results.

Compliance monitoring and promotion

In line with international trends, Norway uses risk-based targeting of compliance monitoring. This approach means that high-risk installations with major environmental impacts and installations with risk for non-compliance are inspected more often. The frequency depends on various factors (emission levels, results from previous inspections and audits, recidivism, etc.). As a consequence, non-compliance detection is higher and does not necessarily represent the general compliance behaviour in the regulated community. In addition, approximately 30% of site inspections are conducted without prior notice. The threat of unannounced site visits has a dissuasive effect and encourages businesses to take steps to ensure compliance throughout the year.

Between 2015-20, Norway conducted about 5 500 inspections of land-based industry; offshore petroleum industry; products and chemicals; regulated species; and various municipal activities. Compliance monitoring also includes desk verification of self-monitoring reports and online checks of products. E-commerce non-compliance is particularly high and requires continued attention.[6] There are fewer inspections than a decade ago (about 2 000 inspections per year) but still more than in the 1990s (about 275 inspections per year) (OECD, 2011[27]). Due to mobility restrictions related to COVID-19, the number of inspections decreased in 2020 (Table 1.2). Businesses fully cover the costs related to the preparation, implementation and follow-up of inspections. Standard rates are specified in the Pollution Control Act.

Table 1.2. Inspections conducted by the Norwegian Environment Agency and at county level

Number of inspections	2015	2016	2017	2018	2019	2020
Inspections conducted at county level	660	705	491	697	683	410
Inspections conducted by the Norwegian Environment Agency	288	285	392	366	284	250
Total number of inspections	948	990	883	1 063	967	660
Inspections with non-compliance*	840	856	718	876	834	561

Note: The number of inspections does not include audits, other control measures or emergency inspections.
*About two-thirds of breaches are related to weaknesses of self-monitoring systems.
Source: Country submission.

Norway has a high rate of non-compliance (60-70% of the checks, including 10% of serious violations). About two-thirds of breaches are related to weaknesses of self-monitoring systems. The high non-compliance rate confirms the quality of Norway's monitoring system and its capacity to detect violations. However, it also underlines a need for stronger compliance monitoring. Moreover, Norway's inspection results need to be interpreted in light of more in-depth compliance monitoring. Such monitoring checks the performance of company-internal environmental management systems whose elements are mandated by law. This makes the Norwegian system unique in the OECD area. The requirements are challenging for smaller companies; many have not sufficiently invested to meet them. They still lack routine checks and knowledge about safety standards and environmental requirements, including for chemical management for imported products. This underlines the importance of inspection campaigns and compliance promotion, which need to be pursued.

Compliance promotion is critical for closing the implementation gap. While the Norwegian Environment Agency primarily monitors compliance, it also publishes various guidelines and provides advice. Inspection activities also contributed to improving the enterprises' knowledge on regulations and compliance. The impact of these activities could be more systematically monitored, beyond the annual reporting of the Norwegian Environment Agency.

Enforcement

Enforcement authorities usually give the offender time to correct the violation before considering sanctions. Administrative penalties are applied in only 2% of inspected cases. Depending on what is considered to be most effective, a combination of administrative and criminal sanctions may be applied. Norway is one of the few OECD countries using coercive fines. This means the fine is only payable if the operator fails to implement prescribed corrective action in a mandated timeframe. This has proven to be an effective enforcement instrument. Over 2016-20, on average, only about 10% of fines need to be paid (13 out of 130 fine notifications); in 90% of cases, operators complied in time.

The government intends to sharpen focus on crime prevention. New measures have been proposed to strengthen criminal prosecution through better review practices, higher penalties, increased use of confiscation and digital solutions. Severe violations are subject to criminal sanctions, including imprisonment. They are handled by the police districts and Økokrim, Norway's specialised agency for combating economic and environmental crime. Established in 1989, Økokrim is being reformed to remove organisational silos and make it more flexible and reactive. It will also have a stronger focus on crime prevention. New measures are also put forward in a white paper (Ministry of Climate and Environment, 2019[49]), which aims at strengthening criminal prosecution through better review practices, higher penalties, increased use of confiscation and digital solutions.

1.5. Environment-related taxes and fossil fuel support

1.5.1. Greening the tax system

Like other Scandinavian countries, Norway is a high tax country with a broad tax base, which allows it to finance its broad social safety net with universal health care and higher education. Norway has a high tax-to-GDP ratio of 38.6% in 2020 and a high value-added tax (VAT) rate of 25% (OECD, 2021[50]).

Norway is a pioneer in using economic instruments for environmental protection to encourage innovation and internalise some of the environmental costs of harmful activities in line with the polluter-pays principle. It was among the first countries to introduce a carbon tax in 1991. Since then, the country has introduced many other environment-related taxes in response to recommendations from green tax commissions and inter-departmental working groups. All per-unit rates of excise duties are adjusted annually in line with estimated inflation, reflecting good practices to maintain their incentive function and revenue. Relevant ministries help design taxes within the annual budget proposals.

According to preliminary 2020 data, the government collected environmental tax revenue of NOK 67.5 billion (USD 7.2 billion), representing 2% of GDP and 5.1% of total government revenue from taxes and social contributions (TSC) (Figure 1.19). This is relatively low compared to the OECD Europe average because of the high weight of other sources of tax revenue, as well as to the environmental tax incentives for EV uptake. However, if environmental taxes work as intended, environmental tax revenue as a share of GDP (and total taxes) should decrease and gradually approach zero. In Norway's case, environmental taxes contributed effectively to reducing environmentally harmful activities. This success, however, undermined the tax base, as illustrated in the example of forgone tax revenues in relation to EVs (Section 1.5.3). As in other OECD countries, energy-related taxes, including taxes on road transport energy, make up the bulk of environment-related taxes (65%), followed by transport taxes (30%); only a small portion comes from waste and other pollution and resource taxes (5%).

Figure 1.19. Norway's share of green taxes has declined, due to a shrinking transport tax base

Environment-related tax revenue by tax base, 2005-20

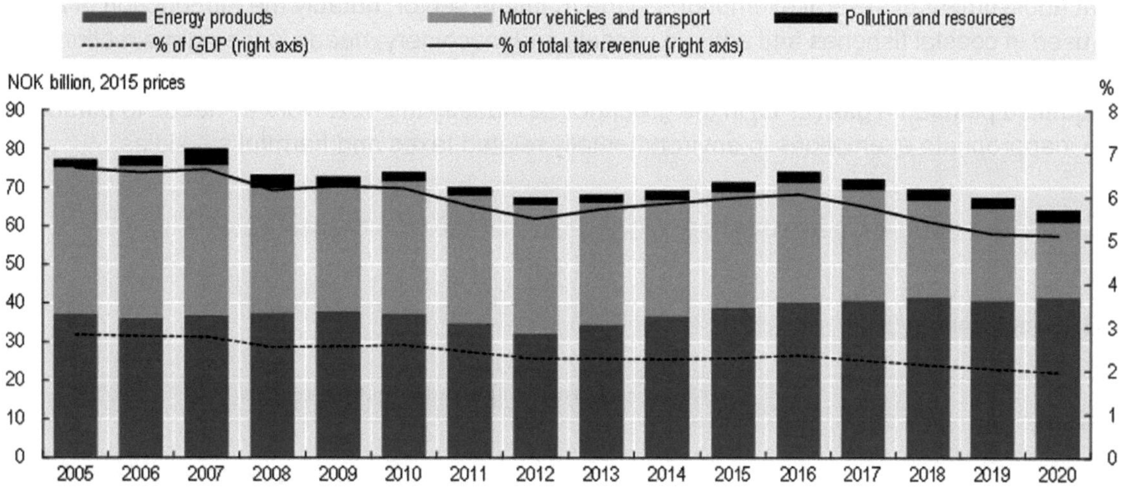

Note: Data include estimates and preliminary data.
Source: OECD (2022), "Environmental policy instruments", *OECD Environment Statistics* (database); Statistics Norway (2022), "Environmental taxes – 10645", *StatBank* (database).

StatLink https://stat.link/9x218m

The share of green taxes in Norway's TSC declined over the past decade from 6.7% in 2005 to 5.1% in 2020 (Figure 1.19). However, a closer look at the breakdown of environmental tax revenue reveals that energy and pollution-related taxes have both increased since 2005. In contrast, transport-related taxes declined slowly from about 50% in 2005 to 42% in 2016, and then recorded a sharp drop reaching about 30% in 2020. This reflects forgone tax revenues in relation to Norway's generous tax incentives for EVs (Table 1.3). While policy measures triggered a strong increase in the purchase of EVs, the related tax revenue losses represented close to a third of environmental tax revenue (Section 1.5.3).

1.5.2. Carbon pricing and taxes on energy use

Norway applies a series of taxes on GHG emissions and energy use. The former include a CO_2 tax on mineral products, a tax on CO_2 emissions from petroleum activities on the continental shelf and taxes for other GHG emissions (e.g. hydrofluorocarbons and perfluorocarbons).[7] Energy taxes include excise taxes on engine fuel, a base tax on mineral oil, a tax on lubricating oil and an electricity tax. In addition, Norway has fully taken part in the EU ETS since 2008 and intends to align with EU measures for the non-ETS sector, with sometimes more stringent targets.[8] According to national assessments, CO_2 taxes and emissions trading cover approximately 85% of national GHG emissions, including offshore production.

Norway's nominal carbon tax rate is among the highest in Europe (NOK 766 [about USD 89]/tonne of CO_2-eq as of 2022) covering 83% of national emissions. Figure 1.20 provides an overview of how energy and carbon taxes apply across the economy. Effective tax rates are high compared to other European OECD countries, especially outside the road transport sector.

Norway ranks among the top OECD countries in carbon pricing. In 2018, it was ranked third on the OECD Carbon Pricing Score based largely on three factors. It has a highly decarbonised electricity supply. It also charges significant taxes on fossil fuels in the residential and commercial sector. Finally, it double taxes emissions from petroleum extraction and aviation via a national carbon tax and the EU ETS (OECD, 2021[51]).

Nevertheless, it should pursue efforts to ensure uniform application of the carbon tax across all sectors. The recent abolishment of several exemptions in the maritime sector, notably the introduction of a CO_2 tax on diesel used in coastal fisheries and antique vessels and machinery, heads in the right direction. Norway has also introduced a carbon tax on waste incineration and abolished the exemption for the use of natural gas and liquefied petroleum gas (LPG) in the greenhouse industry in 2022. Norway needs to pursue efforts to remove inappropriate exemptions in environmentally related taxes and harmful subsidies.

Figure 1.20. Norway applies a nominal carbon tax rate of NOK 766 to over 80% of national emissions

Prices of GHG emissions in 2022

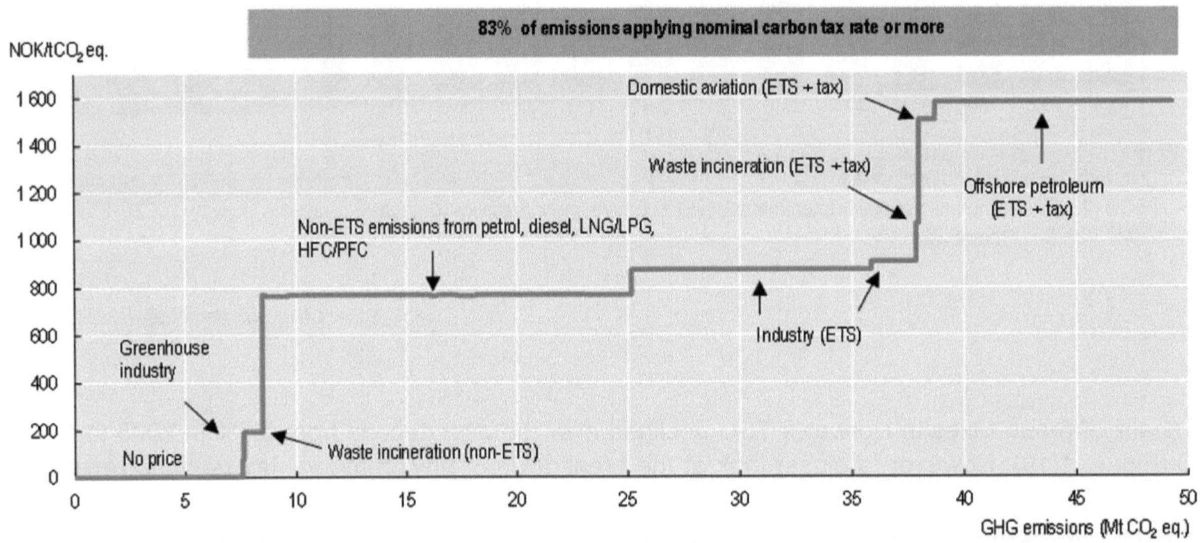

Note: Tax rates applicable in 2022 and ETS allowance price of NOK 817 per tonne of CO_2. GHG emissions data, excluding LULUCF, refer to 2020.
Source: Country submission.

StatLink https://stat.link/eljr7u

Norway's Climate Action Plan 2021-30 proposes to gradually raise the carbon tax on non-ETS emissions from NOK 590 per tonne of CO_2-eq in 2021 to NOK 2 000 by 2030 (from USD 69 to USD 234). The precise arrangements to operationalise the required tax shift will be part of a negotiation process and are expected to be approved by Parliament within its annual budget cycle. A first step was taken in 2022, when the general tax rate on non-ETS emissions was increased by 28% (in real value). By 2030, the scheduled increase in carbon prices is expected to reduce emissions by an estimated 8 million tonnes of CO_2-eq. Norway's gradual carbon tax increase would provide a long-term perspective on carbon pricing and a strong price signal to encourage increased investments in renewable energy and low-carbon technologies.

Social equity concerns have gained prominence in the public debate. The 2022 budget shields motorists from large parts of the tax increase through reductions in the motor insurance tax and road usage tax.[9] This general measure may be easy to administer as it applies to all road users across the country in the same way. However, it weakens the intended carbon-price signal and the incentives to reduce driving and moving to low-carbon transport alternatives. It would make sense to analyse the social and distributional consequences of the proposed CO_2 tax increase. Subsequently, Norway should develop more targeted and time-bound transitional support for vulnerable groups and regions.

Excise taxes on fossil fuels

Norway applies excise taxes on petrol, diesel, bioethanol, biodiesel, natural gas and LPG. Tax rates vary depending on sulphur content and other criteria. Any biogas contained in natural gas or LPG is exempted from taxation. The retail fuel prices per litre rank among the world's most expensive prices. While the CO_2-tax rate (NOK 766 per tonne of CO_2) is the same across all fossil fuels for road transport, Norway's road usage tax rate on petrol is higher than the rate applied to other fuels, measured in NOK per litre.[10] Norway standardises the different tax rates for biofuels, diesel and petrol based on the energy content to estimate how much car usage can be gained from one litre of fuel and to measure related externalities. The lower rate for diesel can be partially justified by the lower energy content in diesel. However, diesel engines emit higher levels of local air pollutants than petrol engines, and the road usage tax primarily intends to price externalities related to road transport. The share of diesel vehicles in new car sales has declined sharply, but diesel vehicles still represent 45% of Norway's passenger car fleet (Figure 1.25). There are trade-offs between environmental goals and distributional impacts, which are part of the political debate.

Biofuel quotas

Norway has put in place a progressive biofuel policy over the past decade. The mandatory quota for biofuels, introduced in 2009, has been progressively increased. As of January 2021, economic operations must sell at least 24.5% biofuels as a share of the total annual amount of fuel sold for road transport, including double counting of advanced biofuels (minimum of 9% within this quota). The Climate Action Plan 2021-30 proposes to further strengthen incentives to choose biofuels. However, biofuel production can also have negative impacts on global food security with limited reductions of CO_2 emissions. Most of the biofuel used in Norway is imported, also generating transport-related emissions. The use of palm oil-based biofuels, associated with high deforestation, has been reduced since 2017. Crop-based biofuels have been restricted.

Off-road

Fuels used in maritime transport and fisheries were for a long time exempted from the excise tax or benefited from reduced rates. This policy did not encourage any efficiency gains. Several exemptions have therefore been abolished. For example, the CO_2 tax now applies to all fossil fuels used in domestic waters. Norway should continue to remove harmful subsidies and inappropriate exemptions from environment-related taxes. An analysis of possible negative effects of subsidies on biodiversity (Aichi Target 3) is underway. Green solutions have become more competitive thanks to economic instruments like the carbon tax, a lower electricity tax rate for commercial vessels and environment-related differentiation of port fees. Similarly, a higher carbon price provides incentives for the aquaculture industry to develop and deploy low- and zero-emission solutions.

Norway applies excise taxes on jet fuel to domestic aviation (NOK 1.51 per litre). International aviation to destinations outside the EEA is only taxed with a passenger tax (USD 9 on flights to European destinations and USD 24 for intercontinental flights). However, domestic aviation is taxed multiple times through a national carbon tax, carbon pricing within the EU ETS and a passenger tax of about USD 9 (temporarily suspended from 2020 to July 2022 due to the COVID-19 pandemic). Double taxation under the EU ETS will not help reduce European-wide CO_2 emissions significantly. However, higher flight prices can contribute to reducing domestic demand and make other more environmentally friendly options such as rail more competitive. However, travel time is also a major factor that determines customer choices.

Electricity tax

Norway's tax on electricity consumption has a relatively limited impact on emission reduction since electricity generation is almost exclusively based on renewable energy. The electricity consumption tax can, however, encourage more efficient energy use and thus contribute to reducing total energy use. It also contributes to raising tax revenues. Although Norway is an energy exporter, Norwegians have by far the highest electricity bills in Europe, representing close to EUR 2 500 per year, compared to Sweden (rank 2, EUR 1 800) and Finland (rank 4, EUR 1 500 (Eurostat, 2021[52]). Due to soaring electricity prices, the government has announced plans to subsidise household electricity bills during the winter. Tax rate cuts in the electricity tax for 2022 are estimated at NOK 2.9 billion (USD 337 million). However, most industries and consumers in northern Norway already benefit from a reduced tax rate. Energy-intensive industrial processes, the greenhouse industry and railways are also exempted.

1.5.3. Transport-related taxes and charges

Vehicle taxes

Vehicle taxation – including taxes on registration, ownership and usage of cars – is a key policy instrument for encouraging the purchase of low-emission vehicles. This, in turn, helps reduce GHG emissions in the transport sector. Norway levies several taxes on internal combustion vehicles, applying rates higher than in most OECD countries. This is one of the measures that helped substantially reduce Norway's average CO_2 emission levels from newly registered cars. Norway has already reached the EU target of 95 g CO_2/km for 2020-24. In 2020, the average CO_2 emission level of new passenger cars was less than 50 g CO_2/km (OFV, 2022[53]).

The taxation of vehicles and road usage has two main challenges. First, the tax does not largely apply to zero-emission vehicles. Second, it does not reflect differences in externalities depending on where and when the driving takes place. An introduction of a time- and place-based road use tax would allow for more accurate pricing of various externalities and would thus be a welcome development (van Dender, 2019[54]). The government started exploring a satellite-based, location and time-contingent, road usage charge system. This would allow a more coherent vehicle tax system based on the actual use of vehicles and related environmental costs.

The National Budget paper presented to Parliament in 2021 included a discussion of principles for a sustainable car taxation system in Norway, in terms of both the environment and revenue. The government emphasised that a sustainable vehicle taxation system must put a price on the negative external impacts caused by use of all vehicles. A sustainable car tax system will also need to include taxes on vehicle purchase and ownership, primarily for fiscal reasons. By outlining the principles above, which seem well founded and balanced, the government intended to provide some predictability for households and car importers. Norway should prioritise preparation of a place-based road-pricing system, covering all passenger and light-duty vehicle categories, while considering the needs of people in remote areas.

Motor vehicle registration tax

Norway has a one-off tax on motor vehicle registrations, using environmentally differentiated rates since 2008. This major tax on the sale of new cars has greatly contributed to cleaning Norway's vehicle fleet. For passenger cars, the tax rate depends on the weight of the vehicle, as well as on its CO_2 and NO_x emissions. Compared to other Scandinavian countries, the Norwegian fiscal regime has by far the strongest CO_2 abatement effect (Østli et al., 2021[55]). EVs are fully exempt from the motor vehicle registration tax. Consequently, fiscal revenues from the motor vehicle registration tax were halved within the past five years and were estimated at NOK 8.5 billion (about USD 1 billion) in 2021 (Figure 1.21).

Norway also applies a scrapping deposit fee as an integral part of the motor vehicle registration tax. The measure aims to limit waste from end-of-life vehicles.

Commuting allowances

In 2022, Norway introduced a fixed rate of NOK 1.65 (USD 0.2) per kilometre. This was an increase from the previous NOK 1.56 for up to 50 000 km and NOK 0.76 for over 50 000 km (Ministry of Finance, 2021[34]). The allowance benefits long-distance travelling, regardless of transport. The threshold amount was reduced from NOK 23 900 (USD 2 780) to NOK 14 000 (USD 1 600) to compensate people with long commutes. It does not include an environmental component as transportation is already taxed through the CO_2-tax. It is unclear whether people in sparsely populated areas have on average a longer commuting distance than people living in more centrally located areas. According to national statistics, there is no clear correlation between driving distance and remote areas.

Support to zero-emission vehicles

In 2021, about two-thirds of new passenger vehicles sold were fully electric. Several factors have contributed to this trend, including the exemption of zero-emission vehicles (ZEVs) from the registration tax, VAT and motor fuel taxes, as well as at least a 50% reduction in road taxes, ferry and parking fees (Table 1.3). These fiscal incentives contributed to shifting demand towards ZEVs (which are now cheaper than petrol or diesel cars) and increasing the share of ZEVs in the car fleet. However, it has also strongly reduced tax revenues. The tax expenditure from the VAT exemption reached NOK 11.3 billion (USD 1.3 billion) in 2021. The overall advantage of EVs (fully battery electric and plug-in hybrid) was estimated at NOK 30 billion (USD 3.5 billion) in 2021 (Figure 1.21). Revenue from car-related taxation is declining.

Figure 1.21. Revenue from car-related taxation is declining

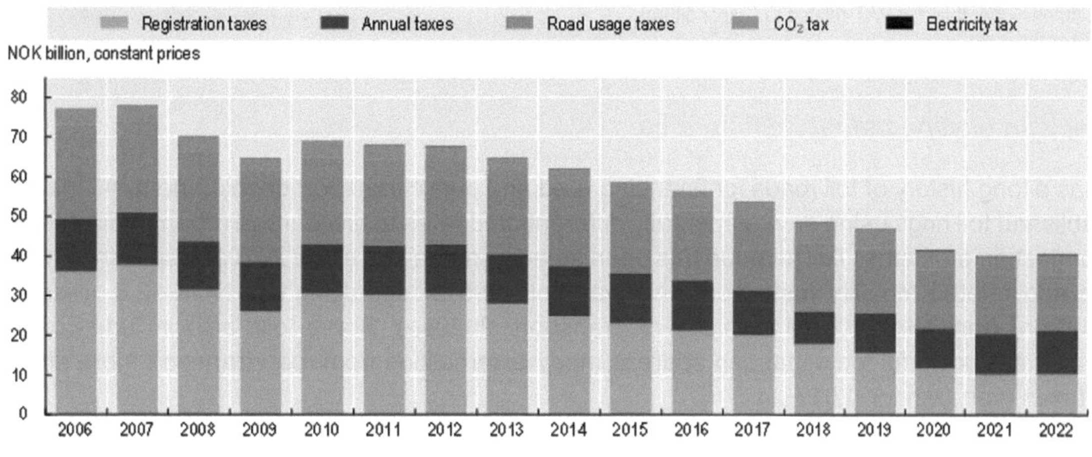

Note: Adjusted for inflation, estimated 2022 NOK values.
Source: OECD (2022), *OECD Economic Surveys: Norway 2022*.

StatLink https://stat.link/prjvgi

As the EV market is maturing, it makes economic sense to reduce tax incentives gradually. As of 2021, the government aligned the annual road tax rate for ZEVs with the amount for motorcycles (NOK 2 135 or USD 248 per year). This rate represents 70% of the traffic insurance tax for petrol and diesel cars. Full road traffic insurance tax for ZEVs will be introduced as of March 2022. The government coalition parties also announced plans to introduce VAT on the most expensive ZEVs (to be applied on the amount over NOK 600 000 or USD 69 775). These are first steps towards sharing the financial burden of road maintenance, infrastructure development and other externalities (congestion, noise, accidents). Other measures may become necessary.

Table 1.3. Norway's incentives for electric vehicles

Type of tax or fees	Level	Timeframe	Estimated tax expenditure (2021)	Estimated additional value of incentives*
Registration tax	Full exemption	1990 – current	NOK 5.8 billion	NOK 10.2 billion (2021)
25% VAT on purchase	Full exemption	2001 – current	NOK 11.3 billion	
Road usage tax for ZEV	n.a.		n.a.	NOK 1.1 billion (2021)
Company car tax	Reduced fee	2000 – current	NOK 340 million	
Re-registration tax	Full exemption	2018 – current	NOK 300 million	
Annual road tax (Traffic insurance tax)	Full exemption 30% reduction No exemption	1996 – 2020 2021 As of March 2022	NOK 950 million	
Charges on toll roads	For free 50% discount min.	1997 – 2017 2018 – current	n.a.	NOK 1.2 billion (2018)
Charges on ferry fares	For free 50% discount min.	1997 – 2017 2018 – current	n.a.	NOK 45 million (2019)
Municipal parking	For free 50% discount min.	1999- 2017 2018 – current	n.a.	
Access to bus lanes	For free Under certain conditions	2005 – 2006 2006 – current	n.a.	

Note: *The estimated tax expenditure does not include the full economic advantage given to low- and zero-emission vehicles. The tax system has been adjusted over many years to promote the uptake of EVs. An average battery electric vehicle has several strong comparative advantages over a conventional car and lower operational costs. The overall advantage is estimated at NOK 30 billion (USD 3.5 billion) in 2021 (nearly three times higher than the VAT-related tax expenditure).
Source: Country submission.

Road tolls with environmentally differentiated rates

Norway has a long history of toll roads for financing road and public transport development. All major cities have established toll rings using environmentally differentiated rates to discourage urban traffic and reduce related congestion problems. Toll revenue has been steadily increasing since 2010. Despite the COVID-19 pandemic and related mobility restrictions, Norway collected a record high of NOK 12.3 billion (about USD 1.3 billion) from tolls in 2020 (Ministry of Transport, 2020[56]). Some tolls also include congestion charges; they are powerful tools that can address many externalities from road transport more effectively than fuel taxes (van Dender, 2019[54]).

In 2021, Norway counted 62 toll road projects, collecting tolls from 332 stations and 4 ferry connections. A recent road toll reform simplified the price and discount schemes through an electronically managed AutoPass; some tolls serve as congestion pricing. For example, the Oslo area has a combined congestion charge and low-emission zone. The toll rate depends on the Euro standard and fuel type, as well as time and distance. EVs no longer benefit from free access. The city of Oslo intends to transform the central area into a zero-emissions zone (ZEZ). Bergen is planning to implement a pilot ZEZ in 2023. Both cities also apply temporary driving bans for diesel-powered vehicles non-compliant with Euro 6 or increased price schemes at times of high pollution.

1.5.4. Taxes on pollution and resource use

As in other OECD countries, pollution and resource taxes play a minor role in generating environment-related tax revenue in Norway. The country applies a tax on plant protection products, which is area-based and differentiated according to the health and environmental risks related to the product. There are seven different tax classes. The environmental tax has helped reduce the use of plant protection products with the highest risks over the years. While products with the highest risks have been used less, pesticides in lower risk categories have been used more.

Norway also applies various waste taxes. It introduced its first beverage packaging plastic tax, for example, as early as the 1970s. Since 1994, it has applied two separate taxes on beverage containers. A basic tax is imposed for single-use containers, while a variable tax depends on packaging return rates. The bottle deposit system is successful, but beverage bottles represent less than 10% of Norway's plastic waste. A plastic bag levy has also been in place since 2017 (Box 1.4).

In 2022, the government introduced a tax on CO_2 emissions from waste incinerators. Given that incinerators are high carbon emitters, the tax could help decarbonise the waste sector. It would be useful to extend the tax to cover air pollutant emissions. When Norway introduced such a tax more than a decade ago, tax rates were set according to estimates of the social costs caused by a large range of pollutants (OECD, 2004[57]). The tax was cancelled in 2010 due to the financial difficulties of some incinerator operators caused, in part, because Sweden abolished its tax on waste incineration the same year. A reintroduction of a more comprehensive emission tax on waste incinerators could be a welcome extension of the CO_2 emission tax.

Better use of taxation and other economic instruments could help Norway make faster progress towards a more resource-efficient, circular economy. Many waste reduction schemes are handled through voluntary agreements with industry, which do not always reflect the full cost of waste to society. Norwegian municipalities made only limited progress in differentiating waste collection fees according to the amount of waste generated (OECD, 2019[58]). Norway has many opportunities to strengthen regulatory frameworks and provide stronger incentives to change business models. According to the "Achieving Circularity" report, "(i)t is not the lack of technical solutions that is preventing a zero-waste circular plastic economy in Norway, but rather insufficiently ambitious regulatory frameworks, business models, incentives, and funding mechanisms" (Systemiq and Norwegian Retailers' Environment Fund, 2021[59]).

Box 1.4. Norway's plastic bag levy needs to be increased

In 2017, the Norwegian retailers' trade association introduced a voluntary levy for plastic bags. Income from bag sales goes to the Norwegian Retailers' Environmental Fund, which promotes behavioural changes to reduce plastic pollution. A fee of NOK 1 per bag is earmarked for the fund. More than 85% of retailers adhere to the scheme. The fund helped reduce the use of plastic carrier bags by 16% between 2016 and 2019 (Norwegian Retailers' Environment Fund, 2021[60]). However, changing eating and consumption habits during the COVID-19 pandemic contributed to use of an additional 39 million plastic carrier bags in 2020 compared to 2019. In 2020, Norwegians bought 782 million plastic carrier bags, which corresponds on average to 146 plastic bags per person (Norwegian Retailers' Environment Fund, 2021[60]). Hang (2018[61]) analysed the average willingness to pay for plastic bags in Norway (estimated at NOK 2.66 or USD 0.3). The study concludes the price per plastic bag should reach at least NOK 3.26 to induce a change in consumers' shopping behaviour. Stronger measures will be needed to put Norway back on track to achieving the EU target (which Norway shares under the EEA Agreement) of using 40 lightweight plastic carrier bags per person per year by 2025. A downstream tax, applied to the end user, proved to be successful in Ireland, which allowed the country to reduce use of plastic bags by 94% (OECD, 2021[62]).

1.5.5. Fossil fuel support

For more than a decade, many OECD countries have prioritised phasing out inefficient fossil fuel support (Box 1.5). They also committed to phasing out environmentally harmful subsidies by 2020 under the Aichi Targets of the UN Convention on Biological Diversity. The Glasgow Agreement at the COP26 in 2021 called upon parties to accelerate efforts towards a phase-out of inefficient fossil fuel subsidies. However, there is still a gap between official declarations and actual support. It is difficult to measure and compare progress among countries without an internationally agreed definition of environmentally harmful subsidies, including fossil fuel subsidies. Norway does not have a national inventory of fossil fuel subsidies and other environmentally harmful or potentially harmful subsidies (Box 1.6).

Norway's fossil fuel support, both forgone tax revenue and direct budgetary transfers, declined over the past decade (Figure 1.22). This decline was thanks to the gradual phase-out of several energy and carbon tax exemptions and reduced consumption of transport fuels with the uptake of EVs (Figure 1.22). Total fossil fuel support represents about 0.2% of tax revenue. In 2020, support for fossil fuels was estimated at USD 328 million (USD 60 per capita) (OECD/IISD, 2021[63]). The lion's share (84%) supported petroleum and the rest natural gas (16%). Norway does not provide any fossil fuel support for end-use electricity. Its electricity comes from 98% renewable energy sources. Consequently, the recently announced government subsidy to help households reduce their electricity bills during the winter will not include any fossil fuel subsidies.

Figure 1.22. Norway's fossil support declined over the past decade

Composition of fossil fuel support, 2010-20

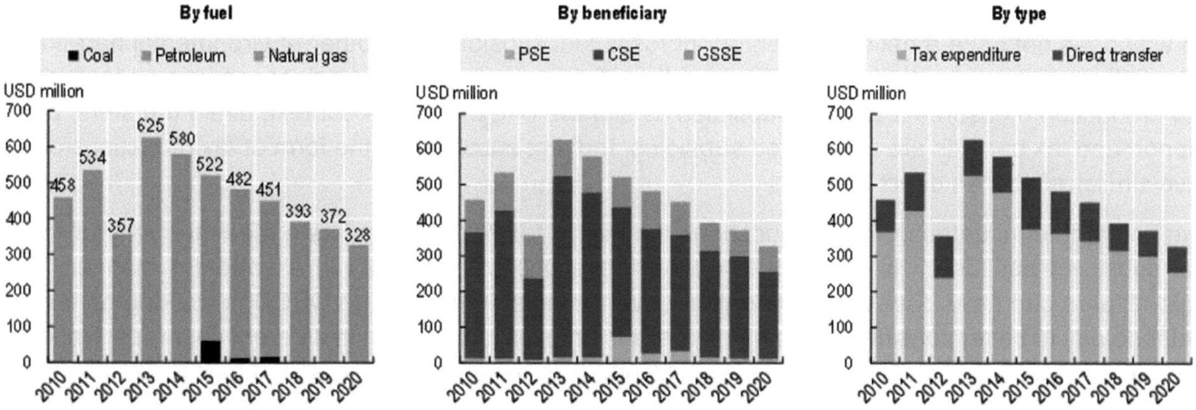

Note: PSE = Producer Support Estimate; CSE = Consumer Support Estimate; GSSE: General Services Support Estimate; fossil fuel subsidy data may be partial. Tax expenditure is an estimate of revenue forgone because the tax system reduces or postpones tax relative to a jurisdiction's benchmark tax system (to the benefit of fossil fuels). Hence, i) tax expenditure estimates could increase due either to greater concessions relative to the benchmark treatment, or to a raise in the benchmark itself; ii) international comparisons of tax expenditure could be misleading, due to country-specific benchmark tax treatments. Definitions of tax expenditure, and the benchmarks used to estimate the size of expenditure, are nationally determined and may hamper international comparisons. The OECD uses a bottom-up method of estimating government support to fossil fuels by identifying and quantifying individual policy measures. This approach measures fossil fuel support as all direct budgetary transfers and tax expenditures (tax reductions, preferential treatment for cost recovery) that provide a benefit or preference for fossil fuel production or consumption.
Source: OECD (2021), "Fossil Fuel Support", *OECD Environmental Indicators* (database).

StatLink https://stat.link/8bn4ea

Most support measures are related to fiscal taxes (e.g. exemptions from the tax on mineral oil used for domestic shipping and fishing and off-road agricultural vehicles). Norway reports on tax expenditures diligently; debate is underway whether it makes sense to consider some of these expenditures as fossil fuel subsidies. Norway should systematically screen actual or proposed subsidies, including tax provisions to identify those that are not justified on economic, social and environmental grounds, and develop a plan to phase out fossil fuel and other environmentally harmful support. The government should also strengthen transparency by disclosing fossil fuel production and support plans in its commitments under the Paris Agreement (SEI et al., 2021[17]).

Box 1.5. Norway's commitments to support national and international reform of fossil fuel support

Norway does not have a national inventory of fossil fuel subsidies and other environmental harmful or potentially harmful subsidies. Calculations of the SDG indicator 12.c.1[11] on responsible consumption and production measures fossil fuel subsidies as a share of GDP. In this context, direct transfers, price support and tax benefits are considered subsidies. Indirect subsidies in the form of tax reductions often have similar effects as direct transfers.

Like some other countries, Norway questions the use of tax expenditures as a measurement for fossil fuel subsidies because it is complex to define the scope of a subsidy in a coherent manner. Tax expenditures can have positive and negative environmental impacts. The OECD is working on a new methodology to better consider the complex realities of fossil fuel support in different countries. National and international reporting of fossil fuel subsidies needs to be further improved and harmonised to make data better comparable.

At the international level, Norway has been supporting various global initiatives to phase out fossil fuel support. The country is a member of the informal grouping of non-G20 countries,[12] known as the "Friends of Fossil-Fuel Subsidy Reform". Established in 2010, the group organised many international events focusing on the links between climate change, trade and sustainable development. On the fifth anniversary of the Paris Agreement, the group issued a joint statement urging governments, businesses and other organisations to accelerate action to eliminate fossil fuel subsidies through a focus on green recovery (OECD/IEA, 2021[64]).

In a 2016 Joint Statement of the US-Nordic Leaders' Summit, Norway committed to "promote access to affordable, reliable, sustainable and modern energy for all by encouraging the reduction of fossil fuel subsidies, promoting renewable energies and fuels, and enhancing energy efficiency". More recently, in November 2021, Norway joined a group of 15 countries of the World Trade Organization that promotes "shared understanding" to achieve "effective disciplines on inefficient fossil fuels subsidies" (WTO, 2021[65]). It notably called for a clear timeline to rationalise and phase out inefficient fossil fuel subsidies that encourage wasteful consumption. The eighth EU Environment Action Programme of December 2021 did not set deadlines. However, it confirmed a collective commitment "to phase out all environmentally harmful subsidies, in particular fossil fuel subsidies, at Union, national, regional and local level without delay". Norway has not yet established quantified time-bound targets.

In response to the COVID-19 pandemic and the oil price drop in spring 2020, the government provided massive support to rescue the petroleum industry and fast-track new projects on the Norwegian continental shelf. The temporary changes to the petroleum tax are estimated to reduce tax revenues over time by about NOK 10 billion (USD 1.2 billion), measured in NOK 2020 terms. In the short term, the tax revenue loss is greater because the change entails a tax deferral. In 2020 and 2021, the accrued tax revenue loss is estimated at NOK 74 billion (USD 8.6 billion) and NOK 57 billion (USD 6.6 billion), respectively (Section 1.7.1). Tax concessions to the petroleum sector allow immediate tax deduction of all investment in 2020 and 2021, as well as investment under new field development plans delivered by 2022 and approved by the government before the end of 2023. In addition, companies benefit from an uplift deduction of 24% of investment costs. The tax breaks did not change the headline tax rate of 78% that oil companies pay on profits but rather increased deductions for new investments. This investment-friendly scheme is expected to be applied until 2028. Taxable profits can thus be reduced for several years. This massive push for Norway's petroleum industry represents more than double the amount of the country's fossil fuel support over the past decade. If these measures persist beyond emergency packages related to

COVID-19, they will become part of a structural policy landscape that needs to change to phase out fossil fuel support.

Furthermore, it would be useful for Norway to engage in a self-review and/or peer review of inefficient fossil fuel support. Such reviews, similar to the ones within the G20, could help identify scalable good practices. In line with its international commitments, Norway should further reduce fossil fuel support and set time-bound targets for such reductions.

1.6. Green investment and practices

1.6.1. National environmental protection expenditure

Like other Scandinavian countries, Norway has a high level of government spending, representing 58% of GDP in 2020 compared to 41% in the OECD area (OECD, 2021[41]). Over the past decade, Norway heavily increased public investment, which was mostly driven by expenditures in the transport sector. Public investment reached 6.2% of national GDP, nearly twice as much as the OECD average (OECD, 2021[41]). Norway also spent nearly twice as much on environmental protection as the OECD average (0.9% of GDP), ranking above the Europe-27 average. Wastewater and waste management made up the bulk of environmental protection spending (Figure 1.23).

Figure 1.23. Norway's environmental protection expenditure is among the highest in Europe

Environmental protection expenditure by environmental media

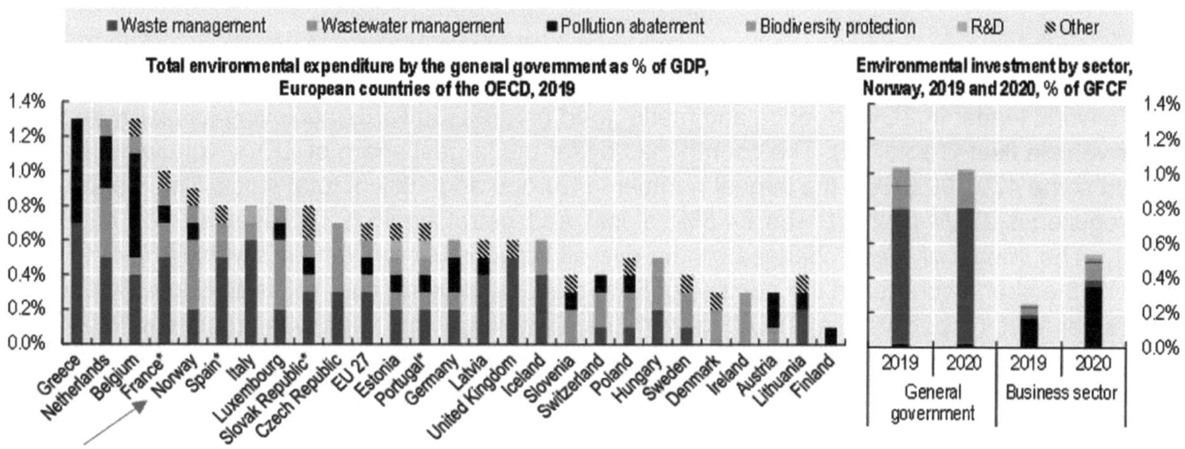

Note: *Provisional data.
Source: Eurostat (2022), "General government expenditure by function (COFOG)", (database).

StatLink https://stat.link/374n95

1.6.2. Investment in water infrastructure

As noted in the previous OECD EPR for Norway (OECD, 2011[27]), the country's ageing water supply and wastewater infrastructure requires substantial upgrades. According to Norsk Vann estimates, NOK 81 billion (USD 9.4 billion) and NOK 114 billion (USD 13.3 billion) will be required for drinking water infrastructure and wastewater infrastructure, respectively, over the next two decades. The rate of improvement in infrastructure has been slow despite substantive investment. In 2020, only 0.7% of the total water pipeline system has been renewed (Environment Norway, 2021[23]). Norway has invested by far the largest share in infrastructure renewal in Europe: EUR 225 per inhabitant per year compared to EUR 82 in other EU member states (five-year average) (EurEau, 2021[66]). Norwegians also pay the largest annual water bill per household (EUR 950 per year, 2017-19 average).

Water is mostly managed by local government departments with sometimes limited capacity. A recent study analyses the potential for rationalisation in the water and wastewater sector, including proposals on how municipalities could renew the pipe networks faster and in a cost-efficient manner. Drawing on key findings, the Ministry of Local Government and Regional Development, the Ministry of Health and Care Services and the Ministry of Climate and Environment work together to identify required action. In 2017, Norway revised its national goals for water and health. It introduced a new drinking water regulation with requirements for operation and maintenance of the drinking water pipe network. As of 2021, the central government offers co-funding for municipalities and market operators to create stronger incentives for upgrading water pipes. Norway could further strengthen incentives to encourage greater efficiency and effectiveness of local service delivery.

1.6.3. Investment in sustainable transport

The government has set requirements for the use of zero- and low-emission technology and promotes strong investment support schemes. A large amount of public investment in sustainable transport and a climate-neutral and circular economy is channelled through Enova. Enova granted a total of NOK 3.7 billion (USD 393 million) in 2020. In addition, funding provided by Enova triggered private investment estimated at NOK 1.6 billion (USD 170 million) in 2020. Enova supports technology development and early market introduction to decarbonise transport, including the road, maritime and air sectors.

Zero-emission vehicle adoption

Norway is a world leader in ZEV adoption and made good progress towards achieving its policy targets to electrify its vehicle fleet (Table 1.4). The country has by far the largest share of ZEVs worldwide. In 2021, Norway had some 470 000 ZEVs, the largest number in Europe and 16% of total stock. The market share of newly registered ZEVs in 2021 was 64.5%; diesel and petrol engines represented 4% and 4.3%, respectively. The impact of these changes on the overall composition of Norway's vehicle fleet will take time. Despite the sharp increase in the number of EVs, diesel and petrol cars still made up 45% and 34% of Norway's car fleet, respectively in 2020 (Figure 1.24). This downward trend was pursued in 2021 when the share of diesel and petrol cars further dropped to 41% and 32%, respectively. The government should place a stronger emphasis on phasing out older, more polluting cars to accelerate changes in the composition of its vehicle fleet rather than encourage additional increases in passenger cars. According to projections (Ministry of Climate and Environment, 2020[67]), the stock of ZEVs might reach 1.25 million by 2030 (compared to 225 000 without incentives). This represents 44.5% of the vehicle fleet. The full greening of the car fleet will take more than a decade.

Figure 1.24. Norway is on track to electrify its vehicle fleet

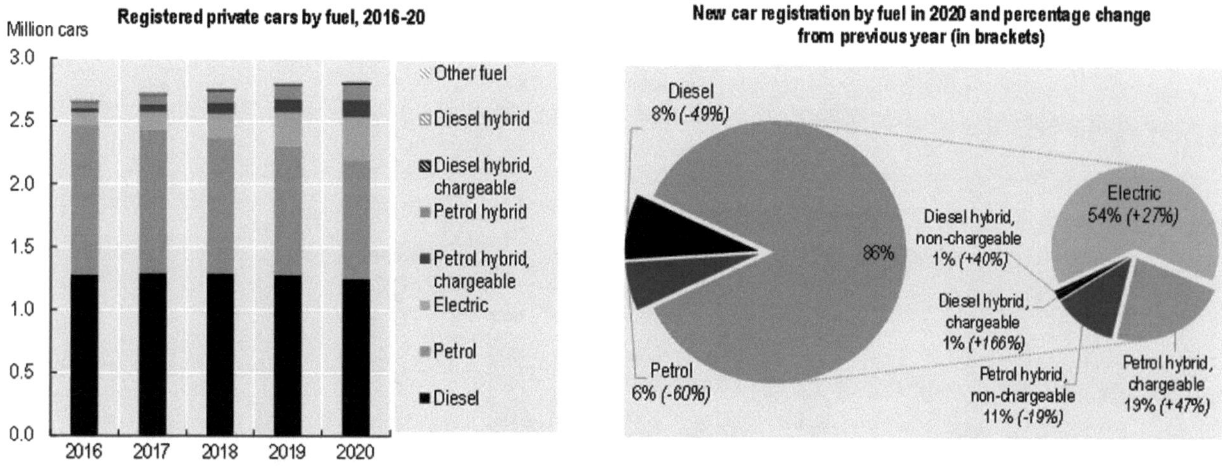

Source: Statistics Norway (2021), *StatBank* (database).

StatLink https://stat.link/yrft1l

Table 1.4. State of progress on selected policy targets of the National Transport Plan 2022-33

Policy target	Year	Status	Comment
All new passenger cars and light vans shall be zero-emission vehicles by 2025	64.5% (2021)	On track	Norway is the world's leader in terms of market share of EVs (16% in 2021).
All new city buses shall be zero-emission vehicles or use biogas by 2025	22.6% (2020)	On track	Proposal for a new regulation is undergoing public consultation. The proposal suggests an exception for city buses that operate with biogas.
All new heavier vans, 75% of new long-distance buses and 50% of new lorries shall be zero-emission vehicles by 2030	Heavier vans: 3% (2020) Long-distance buses: 7.6% (2020) Lorries: 0.5% (2020)	In progress	State aid is available through Enova.
Goods distribution in the biggest city centres shall take place with virtually zero emissions by 2030	n.a.	In progress	Some distribution hubs with zero emissions have been established with support from Enova; for example, the Oslo City Hub.

Source: Country submission.

Norway's success in promoting EVs has mainly been driven by generous tax incentives (Table 1.3). It was also boosted through public investment in the development of a dense network of charging stations, as well as low costs of batteries and related services. In 2020, Norway counted more than 13 000 charging points, including nearly 1 600 high-speed charging points, which were developed with public subsidies (Figure 1.25). Enova has also supported a charging infrastructure for nearly 150 city buses in Oslo. While this infrastructure is increasingly dense, Norway needs to pursue public financial support to establish and maintain public charging stations in areas that lack a commercial market, particularly in the north. The expansion of EVs will require massive investments in the development of a smarter and more flexible charging infrastructure covering the entire territory.

Figure 1.25. Norway has a dense charging infrastructure for electric vehicles

Number of publicly available fast charging points (above 50 kW)

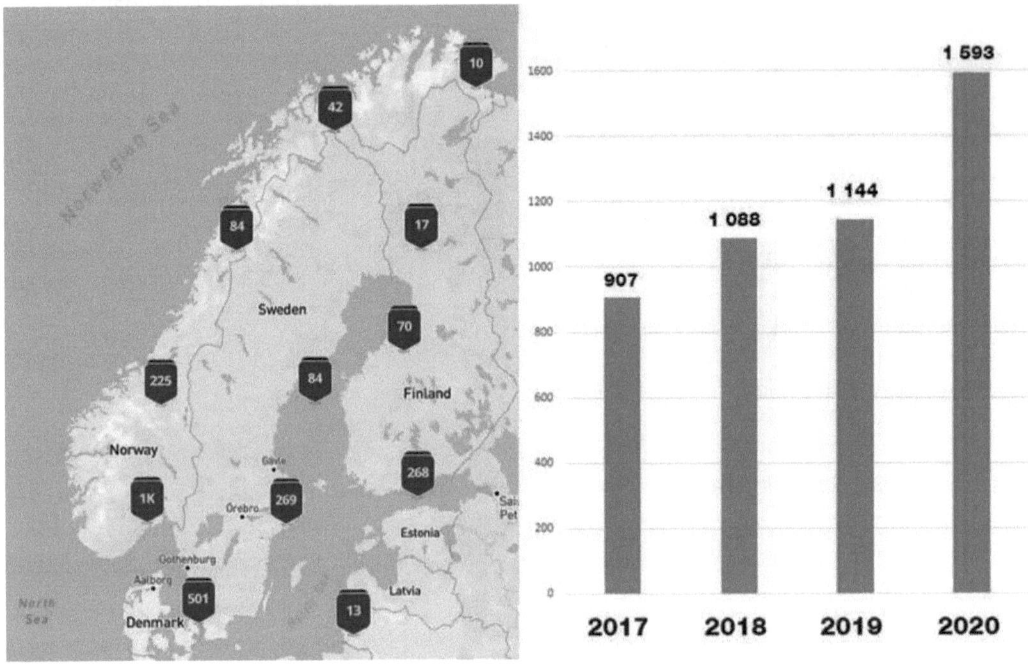

Note: The figure does not include Tesla superchargers, which in 2021 amounted to an additional 1 049 charging points.
Source: Country submission and Elbil, Norway, https://ladekart.elbil.no.

Green shipping

Norway is a pioneer in developing and deploying zero- and low-emission technology in the maritime sector. The country has already electrified a third of its domestic ferries and aims at introducing zero-emission requirements for all new public procurement of ferries in 2023. A first hydrogen-driven ferry will be launched in 2022, and a hydrogen-driven short sea shipping vessel is scheduled to operate as of 2024. However, decarbonising long-distance maritime transport remains a challenge. Close co-operation with the business sector and industry partners will be key. The government supports a series of public support schemes for boosting the competitiveness of the Norwegian maritime industry, as well as the development and uptake of Norwegian environmental technology. Between 2015-19, Enova allocated more than NOK 2.6 billion (USD 294 million) to maritime projects; many projects were also supported by the Business Sector's NO_x Fund or EU funding.

Green aviation technology

Norway is leading the way towards sustainable air travel alongside its Scandinavian neighbours. Avinor, a state-owned company, announced in 2018 that it aims at making all short-haul flights all-electric by 2040. It also intends to make Norway the first country with a significant market share of electric aircrafts. The regional airline Widerøe intends to deploy a first all-electric 11-seater aircraft (P-Volt) by 2026. Norway has a strong comparative advantage in electrification of aviation. This advantage is due to its renewable power production, a well-developed airport network (48 airports and 3 000 docks) with relatively short distances and strong political will to boost electrification of the aviation sector. It will be important to provide clear, predictable, long-term incentives and a regulatory framework to make the electrification of commercial air traffic a success.

1.6.4. Investment for a climate-neutral and circular economy

Carbon capture and storage

Norway is a frontrunner in developing CCS solutions in Europe, together with the Netherlands and the United Kingdom. Norway's Longship project (Box 1.6) aims at kick-starting CCS development both in Norway and Europe, as well as enabling other countries to replicate technological solutions. The project benefits from long-term funding with the government's total investment reaching NOK 3.45 billion (USD 0.4 billion) in 2022 out of NOK 17 billion (USD 2 billion) state aid pledged until 2034, covering the construction phase (2021-24) and the first ten years of operations (2025-34). The practical application of CCS technologies could help set new industrial standards. By 2026-27, the Oslo Varme's facility could become one of the world's first carbon-negative incinerators (Box 1.6). However, there is concern that investment in CCS will privilege end-of-pipe solutions, removing focus from reducing emissions in the first place. For example, CCS-equipped incineration can contribute to a lock-in effect in waste management systems, impeding waste minimisation.

Box 1.6. Longship: Norway's largest-ever industrial climate project

Launched in 2020, Norway's carbon capture and storage project known as "Longship" is the country's largest-ever industrial climate project (total cost of NOK 25 billion – about USD 2.9 billion, including NOK 16.8 billion – close to USD 2 billion – in government funding, 2021-34) (Ministry of Petroleum and Energy, 2019[68]). The project brings together all components to form a complete CCS chain: it covers the capture of CO_2 from Norcem Heidelberg Cement's factory in Brevik and from Fortum Oslo Varme's waste-to-energy plant in Oslo. Northern Lights covers the transport and storage part of the project and is based on a joint venture of Equinor, Shell and Total. If successful, Longship could help scale back the use of emission-intensive construction materials and decarbonise waste. For example, Norcem aims to capture around 400 000 of 800 000 tonnes of CO_2 per year from its cement factory. The post-combustion capture technology of the Fortum Oslo Varme's facility could catch about 90% of Norway's largest "waste-to-energy" plant. This represents up to 14% of Oslo's emissions per year. Longship might also generate many jobs. The government estimates that Norcem and Forum Oslo Varme could directly create up to 3 000 jobs during the construction phase, and many more indirectly. Successful implementation of the Longship project could open other opportunities and provide lessons for research and development support in circular economy initiatives. Synergy could be developed with many other European CO_2 capturing projects that are funded by the EU Innovation Fund (e.g. Kairos@C in Belgium, Eqiom cement factory in France, Neste/Porvoo refinery in Finland and Sweden's largest biofuel heat and power plant). Nevertheless, it is unclear whether societal benefits of this bridging technology will outweigh the high investment costs.

Source: Ministry of Petroleum and Energy (2019), Longship – CCS.

Offshore wind

Norway has a competitive advantage in large-scale deployment of offshore renewables, particularly wind. The government has given a green light to open two new offshore areas – Utsira Nord and Sørlige Nordsjø II – that have a potential 4.5 GW wind power capacity. More active state involvement will be required along the whole value chain to create stronger incentives for private sector investment (Afewerki et al., 2019[69]). As part of the third COVID-19 recovery package, the Research Council of Norway has given NOK 120 million (USD 14 million) the creation of a Norwegian Research Centre on Wind Energy

(NorthWind). It aims to create export opportunities for Norwegian business and industry, and minimise the environmental impacts from wind power development.

Buildings

Energy efficiency of Norway's buildings is excellent in international comparison, with high energy standards for new homes. Enova has already implemented many measures to retrofit buildings. Individual measures should continue to be regularly assessed to check they are delivering anticipated energy savings and remain cost-effective. The revision of the construction products regulation within the European Green Deal could help create a European market for the re-use of building materials.

1.6.5. Environment-related innovation

The total amount of public support for research, development and demonstration (RD&D) has increased by 56% from NOK 9.3 billion (about USD 1 billion) in 2015 to NOK 14.6 billion (about USD 2 billion) in 2020 (Statistics Norway, 2021[70]). Spending for environmental objectives represented about 3% of total public R&D. Public funding in renewables has been increasing since 2010 and was boosted in 2020 by the recovery packages (Figure 1.26). Public funding notably targets the development of energy and climate technology with a view to supporting lasting climate-friendly market changes. Enova provides funding for new technology development in all sectors (NOK 3.7 billion or USD 393 million in 2020, 3 850 projects). A new framework agreement defines new Enova priorities for 2021-24. Moreover, a Green Platform encourages investment and innovation in all sectors (Section 1.7.1). Norway also contributes to finance a partial membership in InvestEU, providing access to European capital investments.

Figure 1.26. Norway's public spending in renewables and energy efficiency has increased

Public spending in energy research, development and demonstration technologies

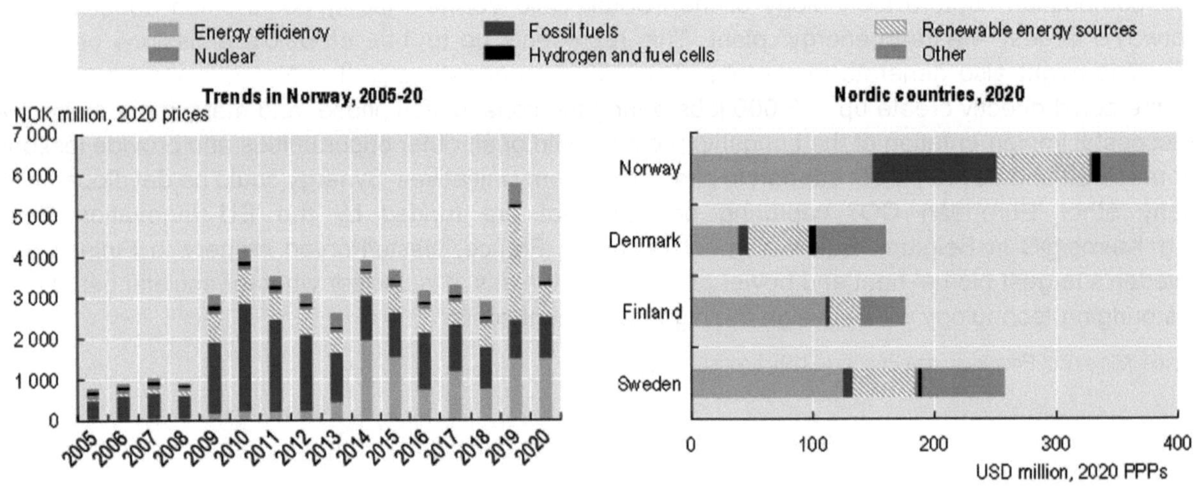

Note: Other includes other power and storage, and other cross-cutting and unallocated technologies. Right panel: data for Finland refer to 2019.
Source: IEA (2021), *Energy Technology RD&D Budgets*.

StatLink https://stat.link/pxz80s

Norway counts a lot on technological developments to achieve its climate goals and strives to reap the gains from innovation. While strong government support for innovation will further boost Norway's green transition, technical solutions alone may not be sufficient. Norway's green transition will also need to involve behavioural changes and require adjustment to consumption patterns.

1.6.6. Voluntary agreements and eco-certifications

Norway applies soft approaches such as voluntary agreements to reduce negative environmental impacts, particularly in the field of agriculture and waste management. Thanks to voluntary commitments with stakeholders from across the food value chain (involving 12 commercial organisations and 5 ministries), Norway reduced food waste by close to 10% between 2015 and 2020. However, NOK 22 billion (about USD 2.3 billion) in food is still wasted each year, representing about 1.3 million tonnes of CO_2-eq emissions. Awareness campaigns to promote better consumer choices and better understanding of best-before dates need to be pursued. Binding measures to reduce food waste may be needed.

The government and Norway's two main agricultural organisations signed a voluntary agreement in 2019 to reduce and enhance removals by a total of 5 million tonnes of CO_2-eq over 2021–30. Moreover, the Business Sector's NO_x Fund provides support and incentives for enterprises to further reduce their NO_x emissions. Voluntary agreements are most effective when combined with a serious threat for regulatory action.

Norway also uses eco-certifications (ISO 14001 and EMAS). The Eco-Lighthouse Certification Programme counts close to 7 500 certified businesses. These firms commit to improving performance in the areas of working environment, waste management, energy use, procurement and transport. Eco-lighthouse certification – the first national scheme in Europe – is also used in green public procurement.

1.6.7. Green public procurement

Norway's general government procurement spending more than doubled over 2011-19 from NOK 275 billion (USD 29.2 billion) to NOK 595 billion (USD 63.2 billion). Public procurement represented 29.3% of government expenditures and 17.1% of GDP in 2020 (OECD, 2020[71]). Consequently, public procurement can be a powerful policy instrument for aligning public expenditure with green objectives, promoting low-emission solutions and reducing GHG emissions.

The promotion of low carbon technologies in the transport sector is a striking example of aligning public spending with green objectives. Within the government's National Transport Plan 2022-33, the country actively uses public procurement regulations to boost the development and uptake of low-emission solutions: about a quarter of city buses are zero-emission vehicles and by 2025, all new city buses shall be zero-emission vehicles or use biogas. Climate requirements for public procurement (construction, vehicles, food/meal services) are also set in the Climate Action Plan 2021-30.

According to the 2016 Public Procurement Act, contracting authorities have a legally binding duty to develop and implement green procurement practices. It encourages a stronger focus on life cycle costs and requires the entire procurement cycle to consider sustainability criteria. There is still room for improvement when it comes to implementation. Norway needs to enhance countrywide uptake and strengthen the accountability framework. Audit and control continue to be weak points in relation to green public procurement in Norway (OECD, 2020[71]). As already noted by the previous OECD EPR (OECD, 2011[27]), there is no systematic approach for monitoring outcomes of sustainable procurement. Availability of data for monitoring purposes remains a challenge. Data on the share of green spending in public procurement could usefully inform decisions but are not yet systematically available. Preliminary findings of the Norwegian Agency for Public and Financial Management indicate an increase in the share of green public procurement spending in food purchases and meal services, as well as in the construction sector, in 2021. A 2021-30 action plan for climate- and environment-friendly public procurement and green innovation proposes measures to increase the share of green public procurement.

1.7. Towards a just and equitable transition

1.7.1. Green recovery

The health and economic impacts of the global COVID-19 pandemic have been less severe in Norway than in other European countries. As elsewhere, local pollution and GHG emissions declined in line with the lower level of activity. While its economy was initially hit hard by slumping oil prices, Norway is recovering quickly and will reach pre-pandemic GDP per capita levels in 2022 (OECD, 2021[3]). Policy makers can now turn more fully to structural challenges (OECD, 2022[20]).

Unemployment in Norway increased from 3.5% in February 2020 to 5.3% in August 2020 – its highest rate during the pandemic. It reached its pre-pandemic level of 3.5% in November 2021.The tourism and transport sectors were hardest hit, even though many job cuts can be classified as temporary due to time-bound containment measures. About 8.5% of Norwegian workers benefited from job retention schemes (OECD, 2022[72]).

Table 1.5. The environmental impact of Norway's recovery measures was mixed

Key measures	Sector	NOK (million)	USD (million)
Increased grant to Enova, which provides R&D funding for industries	Multiple	2 000	233
Increased grants to R&D-funding organisations via Green Platform (2020-22)	Multiple	1 125	131
Grant to "Nysnø", which invests in firms that develop climate-friendly technologies	Multiple	700	81
Grants to Klimasats to support municipalities in GHG emissions reduction efforts	Multiple	50	6
Increased funding for R&D to Norwegian Research Council to research funding programme ENERGIX, PTROMAKS2, DEMO2000 and FME wind	Multiple	120	14
Grants to promote green shipping (R&D and investments in low-emission ships)	Maritime transport	485	56
Loans to support green fleet renewal in the coastal transport and fisheries sectors	Maritime transport	600	70
Income support for commercial bus and ferry companies	Transport	200	23
Grants to stimulate a circular economy	Waste & recycling	100	12
Grants to support gene banks for wild salmon and similar projects	Biodiversity	20	2
Grants to increase the basic funding of environmental research institutions	Biodiversity	30	3
Increased grants to support measures to prevent invasive species	Biodiversity	13	2
Several temporary tax reductions for oil companies operating on the continental shelf, combined with new commitments to reduce emissions	Energy	131 000	15 234
Grant to cover the operating deficit for the last coal mine on Svalbard	Energy	91	11
Loan guarantees to airline companies under some conditions	Air transport	6 000	698
Suspension of the air passengers tax in 2020 and 2021	Air transport	n.a.	n.a.
Purchase of regional air transport services to compensate income losses	Air transport	2 039	237
Purchase of services from airline companies to help citizens return from abroad	Air transport	35	4
Grants to promote ocean-based wind turbines	Energy	55	6
Increased maintenance of road, railway and coastal infrastructure	Transport	1 330	155
Purchase of services from ferry companies operating in connection with national roads, in order to compensate to income losses	Maritime transport	356	41
Purchase of services from railway companies to compensate to income losses	Rail transport	2 575	299
Compensation for income losses for rail and other public transport companies	Transport	8 500	988

Note: Measures cover the period from the beginning of the pandemic in early 2020 until 31 December 2021, at 2021 exchange rates.
Colour code: green = positive impact; red = negative impact; grey = mixed impact; light grey = undetermined.
Source: Country submission and OECD Green Recovery Database (2021).

Economic measures included a mix of time-limited compensation and subsidy schemes, temporary changes in tax rules, income protection, investments in key infrastructure sectors, increased funding in technology development and a green transition package. The cost of these measures was NOK 230 billion in 2020 and 2021 (about USD 26.7 billion), including substantial support for the oil and gas industry and the aviation sector (Table 1.5). In addition, a system of tax concessions allow the immediate tax deduction of current/projected investment spending in the petroleum sector from 2020 to 2028. The temporary changes to the petroleum tax are estimated to reduce tax revenues over time by about NOK 10 billion (USD 1.2 billion), measured in NOK 2020 terms. Thanks to the rebound in oil prices, concessions in the pandemic's early months may have been more generous than necessary (OECD, 2022[20]).

Overall, the government has supported implementation of green restructuring measures and plans. For example, it set up a Green Platform (NOK 1.1 billion, about USD 119 million). The platform aims to stimulate "bigger and more rapid investments from companies in green sustainable solutions and products". The initiative is cross-cutting and involves participation of five ministries. Other measures funded investments in key infrastructure sectors such as green maritime transport. In addition, the government increased funding in technology development and several green conversion packages, the largest of them were channelled through its state-owned enterprise Enova. As in other OECD countries, monitoring and evaluation are needed to ensure that funds are spent in an economically efficient, environmentally sustainable and publicly transparent manner (OECD, 2021[73]).

1.7.2. Foreign investment and climate finance for developing countries

The government intends to better consider emissions associated with foreign investments. The equity-portfolio carbon emissions of Norway's Government Pension Fund Global (GPFG) are estimated to be almost twice the country's total emissions (OMFIF, 2021[74]). The GPFG pioneered ethical guidelines for investment decisions based on active ownership and the exclusion of firms from its portfolio. These guidelines explicitly include carbon emissions. While climate risk is not explicitly anchored in its investment mandate, the fund has started incorporating climate risks in its management. The government should follow through on recommendations from an expert group that has proposed to base the responsible investment management of the GPFG on the Paris Agreement's goals[13] (Ministry of Finance, Expert Group, 2021[75]). At the COP26, Norway's prime minister announced government plans to make the GPFG "(t)he leading fund in responsible investment and the management of climate risk".[14] This would help make the fund's activities more consistent with Norway's commitments under international climate agreements. To date, despite its huge potential, the world's largest sovereign wealth fund plays almost no role in the domestic or global green transition (Kattel et al., 2021[16]).

Norway recognises the critical need for support to developing countries with respect to both climate mitigation and adaptation. So far, the large majority of climate financing for developing countries and emerging economies has been channelled into climate change mitigation. This includes support for the International Climate and Forest Initiative, which is the largest single element in Norway's public climate finance. At COP26, Norway's prime minister confirmed high-level support for this initiative until 2030. The government intends to double its total climate finance to NOK 14 billion (USD 1.6 billion) by 2026 at the latest, including three times more support for climate adaptation. The climate adaptation pillar of Norway's 2021 Strategy for Climate Adaptation, Prevention of Climate-related Disasters and the Fight against Hunger covers five priority areas: i) early warning systems and climate services; ii) nature-based solutions; iii) climate-resilient food production; iv) infrastructure; and v) innovative finance mechanisms (Ministry of Climate and Environment, 2021[76]). Norway is one of the largest donors to the Green Climate Fund, contributing NOK 3.2 billion (about USD 372 million) for 2020-23.

1.7.3. Preparing for a low-carbon future without oil and gas

Norway ranks number one on the Net Zero Readiness Index (KPMG, 2021[77]). It has a better track record than most other oil exporters in diversifying its economy. The country has many comparative advantages in other industries (e.g. low-carbon manufacturing in electricity-intensive industries, offshore wind, aquaculture, CCS). Building on its human capital with high education levels, well-functioning institutions, effective tax system and robust fiscal policy framework, Norway has the capabilities and financial means to accelerate a just transition within its own borders and abroad.

Uncertainty about the future global price of oil and gas due to shifting global energy demand represents a major risk for future investment. With intensifying global awareness of climate change, Norway's transition from oil and gas activities may be faster than previously expected. Norway is likely to face increasing international pressure with the forging of new coalitions such as the Beyond Oil and Gas Alliance. Six countries have already committed to ending new licensing rounds for oil and gas exploration and production. However, the challenges in economic adjustment brought by any such ban would be larger for Norway (OECD, 2022[20]). The European Union announced in October 2021 that it will seek a ban on oil and gas production throughout the Arctic. There is debate whether Norway should announce an end to new licences for oil and gas exploration. The transition to a less petroleum-dependent economy is already underway. The share of the petroleum sector within national GDP shrank from a peak of 25% in 2008 to 15% in 2021.[15] Employment in the petroleum sector dropped following the oil price plunge in 2014-16 and is set to decline in the long term (Figure 1.27). Facilitating the "creation of profitable green jobs through pricing, public procurement, regulations and measures that support technology development" is an official government priority with a view to promoting a just transition (Government of Norway, 2020[78]). A more circular economy could create many new job opportunities. Shifting employment will require strategic planning and co-ordination.

According to the OECD Economic Survey of Norway 2022, the speed of the transition will determine any critical macroeconomic consequences for the Norwegian economy. If labour and capital resources can be reallocated from the oil and gas sector at a speed that avoids massive unemployment or stranded assets, then the transition will be comparatively benign (OECD, 2022[20]). While reduced oil and gas activities will create important economic and societal repercussions, the impact will probably be less than previously feared (Government of Norway, 2021[79]).

Norway has a long-standing system of social protection and institutionalised tripartite dialogue between the government, trade unions and other labour organisations. The country adopted the 2015 Guidelines for a Just Transition[16] of the International Labour Organization and signed the COP26 "Just Transition" Declaration to ensure that no one is left behind in the transition to net zero economies. Beyond Norway's general system of workers' rights, the government has not yet developed an action plan for a "just and equitable transition" from fossil fuel production (SEI et al., 2021[17]). More clarity about the "fair and equitable" transition in the Norwegian context would be useful. The government also needs to show it will address economic, social, spatial and gender inequalities beyond traditional support for affected communities or unemployment relief for workers. This involves a reflection on root causes to address structural changes and avoid replicating the same inequality patterns in new green industries. Equity issues concern uneven exposure to risk, uneven ability to capture the benefits and uneven responsibility for damage.

Figure 1.27. Employment in the Norwegian petroleum sector

Direct employment in the oil and gas industry

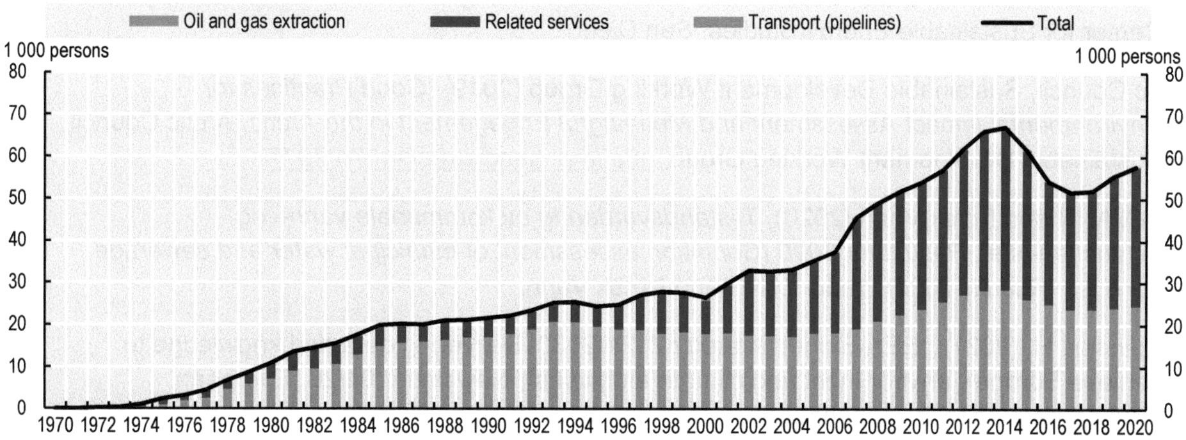

Note: 2019 and 2020 data are preliminary.
Source: Statistics Norway (2021), "Annual National Accounts", *StatBank* (database).

StatLink https://stat.link/wme8cb

Furthermore, the rate of change towards a more sustainable future could be accelerated. Achieving the 2050 targets of a low-carbon society will require government support, stronger private sector investment and civil society engagement. To that end, the government needs to pursue its efforts to help create profitable green jobs through pricing, public procurement, regulations and measures that support technology development (Government of Norway, 2020[78]). It should also ensure attractive conditions for business start-ups along with smooth insolvency processes, remain responsive to evolving skills requirements, and promote education and digitalisation.

The role of the private sector could be further leveraged by better integrating sustainability into business models. A recent survey found that about half of participating companies have a sustainability focus with a publicly stated commitment towards a net zero framework (S-Hub, 2021[80]). While awareness among senior management has increased, middle management needs to be more strongly involved in operationalising new strategies towards a green transition. Efforts to improve the level of competence in different parts of companies need to be pursued. Taxonomy via a common classification system could address greenwashing, promote sustainable investment practices and help companies improve their respective environmental performance.

Civil society groups, communities and – more broadly – citizens are important sources of creativity and innovation, which policy makers could engage more strategically (Bruyninckx, 2021[81]). Transformative change necessarily impacts lifestyle and consumption patterns. Today's children can drive the behavioural and lifestyle changes of tomorrow. Environmental education is of paramount importance.

References

Afewerki, S. et al. (2019), *Conditions for Growth in the Norwegian Offshore Wind Industry*, Center for Sustainable Energy Studies, San Diego. [69]

Arctic Council, Sustainable Development Working Group (2019), *Good Practices for Environmental Impact Assessment and Meaningful Engagement in the Arctic*, Arctic Council, Sustainable Development Working Group, http://hdl.handle.net/11374/2377. [46]

bedreVANN and Norsk Vann (2020), *Tilstandsvurdering av kommunale vann– og avløpstjenester. Resultater 2020 (Condition assessment of municipal water and sewerage services. Results 2020)*, bedreVANN and Norsk Vann. [24]

Bruyninckx, H. (2021), "EEA-Eionet Strategy 2021-2030: Delivering data and knowledge to achieve Europe's environment and climate ambitions", Newsletter 04/20, European Environment Agency, Copenhagen. [81]

Circular Norway (2020), *Norway's Circularity Gap Report 2020*, Circular Norway, Oslo. [30]

City of Oslo (2020), *Climate Strategy for Oslo towards 2030*, City of Oslo. [42]

Climate Action Tracker (2021), *Climate Action Tracker*, website, https://climateactiontracker.org/countries/norway (accessed on 3 December 2021). [35]

Eckstein, D. et al. (2019), *Global Climate Risk Index 2020*, GermanWatch, Bonn. [40]

EEA (2021), *Member States' Greenhouse Gas Emission Projections*, (database), https://www.eea.europa.eu/data-and-maps/data/greenhouse-gas-emission-projections-for-8 (accessed on 3 December 2021). [89]

EEB (2017), *Burning the Evidence. How European Countries Share Industrial Pollution Permit Information Online: A Case Study on Large Combustion Plants*, EEB, Brussels. [48]

Environment Norway (2021), "Freshwater", webpage, https://www.environment.no/topics/freshwater (accessed on 3 December 2021). [23]

EurEau (2021), *Europe's Water in Figures. An Overview of the European Drinking Water and Waste Water Sectors*, EurEau, Brussels. [66]

European Commission (2020), *EU Circular Economy Action Plan 2020*, European Commission, Brussels. [29]

European Commission (2019), "The European Green Deal", webpage, https://ec.europa.eu/info/strategy/priorities-2019-2024/european-green-deal_en (accessed on 10 October 2021). [5]

European Commission (2000), *EU Water Framework Directive, Directive 2000/60/EC*, European Commission, Brussels. [85]

European Environment Agency (2021), *European City Air Quality Viewer*, (database), https://airindex.eea.europa.eu/Map/AQI/Viewer (accessed on 7 December 2021). [87]

Eurostat (2021), *Electricity Price Statistics*, (database), https://ec.europa.eu/eurostat/statistics-explained/index.php?title=Electricity_price_statistics (accessed on 10 November 2021). [52]

Government of Norway (2021), *Norway's Long-term Low-emission Strategy for 2050 Report to the Storting*, Government of Norway, Oslo. [79]

Government of Norway (2020), *Nationally Determined Contribution – Updated Version*, Government of Norway, Oslo. [78]

Government of Norway (2019), *The Government's Action Plan for Green Shipping*, Government of Norway, Oslo. [95]

Hang, W. (2018), "An additional fee on plastic bag: Norwegian consumers' choice on tax or fund based on willingness to pay study", Master's Thesis 2018 30 ECTS, Norwegian University of Life Sciences, https://nmbu.brage.unit.no/nmbu-xmlui. [61]

Hanssen-Bauer, I. et al. (2017), *Climate in Norway 2100 – A Knowledge Base for Climate Adaptation*, Norwegian Centre for Climate Services, Oslo. [39]

Hjorth-Johansen, K. et al. (2021), *Voluntary Subnational Review – Norway: Implementation of the UN's Sustainable Development Goals in Local and Regional Governments in Norway*, Norwegian Association of Local and Regional Authorities, Oslo. [8]

IEA (2021), *Net Zero by 2050*, IEA, Paris, https://www.iea.org/reports/net-zero-by-2050. [19]

IEA (2021), *World Energy Balances*, (database), https://doi.org/10.1787/data-00512-en (accessed on 15 October 2021). [11]

IEA (2021), *World Greenhouse Gas Emissions from Energy*, (database), https://www.iea.org/data-and-statistics/data-product/greenhouse-gas-emissions-from-energy (accessed on 3 December 2021). [90]

IEA (2019), *World Energy Outlook 2019*, IEA, Paris, https://www.iea.org/reports/world-energy-outlook-2019. [12]

Kantar (2020), *Kantar's Climate Barometer*, website, https://www.kantar.com (accessed on 20 September 2021). [31]

Kattel, R. et al. (2021), "The Green Giant: New Industrial Strategy for Norway", *IIPP Policy Report*, No. PR 21/01, UCL Institute for Innovation and Public Purpose, London, https://www.ucl.ac.uk/bartlett/public-purpose/pr21-01. [16]

KPMG (2021), *Net Zero Readiness Index: Norway*, website, https://home.kpmg/xx/en/home/insights/2021/09/nzri-norway.html (accessed on 1 December 2021). [77]

Ministry of Climate and Environment (2021), *Climate Action Plan 2021-30, Meld. St. 13 (2020 – 2021)*, Norwegian Ministry of Climate and the Environment, Oslo. [15]

Ministry of Climate and Environment (2021), *Klima, sult og sårbarhet.Strategi for klimatilpasning, forebygging av klimarelaterte katastrofer og sultbekjempelse*, [Climate, Hunger and Vulnerability – Strategy for Climate Adaptation, Prevention of Climate-Related Disasters and Hunger Fighting], Ministry of Climate and Environment, Oslo. [76]

Ministry of Climate and Environment (2021), *Norway's Strategy for Developing a Green, Circular Economy*, Ministry of Climate and Environment, Oslo. [28]

Ministry of Climate and Environment (2020), *Norway's Fourth Biennial Report Under the Framework Convention on Climate Change*, Ministry of Climate and Environment, Oslo. [67]

Ministry of Climate and Environment (2019), *Miljøkriminalitet (Environmental Crime), Meld. St. 19 - 2019-20*, Ministry of Climate and Environment, Oslo. [49]

Ministry of Climate and Environment (2017), "Regulations on Impact Assessments", No. 854, Ministry of Climate and Environment, Oslo. [44]

Ministry of Energy and Petroleum (2022), "Oil and Gas", webpage, https://www.norskpetroleum.no/en/economy/governments-revenues (accessed on 3 March 2022). [4]

Ministry of Finance (2021), *Nasjonalbudsjettet 2022 (The National Budget 2022)*, Ministry of Finance, Oslo, https://www.regjeringen.no/contentassets/57a14a2bcf0e4970a23d4199714d0001/no/pdfs/stm202120220001000dddpdfs.pdf. [34]

Ministry of Finance, Expert Group (2021), *Climate Risk and the Government Pension Fund Global*, 15 August, Norwegian Minstry of Finance, Expert Group, Oslo, https://www.regjeringen.no/contentassets/fb49a0e957324d7caadb625c6ec4490c/en-gb/pdfs/r-0655-e-klimarisiko-og-oljefondet.pdf. [75]

Ministry of Local Government and Modernisation (2021), *Voluntary National Review 2021 Norway: Report on the Implementation of the 2030 Agenda for Sustainable Development*, Ministry of Local Government and Modernisation, Oslo. [7]

Ministry of Local Government and Modernisation (2019), *National Expectations regarding Regional and Municipal Planning 2019–23*, Ministry of Local Government and Modernisation, Oslo. [43]

Ministry of Petroleum and Energy (2021), *Energi til arbeid – langsiktig verdiskapning fra norske energiressurser (Energy to work – long-term value creation from Norwegian energy resources)*, Ministry of Petroleum and Energy, Oslo. [14]

Ministry of Petroleum and Energy (2019), *Longship – Carbon Capture and Storage*, Ministry of Petroleum and Energy, Oslo. [68]

Ministry of Transport (2021), *National Transport Plan 2022-33*, Ministry of Transport, Oslo. [36]

Ministry of Transport (2020), *Road Toll Revenues*, Ministry of Transport, Oslo. [56]

Norsk Elbilforening (2021), "Norwegian EV Policy", webpage, https://elbil.no/english/norwegian-ev-policy (accessed on 15 January 2021). [94]

Norsk Industri (2020), *Energy Transition Norway 2020: A National Forecast to 2050*, Norsk Industri, Oslo, https://www.norskindustri.no/siteassets/dokumenter/rapporter-og-brosjyrer/energy-transiton-norway-2020.pdf. [84]

Norway Statistics (2021), "Emissions to Air", *Pollution and Climate*, https://www.ssb.no/en/natur-og-miljo/forurensning-og-klima/statistikk/utslipp-til-luft (accessed on 5 December 2021). [21]

Norwegian Environment Agency (2021), *Klimatilpasning.no*, http://Klimatilpasning.no. [82]

Norwegian Environment Agency (2021), *Pollution Release and Transfer Register*, https://www.norskeutslipp.no/en/Frontpage (accessed on 15 November 2021). [47]

Norwegian Environment Agency (2021), "Wastewater treatment plants", *The Norwegian PRTR*, (database), https://www.norskeutslipp.no/en/Wastewater-treatment-plants-/?SectorID=100 (accessed on 1 December 2021). [25]

Norwegian Retailers' Environment Fund (2021), "Facts and Knowledge about Plastics", webpage, https://handelensmiljofond.no (accessed on 27 December 2021). [60]

OECD (2022), *Environment at a Glance Indicators*, OECD Publishing, Paris, https://doi.org/10.1787/ac4b8b89-en. [32]

OECD (2022), "Focus on Green Recovery", *The OECD Green Recovery Database*, https://www.oecd.org/coronavirus/en/themes/green-recovery (accessed on 15 January 2022). [72]

OECD (2022), *OECD Economic Surveys: Norway 2022*, OECD Publishing, Paris, https://doi.org/10.1787/df7b87ab-en. [20]

OECD (2022), *OECD How's Life? Well-being database*, https://stats.oecd.org/Index.aspx?DataSetCode=HSL (accessed on 15 January 2022). [88]

OECD (2021), "Economic Forecast Summary (December 2021)", *Norway Economic Snapshot*, OECD, Paris, https://www.oecd.org/economy/norway-economic-snapshot/. [3]

OECD (2021), "Effective Carbon Rates 2021", (brochure), OECD, Paris, https://www.oecd.org/tax/tax-policy/effective-carbon-rates-2021-brochure.pdf. [51]

OECD (2021), *Environmental Performance Reviews: Ireland 2021*, OECD Environmental Performance Reviews, OECD Publishing, Paris, https://doi.org/10.1787/9ef10b4f-en. [62]

OECD (2021), *Fisheries and Aquaculture in Norway January 2021*, OECD, Paris, https://www.oecd.org/agriculture/topics/fisheries-and-aquaculture/documents/report_cn_fish_nor.pdf. [6]

OECD (2021), *Government at a Glance 2021*, OECD Publishing, Paris, https://doi.org/10.1787/1c258f55-en. [41]

OECD (2021), "Key findings from the update of the OECD Green Recovery Database", *OECD Policy Responses to Coronavirus (COVID-19)*, 30 September, OECD, Paris, https://www.oecd.org/coronavirus/policy-responses/key-findings-from-the-update-of-the-oecd-green-recovery-database-55b8abba/. [73]

OECD (2021), *Measuring the Distance to the SDGs in Regions and Cities*, (database), https://www.oecd-local-sdgs.org (accessed on 20 November 2021). [10]

OECD (2021), *OECD Economic Outlook, Volume 2021 Issue 2*, OECD Publishing, Paris, https://doi.org/10.1787/66c5ac2c-en. [98]

OECD (2021), *OECD Regulatory Policy Outlook 2021*, OECD Publishing, Paris, https://doi.org/10.1787/38b0fdb1-en. [99]

OECD (2021), *Policies for the Future of Farming and Food in Norway*, OECD Agriculture and Food Policy Reviews, OECD Publishing, Paris, https://doi.org/10.1787/20b14991-en. [22]

OECD (2021), *Revenue Statistics 2021: The Initial Impact of COVID-19 on OECD Tax Revenues*, OECD Publishing, Paris, https://doi.org/10.1787/6e87f932-en. [50]

OECD (2020), "A territorial approach to the Sustainable Development Goals in Viken, Norway", *OECD Regional Development Papers*, No. 03, OECD Publishing, Paris, https://doi.org/10.1787/dc1b182d-en. [9]

OECD (2020), *Sustainable Public Procurement in Norway 2020. MAPS Initiative*, OECD, Paris, https://www.mapsinitiative.org/assessments/MAPS%20Norway%20SPP.pdf. [71]

OECD (2019), *Taxing Energy Use 2019: Using Taxes for Climate Action*, OECD Publishing, Paris, https://doi.org/10.1787/058ca239-en. [97]

OECD (2019), *Waste Management and the Circular Economy in Selected OECD Countries: Evidence from Environmental Performance Reviews*, OECD Environmental Performance Reviews, OECD Publishing, Paris, https://doi.org/10.1787/9789264309395-en. [58]

OECD (2013), *Water and Climate Change Adaptation: Policies to Navigate Uncharted Waters*, OECD Studies on Water, OECD Publishing, Paris, https://doi.org/10.1787/9789264200449-en. [38]

OECD (2011), *OECD Environmental Performance Reviews: Norway 2011*, OECD Environmental Performance Reviews, OECD Publishing, Paris, https://doi.org/10.1787/9789264098473-en. [27]

OECD (2004), *Addressing the Economics of Waste*, OECD Publishing, Paris, https://doi.org/10.1787/9789264106192-en. [57]

OECD/IEA (2021), *Update on recent progress in reform of inefficient fossil-fuel subsidies that encourage wasteful consumption 2021*, https://www.oecd.org/fossil-fuels/publicationsandfurtherreading/OECD-IEA-G20-Fossil-Fuel-Subsidies-Reform-Update-2021.pdf. [64]

OECD/IISD (2021), *The Fossil Fuel Subsidy Tracker*, website, https://fossilfuelsubsidytracker.org (accessed on 5 December 2021). [63]

OFV (2022), "CO2 Emissions New Passenger Cars Per Fuel – January through October 2020", webpage, https://ofv.no/CO2-utslippet/co2-utslippet-januar-til-oktober-2020 (accessed on 4 March 2022). [53]

OFV (2021), "Information on Vehicles", webpage, https://ofv.no (accessed on 15 October 2021). [96]

OMFIF (2021), "Norway's GPFG should join the Net-Zero Asset Owner Alliance", 3 August, Official Monetary and Financial Institutions Forum, https://www.omfif.org/2021/08/norways-gpfg-should-join-the-net-zero-asset-owner-alliance/. [74]

Onstad, G. (2021), *Kommunale avløp 2020. Ressursinnsats, gebyrer, utslipp, rensing og slamdisponering (Municipal Sewers 2020. Resource input, fees, discharges, treatment and sludge disposal)*, Statistics Norway, Oslo, https://www.ssb.no/natur-og-miljo/vann-og-avlop/artikler/kommunale-avlop-2020.ressursinnsats-gebyrer-utslipp-rensing-og-slamdisponering/_/attachment/inline/afc55bc5-66d2-4b47-990f-f4a69a04470c:8845f84ba72f4b3d1cc7eda28ee278f11e517350/RAPP2021-39.pdf. [26]

Østli, V. et al. (2021), "Comparing the Scandinavian automobile taxation systems and their CO2 mitigation effects", *International Journal on Sustainable Transportation*, https://doi.org/10.1080/15568318.2021.1949763. [55]

Sachs, J. et al. (2021), *Sustainable Development Report 2021. The Decade of Action for the Sustainable Development Goals*, Cambridge University Press, United Kingdom, https://doi.org/doi.org/10.1017/9781009106559. [86]

Sanner, J. and T. Bru (2021), *FNs klimarapport og norsk olje- og gassproduksjon (UN Climate Report and Norwegian oil and gas production)*, EnerWe Partner. [13]

SDWG (2019), *Good Practices For Environmental Impact Assessment and Meaningful Engagement in the Arctic*, Arctic Council, Sustainable Development Working Group, http://hdl.handle.net/11374/2377. [45]

SEI et al. (2021), *The Production Gap Report 2021*, Stockholm Institute; International Institute for Sustainable Development, Winnipeg; Overseas Development Institute, London; E3G, London; United Nations Environment Programme, Nairobi. [17]

S-Hub (2021), *The State of Sustainability Norway 2021*, S-Hub, https://www.sustainabilityhub.no. [80]

Statistics Norway (2021), "Electricity", *Energy*, (database), https://www.ssb.no/en/energi-og-industri/energi/statistikk/elektrisitet (accessed on 3 December 2021). [18]

Statistics Norway (2021), "Key Figures for the Population", *Population*, (database), https://www.ssb.no/en/befolkning/nokkeltall/population (accessed on 15 September 2021). [1]

Statistics Norway (2021), "Registered Vehicles", in *Land Transport*, (database), https://www.ssb.no/en/transport-og-reiseliv/landtransport/statistikk/bilparken (accessed on 20 November 2021). [37]

Statistics Norway (2021), "Research and Innovation", in *Technology and Innovation*, (database), https://www.ssb.no/en/teknologi-og-innovasjon/forskning-og-innovasjon-i-naeringslivet (accessed on 3 December 2021). [70]

Statistics Norway (2021), *Table 08940*, (database), https://www.ssb.no/en/statbank/table/08940 (accessed on 3 December 2021). [92]

Statistics Norway (2021), "Table 08940", *StatBank*, (database), http://www.website (accessed on 1 December 2021). [33]

Statistics Norway (2020), *Pollution and Climate*, (database), https://www.ssb.no/en/natur-og-miljo/forurensning-og-klima (accessed on 30 September 2021). [2]

Systemiq and Norwegian Retailers' Environment Fund (2021), *Achieving Circularity. A Zero-Waste Circular Plastic Economy in Norway*, Systemiq, London, Norwegian Retailers' Environment Fund, https://www.systemiq.earth/wp-content/uploads/2021/06/AchievingCircularity-MainReport-June2021.pdf. [59]

Tax Foundation (2021), *Gas taxes in Europe*, https://taxfoundation.org/gas-taxes-in-europe/. [83]

Tax Foundation (2021), "Gas Taxes in Europe", webpage, https://taxfoundation.org/gas-taxes-in-europe (accessed on 28 December 2021). [93]

UNFCCC (2021), *Greenhouse Gas Inventory*, (database), https://unfccc.int/process-and-meetings/transparency-and-reporting/greenhouse-gas-data/ghg-data-unfccc/ghg-data-from-unfccc (accessed on 3 December 2021). [91]

van Dender, K. (2019), "Taxing vehicles, fuels, and road use: Opportunities for improving transport tax practice", *OECD Taxation Working Papers*, No. 44, OECD Publishing, Paris, https://doi.org/10.1787/e7f1d771-en. [54]

WTO (2021), "Proposed fossil fuel subsidies ministerial statement", JOB/GC/264/Rev.3, World Trade Organization, Geneva, https://docs.wto.org/dol2fe/Pages/SS/directdoc.aspx?filename=q:/Jobs/GC/264R3.pdf&Open=True. [65]

Notes

[1] Norway does not formally register the number of Sami people. According to the Sami Parliament census/electoral roll, the number of registered Sami voters has increased from 12 500 people in 2005 to 20 500 in 2021. However, this does not reflect the total number of Sami living in Norway as the census excludes children and Sami people who did not register.

[2] Norway's oil production has been increasing over recent years, notably due to Johan Sverdrup, the country's third largest field coming on stream with record-low CO_2 emissions – 4% of the world average. In addition, despite delays, Johan Castberg fields are expected to become operational by the end of 2023.

[3] Norway starts the second cycle while other EU member countries will already be launching the third cycle. The timeline for Norway under the EEA is different.

[4] Due to long distances and low population density, Norway's sparsely populated areas have a natural disadvantage. For example, the north faces high transport costs and unpredictable weather conditions during the winter. These pose obstacles to business development and make the region less attractive.

[5] EEA regulation does not apply on Svalbard; projects on Svalbard are implemented in accordance with the Svalbard Environmental Protection Act.

[6] In most OECD member countries, non-compliance detection numbers cover only site inspections. In Norway, the coverage is much broader, which makes comparison with other countries difficult.

[7] Norway applies taxes on other GHG emissions, namely hydrofluorocarbons (HFCs) and perfluorocarbons (PFCs), which both can cause harm to human health and the environment. The tax rate in 2021 is NOK 0.591 per kg for each gas, multiplied by their respective global warming potential.

[8] As of July 2021, the price of an allowance permitting 1 tonne of CO_2 to be emitted had increased to slightly above EUR 50. The overall cap on emissions has gradually decreased, which is likely to cause allowance prices to increase further. Energy use subject to the EU ETS is generally exempt from the CO_2 tax on mineral products or benefits from a reduced carbon tax rate. For instance, most of the industry sector is exempted from taxes as it is assumed the EU ETS fully covers fossil fuel use in this sector. Natural gas used by the offshore industry is a notable exception: it is subject to both a carbon tax and EU ETS. Norway's domestic aviation is also covered by both the EU ETS and CO_2 taxes.

[9] This would entail a reduction in the pump price of NOK 0.31 for diesel and NOK 0.28 for petrol compared with the previous government proposal.

[10] Norway applies two taxes on petrol and diesel: the CO_2-tax and the road usage tax. In 2021, these taxes amounted to NOK 6.38 per litre of petrol (NOK 1.37 + NOK 5.01) and NOK 5.16 per litre of diesel (NOK 1.57+3.58 NOK). Norway's road usage tax rate on petrol is higher than the rate applied to other fuels, measured in NOK per litre. The lower rate for diesel is partially justified by the lower energy content, but petrol also has a higher tax rate measured in NOK per megajoule. The same CO_2-tax rate (NOK 766 per tonne of CO_2) applies to all fossil fuels for all road transport.

[11] SDG target 12c aims to "rationalize inefficient fossil-fuel subsidies that encourage wasteful consumption by removing market distortions".

[12] Members include Costa Rica, Denmark, Ethiopia, Finland, New Zealand, Norway, Sweden, Switzerland and Uruguay.

[13] "Climate risk can affect all sectors of the economy in different ways, and a large fund that is broadly invested has nowhere to hide. The fund thus benefits from, and, based on its mandate, should contribute to the achievement of the targets of the Paris Agreement, and [make sure] that the transition to a zero-emission society takes place in an orderly manner".

[14] Statement by Prime Minister Jonas Gahr Støre at the UN Climate Change Conference in Glasgow, 2 November 2021: www.regjeringen.no/en/aktuelt/statement-at-the-un-climate-change-conference-in-glasgow/id2882242

[15] In 2021, the petroleum sector represented 41% of total exports, 19% of total investments and 5.8% of employment (Norwegian Ministry of Energy and Petroleum, 2021).

[16] Key elements of a just transition include social protection for people who are adversely affected by the green transition and support for a green transition in the business sector; skills development for everyone; and a green transition based on social dialogue.

Chapter 2. Land use and biodiversity management

This chapter discusses the status and trends for land use and biodiversity management in Norway. It assesses related policies and processes and provides recommendations. Norway's ecosystems are rich and diverse but under threat. The chapter examines how the situation has evolved over the past decade. It points out many worrying trends are likely to continue unless development pressures are addressed and the protected areas network completed. It highlights the need to integrate specific, measurable and time-bound objectives for species, habitat and landscape protection into local planning, including through improved information systems. Finally, the chapter suggests local capacity needs to be strengthened and cross-sector co-ordination improved to achieve national objectives for conservation and sustainable use of land.

2.1. Geography and ecosystems

2.1.1. Norway contains a rich and diverse set of ecosystems

Norway is located on the northwest coast of the Scandinavian Peninsula. It is one of the world's northernmost countries, with the mainland reaching beyond the Arctic Circle. It is bounded by the Barents Sea to the north, the North Atlantic Ocean to the west, the North Sea to the southwest and the Skagerrak strait to the south. Norway's primary land border is with Sweden to the east, but it also borders Finland and the Russian Federation (hereafter "Russia").

The archipelago of Svalbard and Jan Mayen Island are also part of Norway. These are sparsely inhabited and subject to special management regimes aimed at conserving their arctic wilderness landscapes of tundra, glacier and bare mountains, as well as their unique cultural environment (Box 2.1).

Box 2.1. Svalbard - conservation of Arctic wilderness under rapid climate change

Svalbard is a group of islands located about 1 000 km from the North Pole, with some of the Earth's northernmost permanent settlements. With the exception of a few areas surrounding the settlements and mining areas, the archipelago still appears as a large Arctic wilderness with no elements of heavy infrastructure development such as roads or power lines. Svalbard also has an abundant and largely intact High Arctic wildlife, which has been restored from historic overharvesting and is now extensively protected. The Svalbard Environmental Protection Act, which entered into force in 2002, serves to preserve a near-pristine environment in Svalbard with regard to contiguous areas of wilderness, landscape, flora, fauna and cultural heritage. Within this framework, the act allows for environmentally sound community, research and business operations. About two-thirds of Svalbard's land area of 60 000 km^2 is protected as national parks and large nature reserves. These protected areas also include 87% of Svalbard's territorial waters, preserving the wildlife of the seasonally ice-covered waters surrounding the archipelago.

With Norwegian coal mining being phased out, the main activities in Svalbard are now tourism, research, higher education and space-related activities. While Svalbard has only about 2 900 permanent residents, it typically receives more than 100 000 tourists each year. Before the COVID-19 pandemic, the number of tourists was increasing rapidly. Following the slow-down during the pandemic, numbers had begun to increase again in early 2022. Despite strict environmental management policy, the massive inflow of tourists and ever-growing tourism demand increase pressure on the environment and infrastructure.

Svalbard and the surrounding marine areas are among the parts of the Arctic where climate change is fastest. These changes are making both nature and cultural heritage sites more vulnerable to human activity and traffic. In addition to the direct environmental impacts of climate change, retreating sea ice is making more of Svalbard's coastal and marine areas accessible much of the year. This presents opportunities for a continued rise in maritime traffic related to cruise tourism and fishing around Svalbard and in the northern Barents Sea. At the same time, it increases the potential for environmental impacts and risks. An important objective, therefore, is to adapt management policy to the rapid climatic and environmental changes Svalbard is facing. Recent measures include expansion of a national park to enhance the protection of key habitats for sea-ice dependent species such as ringed seals and polar bears. Heavy fuel oil has also been banned in Svalbard's territorial waters. A set of additional regulations to reduce the impact from tourism and other human traffic is under discussion.

Source: Country submission.

Rugged mountains and high mountain plateaus divide Norway into oceanic western and continental eastern parts. The mountains are broken by fertile river valleys. There is also Arctic tundra in the northernmost parts of the country. The climate varies from temperate along the south coast to subarctic in the mountains and in the north. Atlantic winds and the Gulf Stream provide for a climate that is more favourable in Norway than is usual for high latitudes, but it is nonetheless typified by a cold and continental climate.

Norway's landscape is dominated by forest and bare mountains. Forests cover 37% of land area, about 70% of which is considered capable of producing more than 1 cubic metre (m^3) of wood biomass per hectare (ha) per year. Above the treeline, mountains consist of bare rocks, as well as of permanent snow and glaciers (7% and 1% of the total area, respectively). Mountain valleys are rich in wetlands, including peatlands and ribbon lakes. The area suitable for farming is scarce, with agricultural land accounting for only 3% of the country's surface (Figure 2.1). Any land not used for agriculture, forests, built-up or traffic areas is known as open firm ground, which may be vegetated or bare. This includes hayfields, pastures and coastal heathlands.

Figure 2.1. Most land is forest or mountains

Land cover by category, 2021

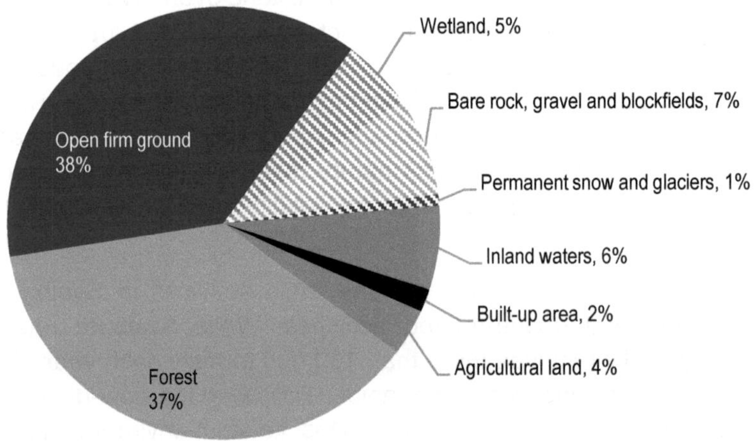

Source: Statistics Norway (2021), "Land use and land cover", *StatBank* (database).

StatLink https://stat.link/tjchi5

Norway has a wide range of climatic conditions, landscapes, vegetation and land use in close proximity, making it one of the most diverse landscapes in Europe (Simensen, Erikstad and Halvorsen, 2021[1]) (Figure 2.2). More than one-third of the bioclimatic variation in all of Europe and North Africa is represented within mainland Norway (Metzger et al., 2005[2]).

Despite being dominated by forest and mountain landscape, Norway has rich landscape diversity, particularly in the southern regions. In addition, it also contains the largest and most pristine representations of many European landscape types. Consequently, Norway plays an important role in landscape and species conservation for the whole continent.

Figure 2.2. Southern Norway has highly diverse landscapes

Share of landscape categories appearing within a 50 km radius of location, average for all classifications used

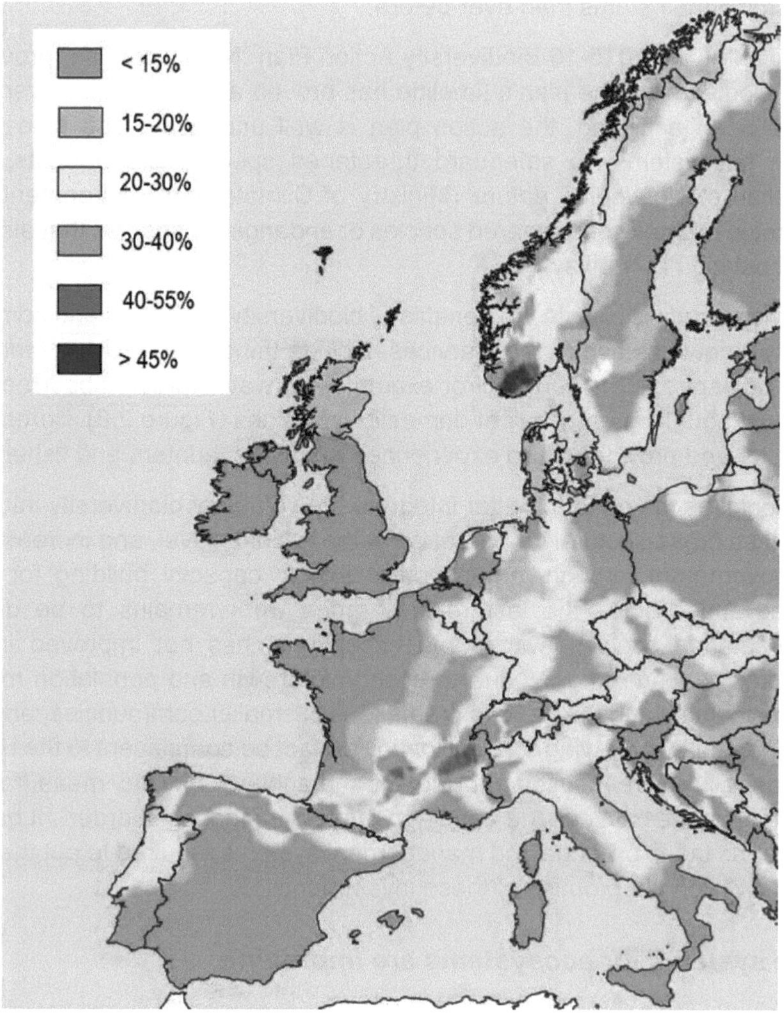

Note: Southern areas of Norway contain representations of more than 45% of all identified European landscape types in close proximity.
Source: Ciglič and Perko (2013), *DragoEurope's landscape hotspots*.

2.1.2. Norway needs to deliver on its ambitious objectives for ecosystem protection

Norway's national objectives cover a range of areas and express a vision of a nation that is environmentally responsible at home and abroad. It aims to protect biodiversity and important landscapes, and maintain a strong economy that is progressively diversified in a just transition from fossil fuel production.

There has been good progress since the last OECD Environmental Performance Review (OECD, 2011[3]). The policy agenda has advanced with the 2009 Nature Diversity Act. National policies have been clarified in the 2019 central government planning guidelines, as well as the Circular T-2/16, which lays out guidance for national priorities and interests (revised in 2021). Government guidance to municipalities for biodiversity plans and environmental impact assessments (EIAs) has been improved. The River Basin Management System has been established to implement the EU Water Framework Directive (WFD). Marine management plans have been continually improved.

Norway has advanced its ability to understand and communicate the status of ecosystems. This is reflected in improvements to the Nature Index for Norway, the Nature in Norway (NiN) system, the *Naturebase* portal and the 3Q monitoring system for agricultural landscapes, among others. This work provides important enabling conditions for better policy making, objective setting and knowledge-based management. Norway has increased the amount of protected areas and reformed their management system. More species have been assessed regarding their status than ever before.

Perhaps most significantly, the 2015-16 Biodiversity Action Plan "Nature for Life" provides a clear agenda for ecosystems and biodiversity. The plan's timeline has proven ambitious. However, while not all of the goals for 2020 have been achieved, the action plan is well underway. The plan set goals for "good ecological status" in ecosystems, to safeguard threatened species and habitats, and to maintain a representative selection of Norwegian nature (Ministry of Climate and Environment, 2015[4]). As a first priority, it seeks to protect critically endangered species or endangered species that also have a substantial proportion of their population in Norway.

The plan also gives increased visibility to the benefits of biodiversity to citizens and communities. The value of nature to humanity, known as ecosystem services, include things that provide food and raw materials, purify air and water, or inspire and entertain. For example, Norway's forests absorb carbon dioxide (CO_2) each year in an amount equal to nearly half of domestic emissions (Figure 2.8). Forests underpin a robust forestry products sector and provide nature experiences for hikers, hunters and fishers, among others.

The government recognises the need to better integrate the values of biodiversity into decision making. It also seeks to strengthen cross-sectoral co-operation at the national level, and increase cohesion between different levels of government through, among other things, capacity building for local governments. However, despite advances since the last review, much work remains to be done. The status of ecosystems and threatened species, with some exceptions, has not improved in the past decade. Development pressures continue to grow due to economic growth and population movement, increased demand for leisure residences and the need to create jobs in smaller communities, among others. Climate change is also an important and growing threat. Norway cannot be complacent to the risks faced by nature. Meeting the challenge will require focused effort to set and achieve specific, measurable and time-limited goals. Most of the action in the past decade has been "getting the house in order". It has established plans and objectives, as well as the knowledge and management systems required to put these plans into action. The next step is to deliver on the promise of these investments.

2.1.3. Knowledge systems for ecosystems are improving

The Nature Index for Norway framework describes the status of ecosystems according to a large number of indicators. The index is updated every five years, most recently in 2020. The Nature Index data and assessments are maturing into a useful tool for setting national objectives related to ecosystem management. The quality status of ecosystems as measured by the index has the potential to become an important policy benchmark.

The Biodiversity Action Plan points to the need for measurement of ecological status to set related objectives:

> One problem for the Norwegian authorities is the lack of clear, agreed management objectives for "good ecological status" in most ecosystems, even though "sustainable" management is specified as a goal in a number of statutes. The exceptions are coastal and freshwater ecosystems and to some extent marine ecosystems. Clearly defined and agreed management objectives for the different ecosystems would provide a better basis for making decisions in cases where a balance needs to be found between different interests and social objectives, and would help to achieve environmentally, socially and economically sustainable development.
>
> *(Ministry of Climate and Environment, 2015[4])*

The Nature Index supports indices of ecosystem quality by different ecosystem types. A value of 1.0 indicates a fully natural condition, while a status of 0.6 or better is considered "good". This index shows that many landforms are in good condition but also points to some worrying areas, especially forests, open lowlands and wetlands (Table 2.1).

Table 2.1. Overview of condition and trends for Norwegian ecosystems

	Nature index value	Overall assessment	Key influencing factors	Trends
Ocean	0.70	Good	Climate Change Acidification Fisheries Litter	Positive development, slight decline over the last few years
Coastal waters	0.67	Fairly good	Pollution Loss of area Harvesting Alien species	Stable slight decline
Fresh water	0.74	Good	Acid rain Eutrophication Hydropower Alien species Interventions and degradation	Stable, slight improvement over the last years
Wetland	0.68	Fairly good	Area loss Overgrowth	Slightly improving
Forest	0.41	Relatively poor	Forestry	Improving
Mountain	0.56	Moderate	Area degradation and fragmentation Climate change	Gradual decline
Open lowlands	0.44	Relatively poor	Overgrowth More intensive farming Alien species	Continued negative development

Note: The Nature Index is a composite index based on the weighted average of scaled indicators representing major ecosystems.
Source: (Norwegian Environment Agency, 2021[5]); trends from (Lier-Hansen et al., 2013[6]).

NiN is a tool to document and develop knowledge about Norwegian natural variation, and can be used to map ecosystems for many purposes. It was developed in 2005 by the Norwegian Biodiversity Information Centre, which also provides financial support for the project. NiN version 1.0 was published in 2009. NiN version 2.0, which began in 2012, was published in 2015.

NiN is central to nature mapping, as called for in the Biodiversity Action Plan (Ministry of Climate and Environment, 2015[4]). It is designed to give professionals and institutions a common set of concepts that describe and map the variation in nature at all levels, and serve as a basis for mapping nature and habitat types. It is an important part of the Red List assessment of habitat types.

NiN is based on the Biodiversity Act's definition of a habitat type: a uniform area type that includes all living organisms that occur together in a given place and the environmental conditions that operate there. It also includes areas with a uniform character caused by systematic patterns in the presence of observable structures and elements. NiN aims to be the most complete system possible for describing biodiversity and ecosystems in Norway (Halvorsen et al., 2015[7]). It operates on many scales that are relevant for national and local planning.

2.1.4. Ecosystem accounting can help integrate nature into decision systems

The Nature Diversity Act aims to protect nature's diversity through conservation and sustainable use to secure a basis for human welfare, now and in the future. To fulfil that purpose, more weight must be attached to nature's use and non-use values, and ecological value. Accounting for these values systematically can allow the status of nature to be tracked over time, providing cross-sectoral knowledge of land-use change and its effects on ecosystems.

Natural capital or ecosystem accounting is an important step for making nature visible in measures of national performance and policy appraisal. It is also a prerequisite for assessing changes in inclusive wealth. Natural capital accounts organise biophysical and economic data on the stock of natural resources and the flows of resources and ecosystem services that support the economy (OECD, 2021[8]).

The UN System of Environmental Economic Accounting–Ecosystem Accounting (SEEA-EA) provides a comprehensive framework that could be applied in Norway (Box 2.2). Using an internationally consistent approach could help Norway to benchmark progress with respect to other countries. Such an approach could be used, for example, with respect to implementation of the Sustainable Development Goals (SDGs). This may be particularly useful in the European context, as the SEEA-EA is applied at European scale by the Joint Research Centre, the European Environment Agency and Eurostat. Important policy areas that are increasingly informed by SEEA-EA include climate change, circular economy, biodiversity and sustainable finance. SEEA-EA could also inform measurement of the environmental and economic impacts of managing COVID-19.

Box 2.2. Valuing ecosystems services highlights the role of nature in the economy

Natural capital accounting is an important step for making nature visible in measures of national performance and policy appraisal. It is also a prerequisite for assessing changes in inclusive wealth. Natural capital accounts organise biophysical and economic data on the stock of natural resources and the flows of resources and ecosystem services that support the economy.

Valuation of ecosystem services and assets in monetary units is of primary importance. This allows consistent comparisons between the UN System of Environmental Economic Accounting–Ecosystem Accounting (SEEA-EA) natural capital accounting and standard economic measures, such as gross national product (GDP) or produced assets, as recorded in the system of national accounts. To that end, the SEEA-EA applies the concept of exchange values, which are the market prices of goods and services exchanged in the markets, or the assumed transaction prices for goods and services that have no market. The SEEA-EA, however, does not include all potential economic values, in particular consumer surplus and non-use values. It acknowledges that alternative valuation concepts, including welfare values and total economic values, may be better suited to some policy contexts (e.g. cost-benefit analysis). Furthermore, the SEEA-EA emphasises that care is needed when analysing large, non-marginal changes, such as the permanent loss of water resources. In these cases, analyses should incorporate the assessment of physical changes in stocks in relation to appropriate thresholds. No matter the valuation approach, a pragmatic and necessary first step is to develop robust accounts of biophysical stocks and flows.

Source: OECD (2021), "Biodiversity, natural capital and the economy: A policy guide for finance, economic and environment ministers", *OECD Environment Policy Papers*, No. 26.

The SEEA-EA system is designed to answer the following questions (United Nations, 2021[9]):

- What is the contribution of ecosystems and their services to the economy, social well-being, jobs and livelihoods?
- How is the condition, health and integrity of ecosystems and biodiversity changing over time and where are the main areas of degradation and enhancement?
- How can natural resources and ecosystems be best managed to ensure continued services and benefits such as energy, food supply, water supply, flood control, carbon storage and recreational opportunities?
- How should conservation efforts be targeted?
- What opportunities exist for development of innovative incentive-based programmes to conserve nature such as payment for ecosystem services?
- What do estimates of a nation's wealth and economic potential look like once the state of its environment is considered?

At least 89 countries have implemented accounts consistent with the SEEE-EA. However, most accounts are incomplete and only 34 countries have developed ecosystem accounts. Adopting a robust SEEA-EA system could put Norway at the forefront of this type of environmental knowledge system.

2.2. Biodiversity

2.2.1. A significant share of assessed species is threatened

The Norwegian Red List of Species includes those assessed as at risk of extinction within Norway, with different risk categories. A large proportion of the red-listed species has declining populations, generally because of habitat loss, degradation or fragmentation as a result of human activity. Due to its long western coast and long north-south mountain range, many species have their most northern or western occurrence in Norway. For this reason, Norway has a high number of rare species or species with naturally small populations.

Of the 2 752 threatened species in Red List 2021, 289 are critically endangered, 959 are endangered and 1 504 are vulnerable (Artsdatabanken, 2021[10]). Moreover, 333 species assessed in 2015 as of least concern are now on the list. At the same time, 309 species have left the Red List owing to improved knowledge and oversight. In addition, 1 839 species have been assessed for the first time. Of the endangered or critically endangered species in 2015, 78 have 25% or more of their European population in Norway.

In 2021, 24% of mammals, 27% of bird species, 22% of mosses and 22% of plants were threatened. The share of threatened species in all four of these categories has increased since 2015. The total number of assessed species has also increased. Norway's profile is overall similar to its Nordic neighbours, with a comparatively large share of threatened birds. Finland is doing better overall but also has a large share of threatened birds (Figure 2.3)

Most threatened species are associated with forest, cultural landscapes (semi-natural areas or open land used for agriculture) and mountains, and to a lesser extent with wetlands and marine and coastal waters (Figure 2.4). More than half of the threatened mountain species (34 of 64 species), and most of the threatened mosses and vascular plants, are found in lime-rich areas (Ministry of Climate and Environment, 2015[4]). Threatened species are found mainly in the southern regions where species diversity is high and human activity widespread (Figure 2.4). These regions also have a large number of threatened habitats.

Figure 2.3. The share of threatened species in Norway is similar to its Nordic neighbours

Threatened species as a percentage of known species, 2015 or latest available data

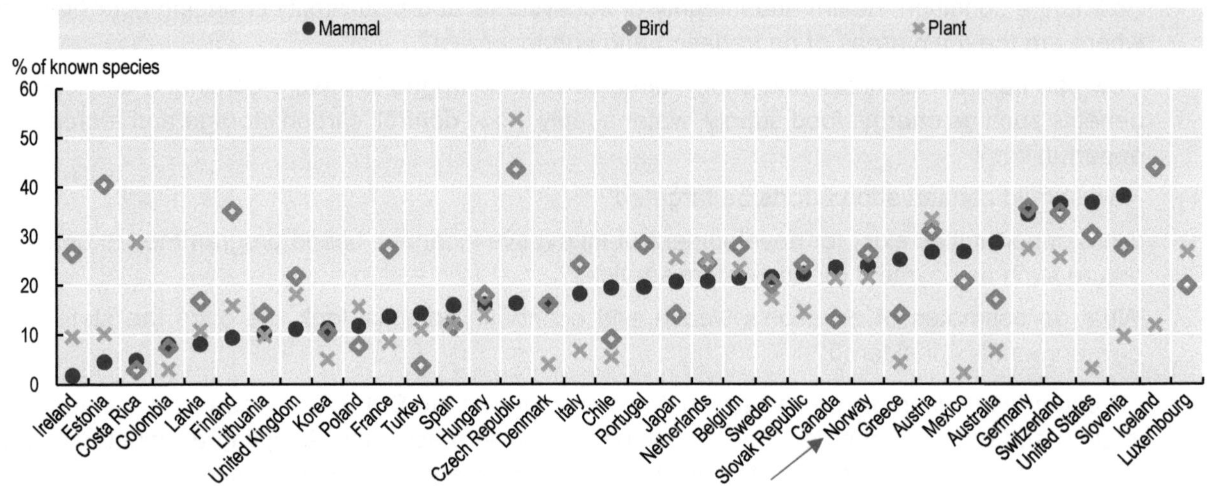

Note: The threatened category refers to critically endangered, endangered and vulnerable species, i.e. those plants and animals that are in danger of extinction or likely soon to be (for further information, see the IUCN Red List Categories and Criteria: Version 3.1, Second edition). Iceland, Luxembourg and Portugal: partial data. Norway: 2021 data.
Source: OECD (2021), "Threatened species", *OECD Environmental Indicators* (database).

StatLink https://stat.link/7r9ngk

Figure 2.4. Most threatened species live in forests or semi-natural areas in southern regions

Threatened species by main habitat

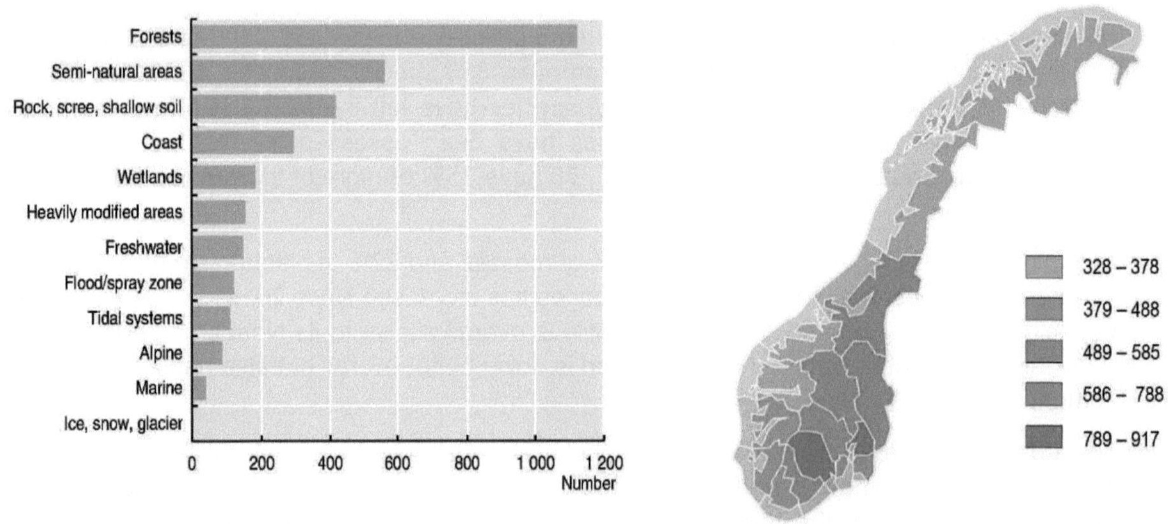

Note: Right panel: number of threatened species on the Red List 2021 with a known occurrence in the various (historical) counties.
Source: Artsdatabanken (2021), *Findings: Norwegian Red List for Species 2021*.

StatLink https://stat.link/pdzbmn

The overall trend in status of Norway's threatened species is worrying. There is a real increase in the number of threatened species, and more species have been moved to a higher risk category than a lower one. Between 2015-21, the status of 1 523 species changed. However, most changes in classification are due to improved information or re-interpretation of data rather than a genuine status change (Figure 2.5). Climate change is an important factor in the increased risk for mountain species.

Figure 2.5. Relatively few species change status due to genuine changes

Reason for transfer between Red List categories, from 2015 to 2021

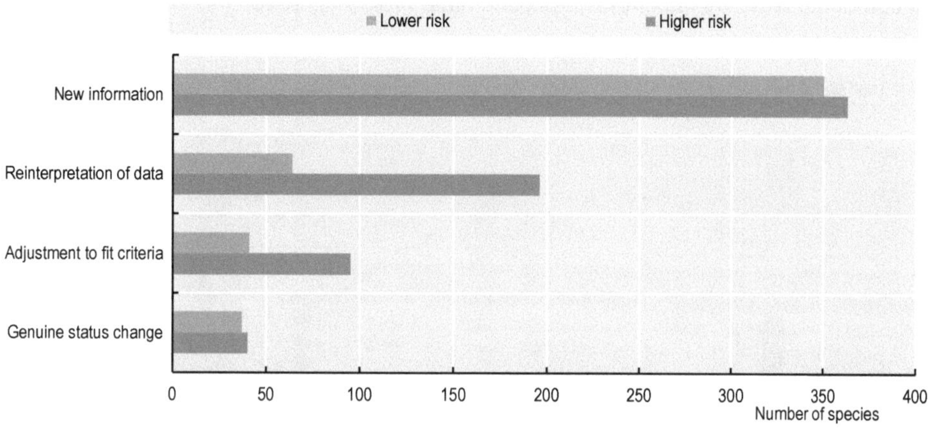

Source: Artsdatabanken (2021), *Endringer fra 2015 til 2021, Norsk rødliste for arter 2021* [Changes from 2015 to 2021, Norwegian Red List for Species 2021] (database).

StatLink https://stat.link/uc0gyw

The trend between 2015 and 2021 is worse than the one observed between 2010 and 2015 (Henriksen and Hilmo, 2015[11]). Efforts over the last decade have not improved the status of threatened species overall. The dependence of a high proportion of species on forested land or cultural landscapes is a particular challenge. These land types are relatively valuable and are implicated in sectoral objectives to maintain or increase commercial exploitation. In particular, forested land is only protected by landowners voluntarily. This limits the government's capacity to act with respect to the most important land category for threatened species.

Protecting the habitats of threatened species via protected area status is the main policy tool to maintain or improve the status of red-listed species. However, the government also undertakes other measures to supplement this tool. For example, it allocated NOK 3.1 million (USD 361 000) in the 2021 budget to supplement measures to protect wild pollinating insects. From 2017, the budget for measures against invasive alien species has increased. About NOK 86 million (about USD 9.1 million) was spent on measures against alien species in the last five years, mainly to combat alien plant species. In 2018-20, the government devoted NOK 27 million (USD 2.9 million) to removing invasive tree species from protected areas.

2.2.2. Land-use change is the most important threat to species and habitats

Habitat loss and degradation of ecosystems are the primary reasons behind biodiversity loss and the loss of ecosystem services globally, and this is true for Norway as well (Figure 2.6). Land-use changes in forestry and in agriculture, as well as for housing and road purposes, are the most important driver of habitat loss in Norway. More than 90% of the threatened or near threatened species are threatened because their habitats disappear or change (Artsdatabanken, 2021[12]).

Figure 2.6. Land use and climate change place the greatest pressure on Norwegian biodiversity

Causes of deviation of the Nature Index from its pristine state (value 1), 2019

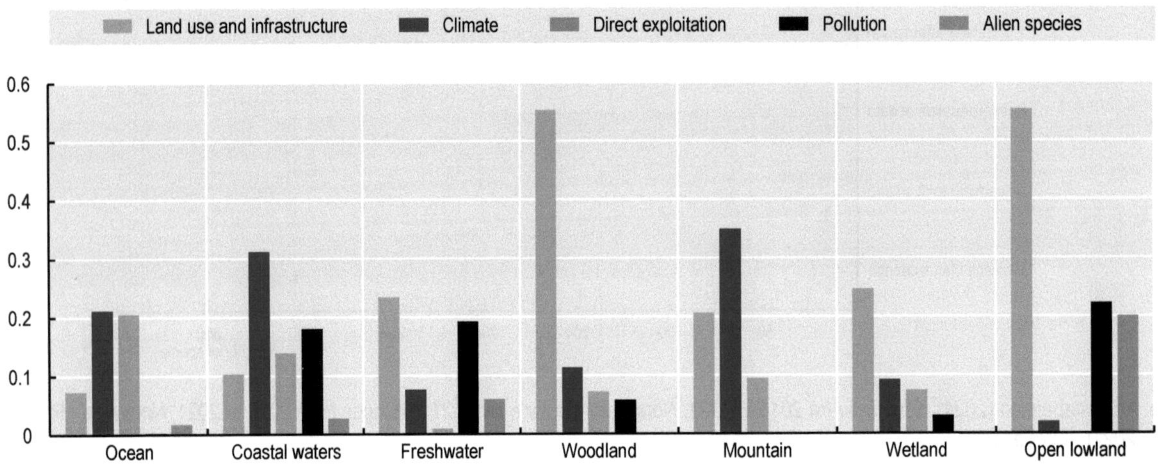

Note: The effect of five pressure categories on the Nature Index value is analysed for each ecosystem. Indicators sensitive to each pressure category have been grouped, and the effect of a pressure has been estimated as the contribution from these indicators to a reduced Nature Index value (deviation from the reference value 1). The effect has been analysed using the Nature Index values from 2019 for each ecosystem. A high value on the y-axis indicates the pressure category has a large negative effect on the ecosystem. The effects of the pressure categories do not sum to a "true" total deviation from 1 for an ecosystem, as indicators may be included in more than one pressure category within the same ecosystem.
Source: Norwegian Environment Agency (2021), *Nature Index* (database), www.naturindeks.no/Pressure.

StatLink https://stat.link/akmodp

Land-use change affects nine out of ten threatened species. In the last 11 years, about 540 km^2 of land have been developed. Overall, this is a small amount, corresponding to 0.16% of the total area over the period and 0.015% per year, but these areas may have high ecosystem value. About 42% of developed land was formerly forest, 17% agricultural land and 2% bog (Kommunal- og moderniseringsdepartementet, 2021[13]).

Despite ongoing efforts to improve the representativeness of the protected area system, existing protected areas do not capture the breadth of variation in Norwegian nature. Further, there is a lack of ecological connection between the areas, which lowers their resilience.

2.2.3. Forest area is in relatively poor condition and challenging to protect

Forest and other wooded land cover approximately 37% of Norway's land area. About 70% of this is considered productive forest, which can produce 1 m^3 or more of wood per hectare each year. The most important commercial wood species are Norway spruce (47%), Scots pine (33%) and birch (18%) (Landbruks- og matdepartementet, 2020[14]).

Norway protects 5% of forest area, which is only half of the government's target. Productive forest land is relatively valuable compared with unproductive forest land, and ownership is diverse with many small landowners. This makes it challenging to increase the amount of protected forest area. Almost uniquely among land types, additional protection of forest area is voluntary, requiring the proactive agreement of landowners. This reduces conflicts with landowners but makes achieving the 10% target difficult without additional measures.

Forest area is largely stable over time, though the ecological condition of forest lands in aggregate is relatively poor. According to the system for assessing ecological condition, the Norwegian forest area has a 0.42 rating. This is significantly lower than 0.6, the limit value for good ecological condition (Figure 2.7).The ecological condition of forests in the coming decades is expected to deteriorate due to the continued influence of forestry activities, buildings and infrastructure development, and to a lesser extent climate change (Framstad et al., 2021[15]).

Figure 2.7. The overall condition of forest lands is relatively poor

Estimated ecological condition of forest area in Norway: scaled indicator values, 1 = pristine, 0.6 = good condition

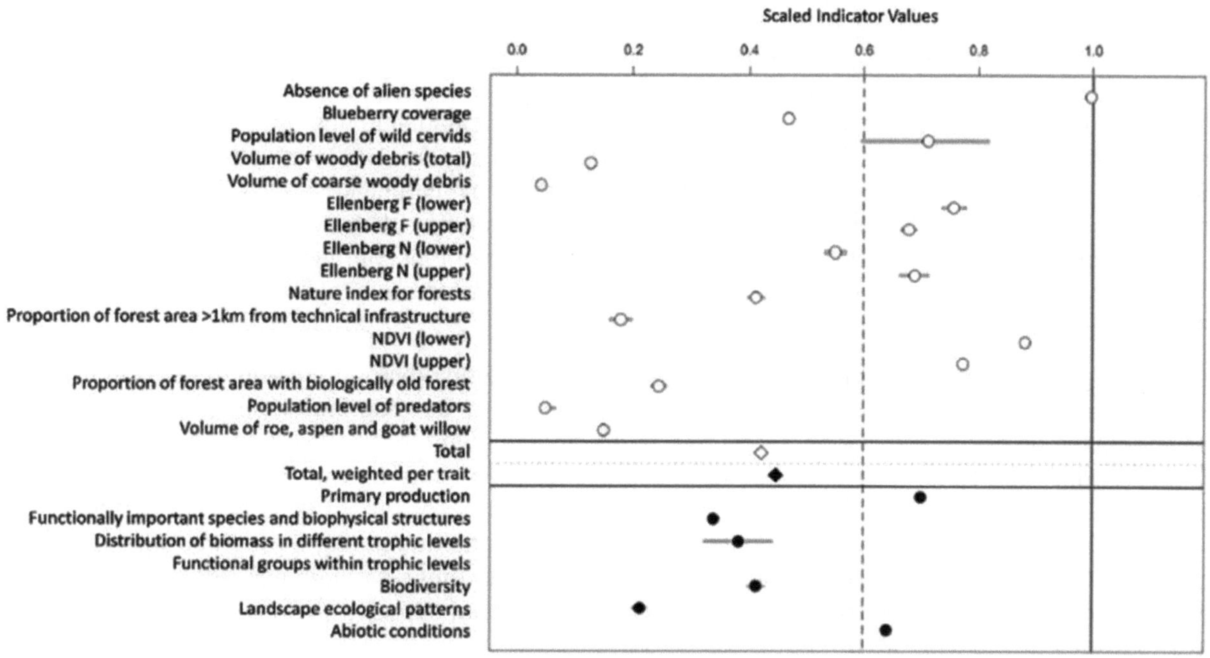

Note: White circles indicate the scaled values for the individual indicators included in the calculation. White diamond shows the total state value of the ecosystem based on these indicators directly, while the black diamond shows the total state value based on the state values of the various properties of the ecosystem (black circles). The symbols show median values for indicators or average state values, while grey and black bars show the 95% confidence interval. Some confidence intervals are so small that they are covered by the symbols. NDVI = Normalised Difference Vegetation index, a measure of vegetation cover. Ellenberg F = indicator of soil moisture. *Ellenberg N = indicator of soil productivity.*
Source: Framstad et al. (2021), Vurdering av økologisk tilstand for skog i Norge i 2020 [Assessment of Ecological Condition for Forests in Norway in 2020].

The state-owned company Statskog SF is the largest forest owner in Norway, with approximately 6% of productive forest area. Approximately 88% of forest area is privately owned, resulting in a diversified sector characterised by small-scale activity. Forestry operations are mostly co-ordinated through the forest owners' co-operative. The average size of clear cuttings is estimated to be approximately 3.2 ha.

Norway is active in intranational forest conservation efforts (Box 2.3). It was one of the earliest participants in the Programme for the Endorsement of Forest Certification (PEFC), an independent third-party certification system for forest products. Norway first joined PEFC in 1999, and its standard was first endorsed in 2000. It has subsequently been reviewed every five years, most recently in 2016. The system is now in its fourth revision, which covers 2020-22. Norway's standard covers activities related to forest management responsibilities and planning, felling and forestry operations and special environmental values (PEFC Norway, 2016[16]).

Box 2.3. Norway is a leader in international forest conservation

Norway's International Climate and Forest Initiative (NICFI) is its biggest development co-operation programme in climate and environment. NICFI makes up more than half of environmental and sustainable development assistance expenditure since 2009. Most of NICFI's activities address forest and land-use policies and planning. This includes law enforcement, Indigenous People's territories and forest protection, combined with sustainable development, global drivers of deforestation and deforestation-free supply chains and financial markets.

Norway's approach to prevention of international deforestation and forest degradation has evolved since NICFI's inception in 2008. NICFI was initially set up as a payment mechanism focused on establishing carbon markets for reduced emissions from deforestation and forest degradation (REDD+). NICFI has also given attention to green development, and sustainable food and land use systems within planetary boundaries. It is one of the three national participants in the Lowering Emissions by Accelerating Forest Finance (LEAF) Coalition, which was set up in April 2021 after the Leaders' Climate Summit. The LEAF Coalition works to halt deforestation by financing large-scale tropical forest protection through a public-private partnership. A growing number of the world's leading companies take part in LEAF. In November 2021, LEAF signed letters of intent with five tropical forest countries (Costa Rica, Ecuador, Ghana, Nepal and Viet Nam) and memoranda of understanding with eight Brazilian states.

Addressing drivers of deforestation requires creating an enabling environment and more incentives for transformational change. This results in a bigger and more development-focused approach than payments for emissions reductions. NICFI has an advantage over other development partners that use annual budgeting: it can take a longer-term perspective on results and make use of results-based finance. It has a portfolio of projects and can redirect funding across them according to performance. In the past, NICFI has tried to increase its impact by leveraging its funding through co-financing with partners. This will continue through the LEAF Coalition and in other partnerships. Future approaches may better focus on its comparative advantages and institutional capacity.

Source: Country submission.

While forest land area is relatively stable, the total forest biomass is growing strongly. Harvests of around 10 million metric tonnes (MMT) per year are significantly below the annual growth rate (25 MMT) (Figure 2.8). The annual growth rate has been at or near its highest recorded amount continually since 2003, nearly double the amount since the start of record keeping in the 1930s. These growth levels are the consequence of longstanding forestry management activities that have reduced the age structure of the forest and promoted large-scale replanting.

The amount of carbon absorbed by forest growth is equivalent to about half of the total annual human-induced greenhouse gas (GHG) emissions in the country (Section 1.3). Norwegian forest policy recognises the important role of forests in combating climate change. Consequently, it aims to maintain a high level of wood production. This, in turn, aims to maintain a high annual growth rate and carbon sequestration in forests, while providing climate-friendly raw materials for a range of applications.

The high annual carbon uptake of forest area does not count towards Norway's Nationally Determined Contribution, as it is part of the policy baseline. However, increases in uptake above this baseline do count towards targets, leading to several actions to increase the forests' capacity to sequester carbon. These include measures for increased seedling density on regeneration sites, enhanced breeding of forest seedlings and fertilisation of forest stands. The amount of extra uptake is small but will increase over time.

Figure 2.8. Forest biomass growth is well above the rate of harvest

1 000 m^3 biomass on left axis, annual increment and harvest on right axis, 2000-19

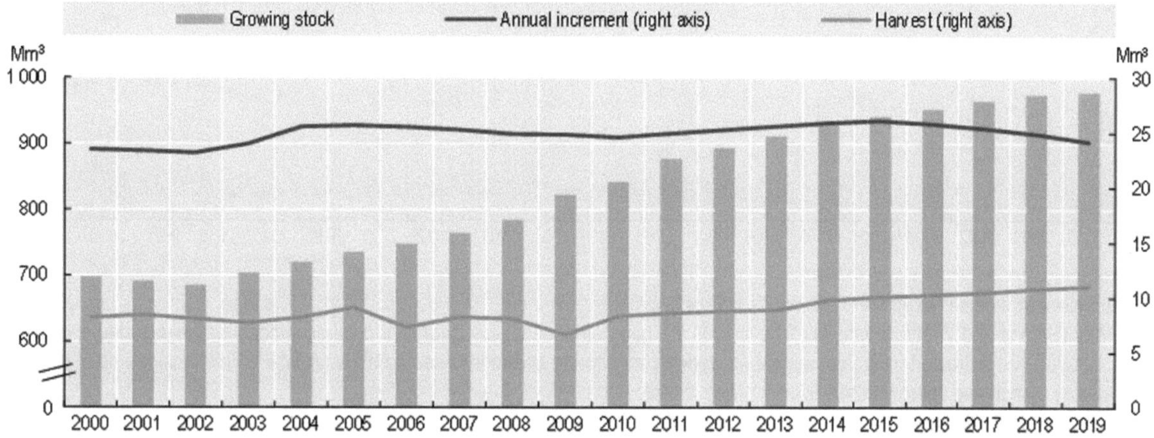

Note: Total biomass and increment, including spruce, pine and broad-leafed forests. One cubic meter of biomass contains approximately one metric tonne of carbon that has been extracted from the atmosphere.
Source: Statistics Norway (2021), "The National Forest Inventory", *StatBank* (database).

StatLink https://stat.link/hbvc91

2.2.4. Changing agriculture practices and the quality of cultural landscapes are closely associated

Agricultural landscapes are important ecosystems that provide services such as food production, animal feed production, pollination and biodiversity. Agricultural activity creates a large number of different semi-natural landscapes. The cultural and ecosystem value of these landscapes depends on how they are used, making this landscape type uniquely intertwined with human activity. Around 50% of threatened species are linked to cultural landscapes and open lowlands. Mowing and grazing help maintain important habitat types in agriculture, such as hay meadows and coastal heaths (Landbruks- og matdepartementet, 2016[17]).

The interplay of ecosystems with human activity can be seen in the rapid decline of farmland bird species compared to other Nordic countries (Figure 2.9). The sector's transformation from low productivity, labour-intensive methods into more capital-intensive systems has altered the way it interacts with the landscape. Some landscape types such as hay fens have been red-listed as a result. This change is just as important as land conversion in terms of the effect on threatened species that depend on agricultural landscapes.

Figure 2.9. Norway's farm bird populations are declining more strongly than in neighbouring countries

Farm Birds index, year 2000=100

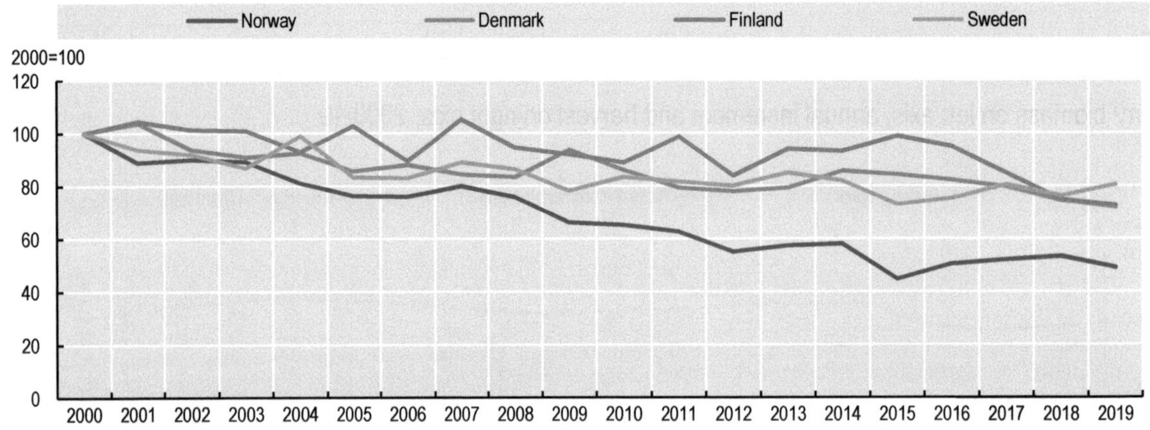

Note: Index for Norway includes eight species: *Alauda arvensis, Emberiza citrinella, Hirundo rustica, Motacilla alba, Numenius arquata, Saxicola rubetra, Sturnus vulgaris* and *Vanellus vanellus.* The indices are geometric means of national population indices for the included species. Since 2009, all data have been extracted from the national network for monitoring common breeding birds (TOV-E). This includes point censoring in a national network comprising approximately 500 sampling routes, https://tov-e.nina.no/hekkefugl.
Source: OECD (2021), *OECD Agri-Environmental Indicators* (database).

StatLink https://stat.link/2h3opf

Roughly one-third of active agricultural area is used to grow arable crops (327 000 ha in 2018, including 500 ha of fallow land), a share that has declined by 5% over the last 20 years (Statistics Norway, 2021[18]). The balance of agricultural land is mainly pastures, meadows and other permanent grasslands typically used for grazing pastures or harvesting of grass. Agricultural land use is largely determined by the small share of land that is technically feasible for farming combined with national policies designed to maintain and distribute production. The agricultural areas with the best growing conditions are dedicated to grain cultivation, while those with less favourable ones are used for animal husbandry. Policies in place maintain this distribution of production types, which maximises grain production.

Norway's levels of nitrogen and phosphorus surpluses, which place pressure on soil water and air quality, are among the highest in the OECD (Figure 2.10).

Figure 2.10. Nutrient surpluses remain high in Norway despite declines across the OECD

Nutrient surpluses per agricultural land area

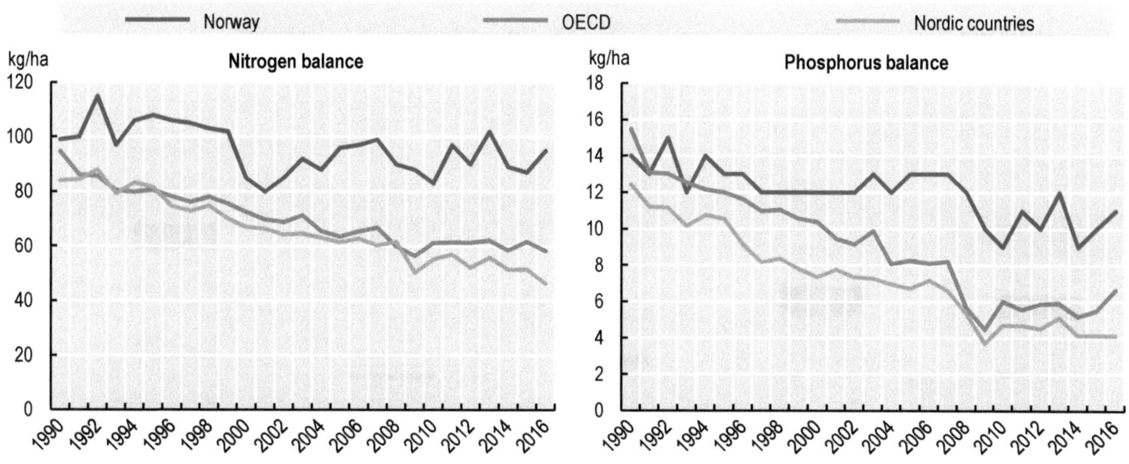

Note: Manure accounts for 57% of phosphorus inputs and 47% of nitrogen inputs. Nutrient surpluses per agricultural land area (in hectares) are measured as the difference between the total quantity of nutrient inputs entering an agricultural system (mainly fertilisers, livestock manure), and the quantity of nutrient outputs leaving the system (mainly uptake of nutrients by crops and grassland).
Source: OECD (2022), "Environmental performance of agriculture – nutrients balances", *OECD Agriculture Statistics* (database).

StatLink https://stat.link/2i9ld3

Total agricultural area has been stable over the long term, varying from a low of 0.90 million ha in 1976 to 1.05 million ha at its height in 2001. It was 0.985 million ha in 2021. Agricultural land used for farming reduced on average by 0.5% per year between 2006 and 2016. Unlike the OECD as whole, which has seen reduction in agricultural lands for all uses, the decrease in Norway affected only cropland (-0.7% per annum), while permanent pasture marginally expanded (0.3% per annum). Agropastoral systems make extensive use of unimproved pasture across the country. Agricultural area under organic certification expanded quickly from 1995 until 2012, reaching a maximum of 50 000 ha. Since then, it slowly declined to 4.7% of the total farm land in use in 2018, below average for the European Union (EU 27.8%) (OECD, 2021[19]).

The most productive agricultural areas are often near towns and are flat, accessible and cost efficient for development. This has led to a strong correlation between conversion of farmland and urban areas. Overall, 23% of the total conversion of farmland took place inside urban areas (Figure 2.11). Furthermore, 27% took place close to, and less than 1 km outside urban areas. Scattered development in rural areas (at least 3 km from the urban areas) accounted for 31%. In 2004-15, as much as 12% of all cultivated land in urban areas was converted to built-up areas. The corresponding share for locations less than 1 km outside urban areas was 1.1%. Residential areas constituted the greatest share of the converted land. A total of 2 530 ha of farmland was converted to residential areas, of which 80% was used for single-unit dwellings and semi-detached houses (Gundersen, Steinnes and Jostein Frydenlund, 2017[20]).

Figure 2.11. Most agricultural land near settlements is converted to residential or recreational use

Converted agricultural area by distance from settlements and purpose, 2004-15

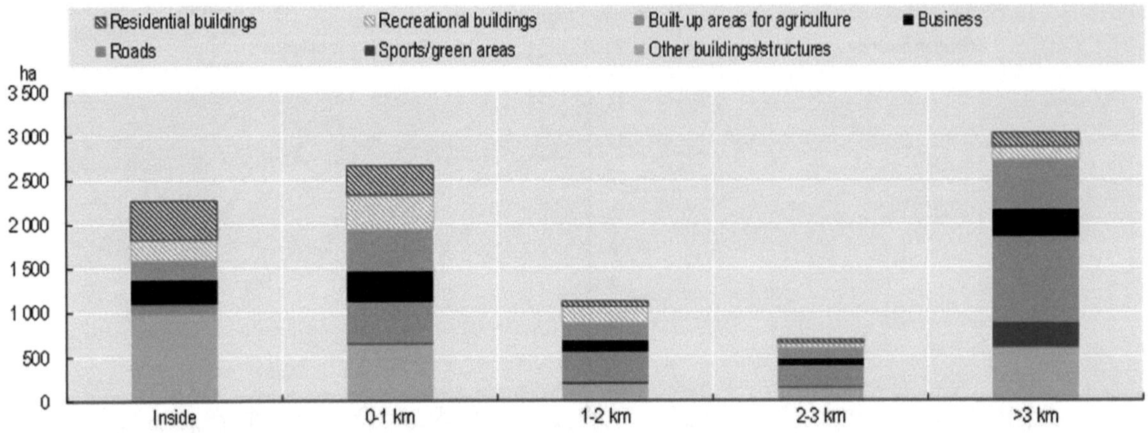

Source: Gundersen et al. (2017), *Nedbygging av jordbruksareal. En kartbasert undersøkelse av nedbygging og bruksendringer av jordbruksareal* [Degradation of Agricultural Land. A Map-based Study of Degradation and Changes in the Use of Agricultural Land].

StatLink https://stat.link/dsfuy4

Agriculture emissions in 2019 were 4.4 million tonnes of CO_2 equivalent (CO_2-eq), a decrease of 6.4% since 1990 (OECD, 2021[19]). GHG emissions from the agricultural sector represent 8.8% of total Norwegian emissions and 18% of non-ETS obligations. Objectives for agriculture are to reduce GHG emissions' intensity in production, increase the uptake of CO_2 and adapt production to a changing climate. The role of agriculture in Norway's climate change reduction plans was outlined in a voluntary agreement between the government and the main farmers' organisations, Norges Bondelag and Norsk Bonde- og Småbrukarlag.

According to the EU Land Use, Land-Use Change and Forestry (LULUCF) Regulation, Norway has committed to ensure that emissions do not exceed removals overall for the land-using sectors. As mentioned earlier, the baseline forest uptake of CO_2 is not counted, which actually makes forestry one of the largest LULUCF emitters under current EU accounting rules (Figure 2.12). Agricultural emissions are largely flat. Limiting conversion of peat bogs to agricultural land is one of the main tools available to control net LULUCF emissions. This would potentially save 450 000 tonnes CO_2-eq for 2021-30, based on an assumption that the restrictions would prevent conversion of 200 ha per year.

Reduced GHG emissions from agriculture are in tension with the goal of increased food production. The potential for carbon leakage is cited as a reason to be less aggressive with respect to mitigation in agriculture [Meld. St. 11 (2016-2017]). For agriculture to continue to be exempt from carbon taxation and other measures applied elsewhere, the sector must make a good-faith effort to reduce emissions. To follow up the 2019 letter of intent, the agricultural organisations drew up a climate action plan for the sector, published in 2020. This sets out how the agricultural sector intends to achieve the target through action in eight defined focus areas.

Figure 2.12. Deforested land is the largest source of GHG emissions from LULUCF

Projected total uptake or emissions from LULUCF, 2021-25

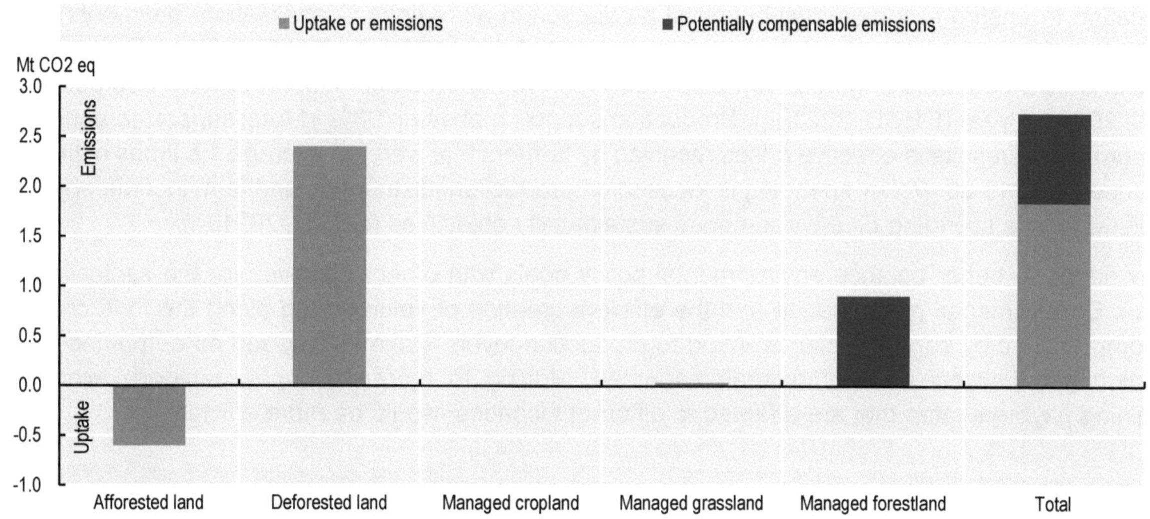

Note: LULUCF: land use, land-use change and forestry. Preliminary calculations of the projections of all land-use categories in the LULUCF sector. Agriculture uses (crop and grassland) have almost no projected impact on the LULUCF total. Under the EU forest management accounting rules, it is possible to exclude managed forest land emissions (so-called compensation) if the European Union has net removals and for countries with plans to increase removals in forest management.
Source: Norwegian Institute of Bioeconomy Research via Ministry of Climate and Environment (2019), *Norway's National Plan related to the Decision of the EEA Joint Committee No. 269/2019 of 25 October 2019*; and Ministry of Climate and Environment (2020).

StatLink https://stat.link/0zvio4

The plan is under the responsibility of the farmers' union and sets a voluntary target of 5 million tonnes of CO_2-eq of abatement of GHG emissions and removals from agriculture between 2021 and 2030. This equals about 10% of 1990 emissions from agriculture on an annual basis. The plan has eight focus areas:

- Deployment of a climate calculator and increased investment in climate advice. By the end of the plan, all farms should be using the climate calculator and have been offered climate advice.
- Targeted efforts to improve roughage quality and use of feed additives, livestock breeding in cattle, sheep and pigs, and improved animal health.
- Adoption of machinery that runs on electricity, biofuels, biogas or hydrogen.
- Adoption of fossil-free heating sources.
- Better use of fertilisers through more environmentally friendly spreading methods, better storage capacity and timing.
- Increased use of livestock manure for biogas production to reduce GHG emissions in both agriculture and other sectors.
- Use of cover crops, biocarbon and grazing to remove carbon from the atmosphere and store it in plant biomass and soil.
- Development and application of new technologies that reduce GHG emissions and increase carbon storage.

Policy implementation regarding production and environmental objectives is not well balanced

Agricultural policy has four overarching goals: food security, agriculture across the country, increased value creation and sustainable agriculture with lower GHG emissions. Support payment rates vary by commodity and location to ensure a certain distribution of production in all regions ("canalisation" payments). State funding strongly shapes the agriculture sector; it accounts for more than half of farm incomes, among the highest in OECD countries (Figure 2.13). Each farm receives an average support of NOK 680 000 (about USD 72 200) per year (OECD, 2021[21]). Production support makes up 93% of total support to agriculture. Border protection results in effective prices received by farmers that were on average 1.8 times higher than world prices in 2018-20. Policy spending is focused on production, distribution and farm income objectives with relatively little spending on environmental sustainability objectives (OECD, 2021[19]).

Norway needs to better balance environmental policy goals with other objectives for the sector (OECD, 2021[21]). Environmental performance and the efficient creation of value added along the food chain are both compromised by support policies linked to production levels. Payments based on output incentivise production and risk over-use of natural resources. Moving to more decoupled support, even while maintaining payment rates that are adapted to different locations, would be more efficient.

Figure 2.13. Producer support in agriculture remains among the highest in the OECD

Producer Support Estimate transfers as a share of gross farm receipts, 2020

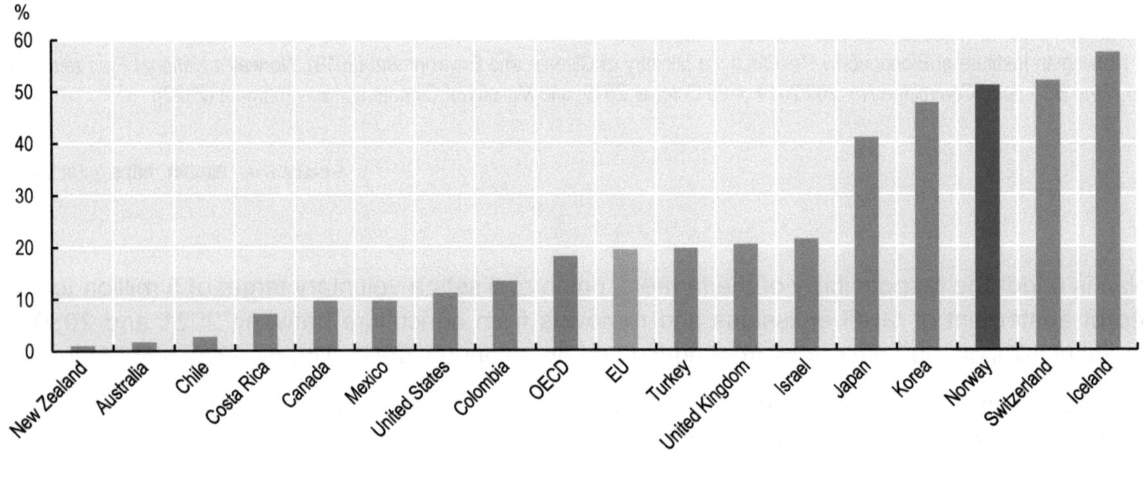

Note: Producer Support Estimate is the annual monetary value of gross transfers from consumers and taxpayers to agricultural producers, measured at the farm gate level, arising from policy measures that support agriculture, regardless of their nature, objectives or impacts on farm production or income. It includes market price support, budgetary payments and budget revenue forgone, i.e. gross transfers from consumers and taxpayers to agricultural producers arising from policy measures based on current output, input use, area planted/animal numbers/receipts/incomes (current, non-current) and non-commodity criteria.
Source: OECD (2021), "Producer and Consumer Support Estimates", *OECD Agriculture Statistics* (database).

StatLink https://stat.link/ximv0t

Direct payments to farmers should be made conditional on proper implementation of an environmental plan. In addition, more can be done to internalise pollution externalities, especially for nutrient surpluses. Farmers can be aided through more targeted advice on sustainable technologies and practices. Moreover,

Norway should provide greater flexibility and stronger incentives for farmers to improve agri-environmental outcomes and develop climate-smart agriculture.

Soil protection policy is aimed at maintaining the resource base for food production. Norway has established a target of converting no more than 400 ha of cultivated land to other uses per year. This goal has been met in the last several years, but conversion rates were higher in the past. In 2004-15, 9 760 ha of agricultural land were converted to other uses. This is equal to just under 1% of total agricultural land area. Total agricultural land is just one factor determining ecosystem services from these landscapes, which depend in part on the way the land is farmed. From this perspective, an overall limit on land conversion is not a precise instrument. Moreover, maintaining agricultural land has important trade-offs for development, especially for housing. More flexibility in those areas where development needs are highest can bring net benefits.

While policies are designed in part to maintain the presence of small farms, average farm sizes have been increasing. Sector participants have invested strongly in capital to increase productivity and counteract the effects of labour outflows from the sector. Policies also exist (such as the Allodial Act) to encourage farmland to remain in the same family. This is intended to maintain family farms, but it leads to fragmentation of farmland ownership and a situation where the inheriting landowner may live in the city with someone else operating the land. This may result in under-use of land or poor land stewardship that leads, in turn, to a decline in the quality of agricultural land and reduced ecosystem services from it.

Maintaining ecosystem services from agricultural land cannot depend on preserving traditional agriculture structures and systems. Modernisation of the sector is desirable and likely inevitable. More flexibility in farmland markets can improve the structure of farm enterprises and the husbandry of farmland, with associated benefits for the environment. These benefits will be contingent in part on the presence of policies that encourage improving the quality of natural capital of farmland and the production of ecosystem services from it.

The Selected Cultural Landscapes in Agriculture (*Utvalgte kulturlandskap i jordbruket, UKL*) initiative supports farmers who want to make an extra effort to care for the cultural landscape in selected areas. The investment is based on voluntary agreements between the state and landowners. Co-ordination of these cultural landscapes nationally is the responsibility of the Norwegian Directorate of Agriculture, in collaboration with the Norwegian Environment Agency and the Norwegian Directorate for Cultural Heritage. Each of the selected areas is co-managed by the municipality, landowners and agricultural enterprises, in collaboration with regional agricultural, natural and cultural heritage management. The initiative had a budget of NOK 37.3 million (about USD 4 million) in 2020 (Landbruksdirektoratet, 2020[22]), an increase from NOK 12 million in 2016 (USD 1.4 million). However, this is only a small part (0.01%) of total agricultural support expenditure, which was NOK 26 billion (USD 2.8 billion) in 2020.

2.2.5. Development pressures on the environment are growing but uneven

Compared with the rest of Europe, Norway's population has a large number of small and medium-sized cities spread over a large geographical area. The most central parts of the country, mostly in Norway's south, have the highest population growth and are the most attractive to immigrants. However, there are two major trends. On the one hand, the urban population in Norway's larger cities and surrounding areas, is rapidly growing (only ten cities have more than 50 000 inhabitants). On the other, the population living in smaller settlements in remote regions (still most people) is shrinking and ageing. This implies two different realities among these groups in terms of environmental impacts and ambitions, and the economic pressures they face. These differences can be expected to manifest in the objectives and outcomes of municipal planning.

Migration from rural to urban zones, particularly to the Oslo region, is expected to change the demand structure for ecosystem services, as urban and rural populations generally have different preferences in this regard (Figure 2.14). Urban populations may favour non-use or indirect ecosystem benefits, while rural populations make more direct use of ecosystems (such as for hunting and fishing).

Figure 2.14. People move from remote regions to larger cities

Drivers of population growth by type of regions, average yearly growth rate, 2016-21

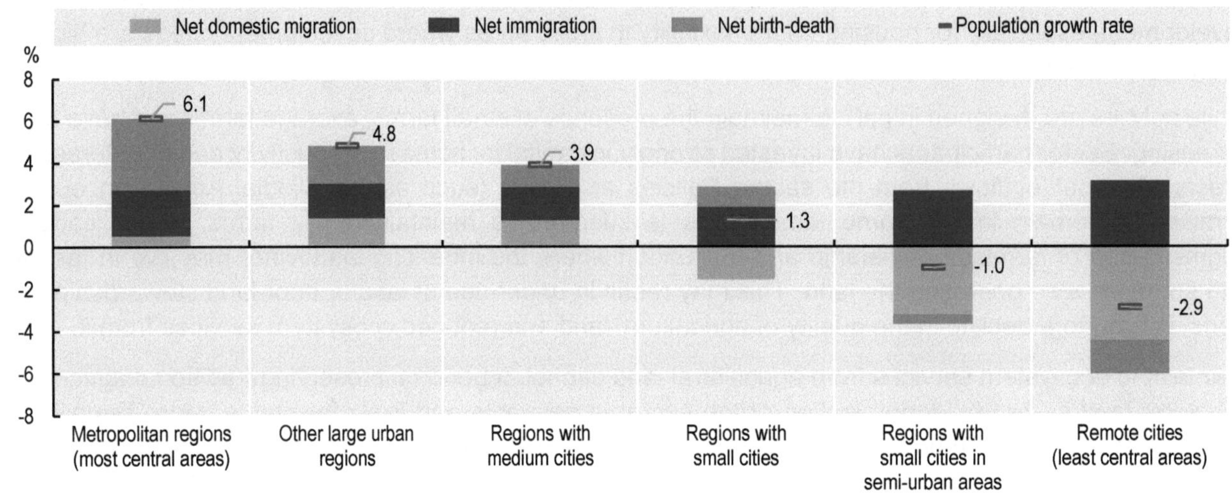

Note: Remote cities include municipalities where the commuting distance to a large or small regional centre is more than a one hour drive.
Source: Ministry of Local Government and Modernisation (2021), *Regional Development Trends 2021*.

StatLink https://stat.link/y90ewa

Demographic changes and population movements can affect ecosystem quality, as land-use changes have been the main driver of changes in ecosystem services and biodiversity (Miljoverndepartementet, 2011[23]). A government objective is to maintain the settlement pattern and slow or stop rural depopulation. Planning is important in this regard, as well-designed communities with connection to green spaces and a vibrant economy can make small towns and rural regions as a whole more attractive to population, visitors and business (Kommunal- og moderniseringsdepartementet, 2021[13]).

Development pressure is reflected in planning guidelines, which call for sufficient housing construction in areas that face housing market pressure. In this regard, the guidelines emphasise good regional solutions across municipal boundaries (Kommunal- og moderniseringsdepartementet, 2014[24]). These guidelines try to strike a balance among addressing pressure on housing markets, providing opportunities for development where needed and maintaining sustainability standards. For example, they prioritise infill development close to the city centre (which also contributes to the zero increase in vehicle traffic objective). They note the objective of agricultural soil protection but state this must be balanced against the needs of society at large. There is more flexibility in areas with low development pressure that need to increase the attractiveness of settlement areas.

Population migration and growing affluence have increased demand for secondary residences for leisure purposes outside of urban areas. The COVID-19 pandemic has amplified this trend. There has been correspondingly large growth in the number of holiday homes being built – in mountain areas but also along the coast. This amount of new home construction is expected to continue. Most of this development is infill of existing areas, but a significant share is in the form of diffuse development of scattered homes or new areas.

Part-time housing can be important for municipalities' finances and for land use. For many shrinking communities, holiday homes are the only realistic development opportunity. Several communities have more part-time than permanent residents (Figure 2.15). Many holiday homes are former farms, signalling an economic transition in the local community from agriculture to services and tourism.

Figure 2.15. Demand for secondary residences is growing

Number of holiday homes by region, 2021

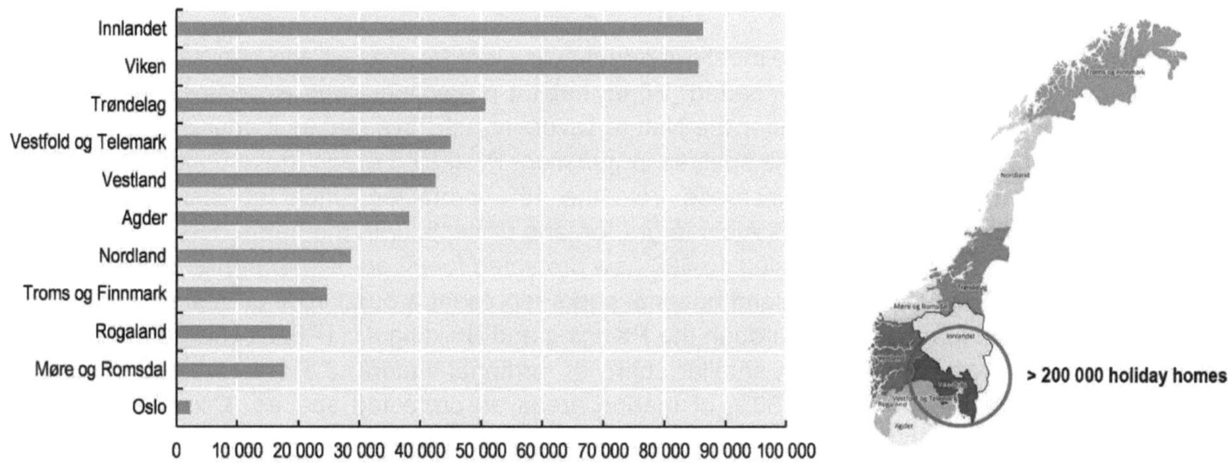

Source: Østlandsforskning (2021), "Knowledge status holiday homes 1 June 2021".

StatLink https://stat.link/9yfexb

The overlap between those area types planned for development and those likely in need of increased protection means that development activities need to be tracked and co-ordinated. This tracking would aim to ensure that development does not prevent achievement of national objectives for threatened species and protected areas. This requires a system that connects diffuse development activities with their expected cumulative environmental impacts. Such a system should feed information on expected impacts into land-use planning to help co-ordinate protection of biodiversity. Municipalities must already send their area plans to a national database in a manner that allows this information to be analysed (Steinnes, 2018[25]). EIA connected to a proposal is the main mechanism to identify these impacts. Regional and municipal plans identify related priorities with respect to land conservation and development. Both of these processes would be improved with greater integration of data on the overall state of the environment and the pressures on it. Chapter 1 also discusses how local EIA can be improved.

2.3. Protected areas

Norwegian protected areas have evolved through devolution of authority to local control. The first large protected areas were established following the Nature Preservation Act (1954) and drawing on national park plans developed by the Nature Conservation Council. Management of protected areas was largely top-down and based on "purist values". These promoted the absence of human influence as the most important reason for protecting nature. The first national parks were established on state property in remote areas where traditional uses were allowed to continue. An amendment to the Nature Conservation Act (1979) that harmonised protected area planning with land-use planning legislation strengthened local participation in protected area management during the 1980s. A two-step process provided for negotiation on the designation, boundaries and regulations of protected areas before sending the plan for local hearings and municipal review (Hausner, Brown and Lægreid, 2015[26]).

Today, protected areas are established under the 2009 Nature Diversity Act, with main emphasis on national parks, protected landscapes and nature reserves. The Act establishes a framework for protected areas, including general purposes and individual categories, general rules on permitted and prohibited actions, and governance (Fauchald and Gulbrandsen, 2012[27]). There will often be conflicts of goals related to protection, with a need to weigh the preservation of natural values against other societal interests (Norwegian Environment Agency, 2017[28]).

Protected marine and land areas are the most important policy tool for species and habitat protection, with other protection actions taken only as needed. When habitat protection alone is deemed insufficient, a species may be given priority status under the Nature Diversity Act. This makes it possible to prohibit all removal, damage to or destruction of the species in question. Protected areas make up just over 17% of Norway's mainland area. This is an increase from the 15% protected since the last Environmental Performance Review, meeting Norway's Aichi target for land protection. In the same period, Norway has added 4 000 km² of protected areas, including 656 new protected forest areas, 10 marine protected areas and 3 new national parks. The 40 mainland national parks represent around 10% of total protected area, with most of the rest managed mainly through the Planning and Building Act (PBA). This comprises more than 3 000 specific sites (Table 2.2). A smaller share of territorial waters, 3.5%, is protected, although Norway has committed to preserving 30% of marine areas as protected spaces. Considerably larger portions of land area in Svalbard (67%) and Jan Mayen (nearly all) are protected. About 87% of Svalbard's territorial waters and all of Jan Mayen's out to 12 nautical miles are protected areas.

Table 2.2. Protected areas in mainland Norway by amount, percentage and count, 2020

	Protected area total (km²)	Protected land area (km²)	Proportion of protected land area (%)	Protected sea area (km²)	Proportion of protected sea area – territorial waters (%)	Number of protected areas
All protection purposes	61 962	56 799	18	5 162	4	3 170
National parks	33 070	31 614	10	1 456	1	40
Nature reserves	9 159	7 554	2	1 606	1	2 457
Landscape protection areas	18 320	17 247	5	1 073	1	196
Marine protected area	1 081	0	0	1 081	1	16
Other protections	643	393	0	250	0	462

Note: Some protected areas belong to several protection categories. Total protected area is therefore smaller than the sum of protected area for all categories.
Source: Statistics Norway (2021), "Protected areas", *StatBank* (database).

The amount of protected land in Norway exceeds the OECD average and many of its Nordic neighbours (Figure 2.16). However, the amount of protected land is less than the EU average. Aichi target 11 covers area-based conservation measures. Norway's corresponding national target is that "a representative selection of Norwegian nature will be maintained for future generations". Promoting the conservation of "the full range of variation of habitats and landscape types" is mentioned in Section 33 of the Nature Diversity Act in a list of the objectives of establishing protected areas. Others include the conservation of endangered natural environments and major intact ecosystems.

Figure 2.16. Protected area in Norway meets its Aichi 2000 target

Terrestrial protected areas as percentage of land area in OECD countries, 2016-21

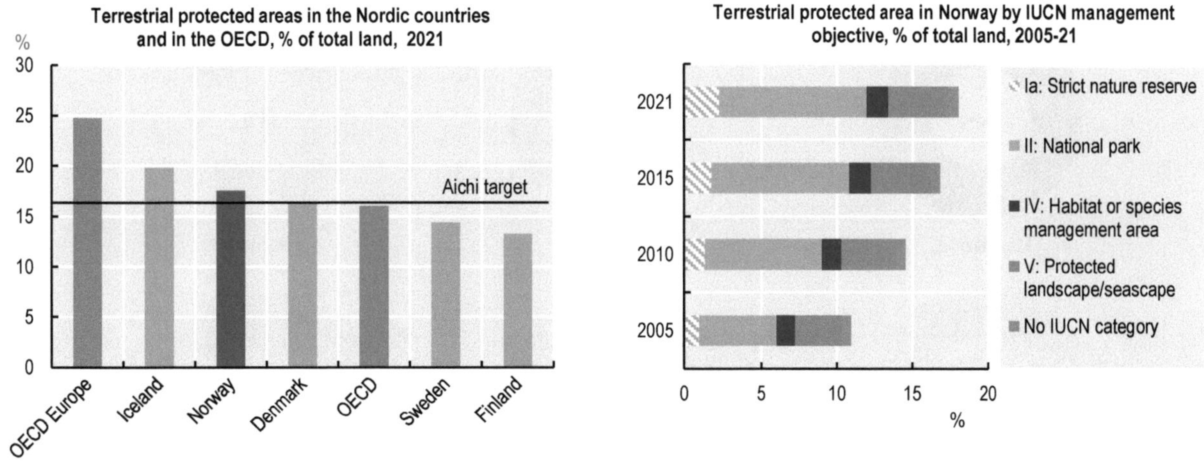

Note: Data exclude protected areas in overseas territories. In Norway, the share of terrestrial area protected, including Jan Mayen and Svalbard, is about 25%. Right panel: Protected areas under management categories of the World Conservation Unit (IUCN) classification. Strict nature reserve and national parks reflect the highest level of protection.
Source: OECD (2021), "Protected areas", *OECD Environmental Indicators* (database).

StatLink https://stat.link/0d2k6v

Protected zones are identified in co-ordination with county governors and local governments, but identification itself does not ensure protection of areas of high merit. For example, some recently proposed national parks were cancelled due to lack of local acceptance (Norwegian Environment Agency, 2021[29]). Local acceptability is important. However, if the designation of an important natural area is purely a negotiation, this can make it more difficult to meet national objectives for conservation. As one sign of the important role of local economic trade-offs, most protected areas are high mountainous areas, with relatively little forest, coast or sea areas protected (Figure 2.17).

Norway is well below the OECD average for marine protected areas and failed to meet the Aichi target. According to the World Database on Protected Areas (WDPA), Norway protects 0.9% of its Exclusive Economic Zone (EEZ), compared to 21.5% (OECD), 18% (Denmark), 15.7% (Sweden) and 12% (Finland). Iceland is the only Nordic country that protects a smaller share of its EEZ, at 0.4%.

Large, contiguous protected zones are more effective at protecting biodiversity and threatened species. Many protected areas in Norway are small, in particular for habitat types most at risk (Norwegian Environment Agency, 2017[28]). In addition, protected areas along the western coast and northern Norway are often isolated from each other, especially wetlands. The protected areas along the mountain range in southern Norway and the Swedish border in the north have good connectivity (Framstad et al., 2012[30]).

Protected areas with a broad range of vegetation zones offer some protection against the effects of climate change, as species can migrate to different climatic zones within the same area. Only 5% of protected areas have climate variation over three vegetation zones or more, while only 8% include more than two vegetation zones. Many smaller protected areas have little variation in climatic conditions (Norwegian Environment Agency, 2017[28]). Including more vegetation zones in a single protected area would make these ecosystems more resilient to climate change and provide better habitat for species requiring large areas.

Figure 2.17. Ocean and forest areas are relatively little protected

Proportion of protected area in Norway 2020

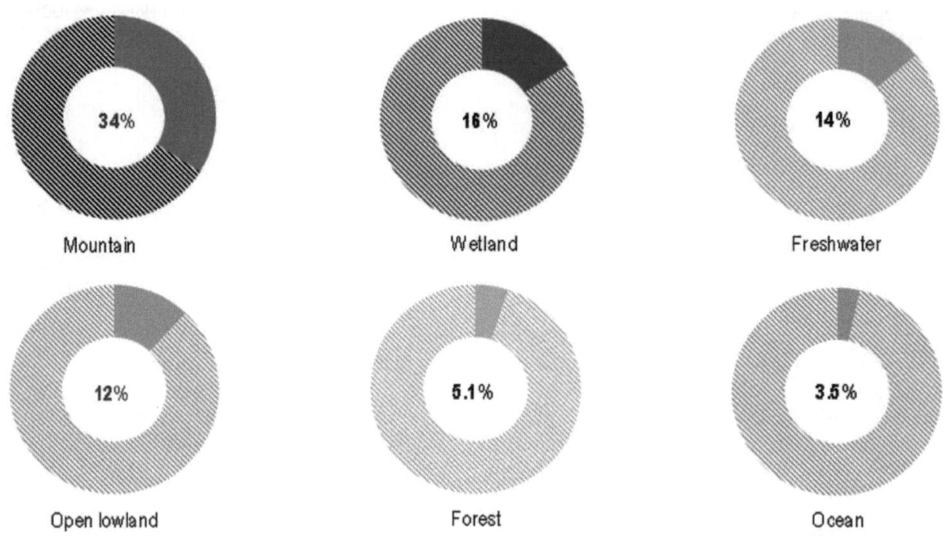

Source: Norwegian Environment Agency (2020), *Norway's environmental status*, https://miljostatus.miljodirektoratet.no/norgesmiljostatus.

Management of larger protected areas is devolved to 48 local management boards, an outcome described as a "grand experiment with delegation of authority" (Fauchald and Gulbrandsen, 2012[27]). This devolution was part of a comprehensive reform of national parks and protected areas. The budget for the management of protected areas (e.g. costs related to the boards, national park managers) has increased from NOK 60.1 million (USD 7 million) to NOK 85 million (USD 9.9 million) over 2014-21.

These protected area boards manage clusters of national parks, protected landscapes and nature reserves. The responsibility for small protected areas has been delegated to many municipalities (Hausner, Brown and Lægreid, 2015[26]). Part of the reason for this devolution is to obtain local buy-in for environmental protection. The earlier, more centralised conservation management approach was viewed as bureaucratic and prioritising nature values over local values and user interests. Local resistance and conflict reduced its effectiveness.

Delegation of responsibility has reduced conflict between governments regarding protected areas. However, it has also led the management of some protected areas to become more responsive to local interests, potentially at the expense of national ones (Hovik and Hongslo, 2016[31]; Falleth and Hovik, 2009[32]). That said, there is evidence these management boards, which report to the Norwegian Environmental Agency, try to fulfil their obligations faithfully and can raise local awareness and anchoring (Hovik and Hongslo, 2016[31]). Thus, the management boards provide a useful balance between local and central government responsibility. The government has established an action plan to strengthen management of protected areas, with emphasis on increased staffing, improved mapping and measurement, and preparation of strategies.

Management boards must address the fundamental challenge of balancing conservation and sustainable use in protected areas. However, they are committed to doing this within the rules set by the government for each protected area. If they consider the board decisions to be in conflict with the established rules, non-governmental organisations and other stakeholders can complain to the Norwegian Environmental Agency. These boards have more promise of finding this balance than either a fully centralised or a fully devolved system. Other forms of co-management of protected areas between different levels of government can be found in Sweden, Scotland and Austria; this approach is also reflected in Norway's River Basin Management System.

2.3.1. Protected area policy focuses on improving quality of coverage rather than increasing overall area

The system was largely established between 1985 and 2000, a period that saw a rapid increase in protected areas (Figure 2.18). After 2000, increases in protected areas have been gradual. They have focused on coverage of areas of special interest, including conserving a representative sample of all landscape types for posterity. In the Nature for Life report, the government indicated that protected areas are largely sufficient and that no major expansion of protected areas was needed (Ministry of Climate and Environment, 2015[4]).

Figure 2.18. The protected area network has been relatively stable since 2011

Trend in protected areas, 2000-20

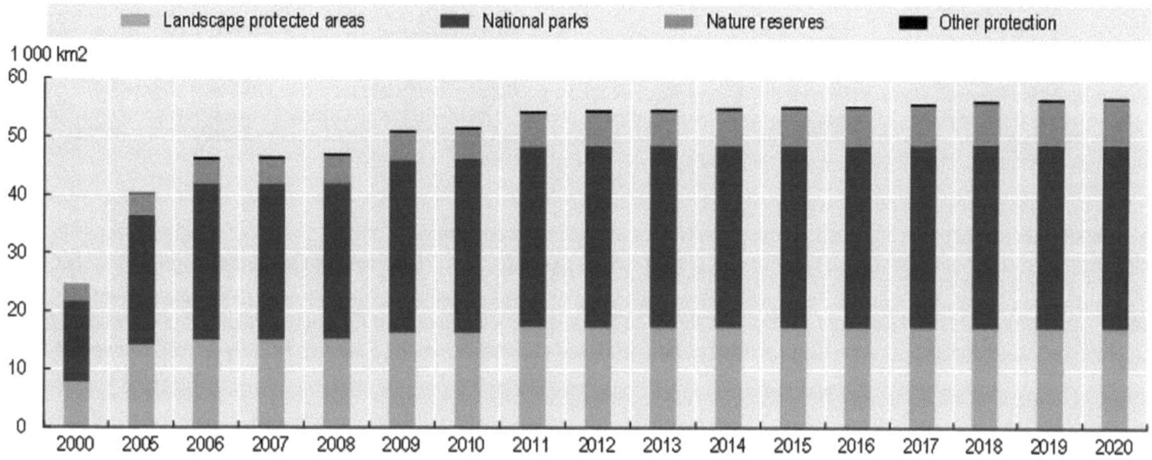

Note: Areas on Svalbard are protected according to the Svalbard Environmental Protection Act and areas on Jan Mayen are protected according to the Act of Jan Mayen and are not included. Landscape protected areas: flora and fauna protected areas. Since 2006 data also include nature relics with an area protection and biotops protected by the Act relating to Salmonids and Fresh-water Fish and the Wildlife Act. Other protection: areas with flora- or fauna protections are also included.
Source: Statistics Norway (2021), "Protected areas", *StatBank* (database).

StatLink https://stat.link/ip42nr

The greatest need for additional terrestrial protection is in coastal areas and the south (Framstad et al., 2010[33]) (Figure 2.19). Several of the less protected habitat types appear on the Red List for habitat types.

Figure 2.19. Most areas needing additional protection are in the south

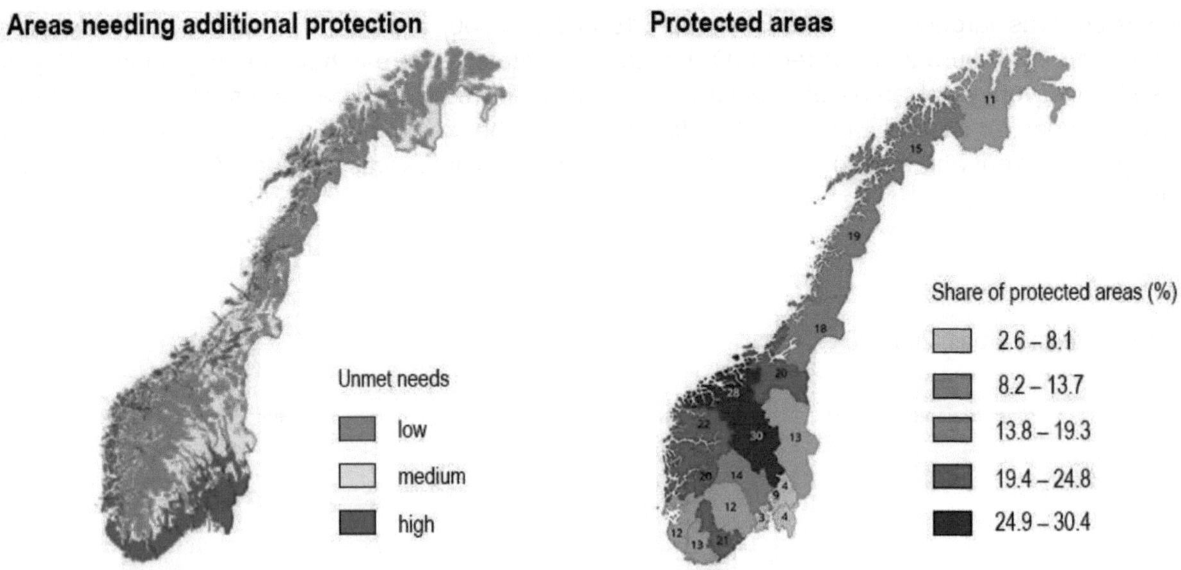

Note: The distribution of unmet protection needs is based on NINA's assessments and derived from the division of vegetation zones in Norway.
Source: Norwegian Environment Agency (2017), *Forslag til plan for supplerende vern - Miljødirektoratets anbefalinge - Proposed plan for supplementary protection* [The Norwegian Environment Agency's recommendations]; Framstad et al. (2012), *Naturfaglig evaluering av norske verneområder. Verneområdenes funksjon som økologisk nettverk og toleranse for klimaendringer* [Scientific evaluation of Norwegian protected areas. The protected areas' function as an ecological network and resilience to climate change]; Statistics Norway (2016), *Norwegian Mapping Authority.*

While there is a need for additional protection of certain areas, this will be challenging. Most potential sites are either small, already affected by human activity or potentially affected (Norwegian Environment Agency, 2017[28]). In municipal area plans, areas set aside for agriculture, nature and outdoor purposes, as well as reindeer husbandry (LNFR areas), make up 87% of total planned area. LNFR areas have special development restrictions and allow only "scattered" dwellings. However, 75% of the remaining area planned for development is forest or open land, the two most important types for endangered species habitats (Steinnes, 2018[25]).

Many areas identified as worth protecting are in densely populated areas with intensive use of land for agriculture, industry, infrastructure and housing construction. This means development pressure will remain, as well as risk of increased fragmentation of associated ecological networks. Without a means of comprehensive and predictable protection of such areas, the national goal of representative conservation of Norway's areas is at risk (Norwegian Environment Agency, 2019[34]). Such areas that are simultaneously valuable for economic development and for a high level of ecosystem services pose a particular challenge for policy makers.

Conflict between social/economic versus environmental objectives may be an unavoidable part of area protection. Much of the land planned for development is of the types most relevant for threatened species. As mentioned, 75% of planned development is on forested or open land. Of this, agricultural land accounts for 6% of all land planned for development but 17% of land planned for residential development. Wetlands account for 9% of planned development area. Most of this is foreseen near urban centres; only 10% of residential development is planned for areas more than 5 km from a town (Steinnes, 2018[25]). Large-scale development of secondary residences is expected to continue, especially in the central municipalities. The total area planned for development as of 2019 was 2 777 km^2. Of this, 56% is forest and 20% is open land composed of agricultural land and wetlands (Rørholt and Steinnes, 2020[35]).

2.3.2. Expanding the protected area network and the voluntary forest protection scheme

According to the Biodiversity Act, habitat types and ecosystems that are poorly represented in the protected area system should be progressively integrated into new or existing areas. This will ensure that threatened areas are conserved and a representative sample of Norwegian nature will be protected for future generations. Additional protection can also increase the robustness of protected areas.

The Norwegian Environmental Agency found deficiencies in area protection in all regions of Norway, including area types on the Red List for habitat types (Norwegian Environment Agency, 2017[28]). Its report found that not all habitat types requiring additional protection had examples worthy of protection, as many were too small or of poor quality.

The 2017 report started a process whereby county governors suggested areas suitable for additional protection. A May 2019 report describes 1 300 new protected sites, plus modification of some existing sites. Of these, 275 sites with a total area of 584 km^2 are ecosystem types that are either under-represented in protected areas or are in parts of the country with low protection coverage. For context, existing protected area is about 24 000 km^2. The report also covers wetland areas in the region of Finnmark and proposed new national park areas as separate categories.

In the second phase, the Ministry of Climate Change and Environment will act on recommendations from the Norwegian Environmental Agency. To that end, it will proceed with protection plans under the Biodiversity Act. Related to the costs of compensation and establishment of new protected areas, the operating budget of the agency was increased by NOK 18 million (USD 1.9 million) in 2020. Grants for the care of endangered species and habitat types increased from NOK 33 million (USD 3.8 million) to NOK 42.8 million (USD 5 million) over 2013-21.

Protected area for forests is expanded through a process separate from other ecosystem types. For other land types, the government has discretion to designate a protected area, paying compensation after the fact (though local opposition may still be a decisive factor). For privately owned forest land, protection is at the discretion of the land owner. As a starting point, the authorities define priorities for the type of forests in the selection process. Private forest owners then suggest potential areas, which authorities evaluate. If the suggested area qualifies for protection, negotiations for compensation begin. If successful, the private owner receives a payment and the land is given long-term protected area status. This is done in co-operation with the Forest Owners' Association. The budget for forest protection has nearly doubled since 2013 and reached NOK 435 million (USD 50.6 million) in 2021.

A voluntary process for forest protection may be a pragmatic approach to this sensitive and often valuable land type, reducing conflict between landowners and government. However, it cedes control over outcomes as the government cannot target specific forest areas for protection, only choose among those sites offered. When threatened species depend on protection of specific forest areas, the government's capacity to act can be significantly constrained (Box 2.4).

Box 2.4. Voluntary protection of forest land can put species at increased risk

Trøndelaven, *Erioderma pedicellatum*, is a rare lichen that is critically endangered both in Norway and in the world. This small lichen is coloured grey-blue to grey-brown with reddish-brown spheres, which are the fruiting bodies. It is only found in places with high humidity, which in Norway means two habitat types: boreal rainforest in Nord-Trøndelag and a brook gorge in Hedmark. Today, the species can be found only in one site: the brook gorge in Hedmark, and this is the only remaining known site in Europe. It can only be saved if the site is not logged and the humidity does not change for other reasons.

Area protection is the only practical policy tool available for this species. However, an inter-directorate group on threatened nature mandated to set out protection plans for endangered species declined to put this species on its priority list. It reasoned the voluntary protection policy was uncertain. This leaves the lichen without a protection plan and subject to landowners' forest harvest decisions for its survival.

Source: (Hovik and Hongslo, 2016[31]; NNV, 2011[36]).

Forests in Norway are vast, complex and diverse ecosystems that contain the largest share of all species. Forest land is the most important habitat for threatened species, where protection is well below targets, and for which the policy tool for protection is weaker than for other area types. This is a troubling combination that puts protection objectives at risk. The approach prioritises reducing conflicts with landowners, but conflict reduction for its own sake should not be a goal, however pragmatic.

2.4. Ecosystem quality outside of protected areas

2.4.1. Restoration, area neutrality or biodiversity offsets can help achieve national objectives for nature protection

As many important nature types are threatened and good candidate areas for protection in acceptable condition are not always available, restoring landscapes can help achieve biodiversity objectives. Until now, bogs, other wetlands and watercourses were the focus of restoration activity. Norway invested NOK 22 million (USD 2.6 million) in 2021 for such restoration measures in water management plans. For 2022, the government more than doubled the budget for restoring wetlands, watercourses, threatened nature and removal of alien species from NOK 17 million (USD 2 million) to NOK 41 million (USD 4.6 million).

The Norwegian Environment Agency has prioritised restoration projects in other ecosystems that can be implemented quickly and with good probability of success (Hovik and Hongslo, 2016[31]). Restoration work on some of these areas will start in 2022. It will begin inside protected areas on beach dune land, southern established beach dune land and open shallow limestone land in the southern boreonemoral zone. An important restoration measure will be removal of invasive alien species.

Area neutrality is an application of biodiversity offsetting that aims at no net loss of land-based natural capital relative to a reference state. The likely cumulative negative impacts of land use and land management decisions can be counterbalanced with measures to achieve equivalent gains elsewhere (Cowie et al., 2018[37]). Such offsetting is appropriate only after all practical steps have been taken to avoid and minimise impacts of the activity requiring offsetting. Area neutrality has been proposed as a solution that could balance development with conservation goals.

Area neutrality should occur only within specific land types to ensure "like for like" exchanges. As part of this, spatial characteristics such as ecosystem connectivity should be considered. Implementation should be managed at the local level as part of land-use planning. Meanwhile, achievement is assessed at national level according to objectives for landscape conservation, perhaps in the context of endangered habitats.

Mandatory biodiversity offset programmes are likely to be a much more powerful instrument than voluntary ones. The former tend to be more stringent, and associated with greater oversight, controls and the possibility of sanctions for non-compliance (OECD, 2016[38]).

There are several examples of such policies, also called biodiversity offsets, in OECD countries. One of the oldest is the US Wetlands Mitigation programme designed to achieve "no net loss" in wetlands (McKenney and Kiesecker, 2010[39]). In Europe, the Biodiversity Strategy to 2020 aims to ensure no net loss of biodiversity and ecosystem services. It foresees "an initiative to ensure there is no net loss of ecosystems and their services (e.g. through compensation or offsetting schemes)" (Tucker, Quétier and Wende, 2020[40]).

Box 2.5. The US Wetlands Mitigation Programme shows area neutrality can work if carefully implemented

Each year, thousands of mitigation projects are undertaken in the United States under Section 404 of the Clean Water Act. Mitigation in the US Wetlands Mitigation Programme has at times been applied in ways that appear arbitrary, to lack transparency or that are seemingly uncoupled from the amount or type of impacts. However, these are fundamentally implementation issues and mitigation "design" challenges rather than any inherent problem with the basic concept or legal underpinnings of mitigation.

Without national policies, mitigation will be decided on a project-by-project, ad hoc basis, which invites arbitrary decision making. Ad hoc approaches are also time consuming for both oversight agencies and developers, and add significant unpredictability for developers.

Mitigation done right can support efficient and defensible government decisions, predictability for project proponents, and positive outcomes for communities and the environment. To achieve these benefits, clear national mitigation policies are needed that provide direction on how to meet the obligations of legal authorities and that establish a framework that can be applied consistently at the local level.

The success of mitigation projects depends on the following:

- carefully defined reference conditions
- a focus on groundcover restoration
- monitoring of plant and animal community structure, not just presence or cover of exotic or nuisance species
- consideration of the sustainability of mitigation within the landscape
- a focus on achieving success criteria and not task completion
- good co-ordination and standardisation across regions
- adequate compliance responsibilities of the regulatory agencies.

Source: (Hough and Harrington, 2019[41]; Chinners Reiss, Hernandez and Brown, 2007[42]).

2.4.2. Quality norms add an additional layer of protection

The Nature Diversity Act allows for establishment of quality norms for biological, geological and landscape diversity when the biodiversity of a species or ecosystem has a negative status or trend. A norm could, for example, set standards for the abundance of a species or nature type, or the ecological state of a species or nature type.

Norms established under the Act are not legally binding but are considered stronger than policy recommendations. A norm can lead to an action plan of measures for its achievement. Two such action plans are in existence, one for salmon and one for wild reindeer. Atlantic salmon are listed as "near threatened" on the Norwegian Red List for Species.

Quality norms can support better decision making by providing a benchmark for planning and objective setting. This can help close gaps between local planning and national objectives as part of an overall system of ecosystem assessment and accounting.

An example of a successful quality norm is that in place for wild reindeer. Norway is subject to an international obligation under the Berne Convention to protect wild reindeer herds and their habitats. As a result, wild reindeer are a national responsibility. They require large areas, and their habitats extend across municipal and county boundaries.

Wild reindeer were originally found in all mountain regions of Norway. However, due to human intervention, Norwegian wild reindeer are now found only in 24 areas in the south, and the population is at risk of fragmentation. Climate change is making grazing conditions for wild reindeer more difficult, and diseases and parasites can have a negative impact on herds. For example, in 2016, the entire wild reindeer herd in Nordfjella zone 1 was culled to fight chronic wasting disease. The quality norm is designed to ensure that viable populations of wild reindeer are maintained in southern Norway, and to contribute to more manageable and cost-effective management of wild reindeer.

The quality norm for reindeer sets values for good, medium and poor quality for wild reindeer in wild reindeer areas. The goal is to maintain or reach medium quality for each reindeer area as soon as possible, with a long-term goal of good quality. This goal may deliberately not be met in the face of important societal interests. The bar for such exceptions is higher in established national wild reindeer areas.

The quality norm has three components: the condition of the herd, grazing availability (especially winter forage) and human interactions with habitat (affecting the range and movement of the herd). Each area is assessed every four years. The overall classification is determined by the worst-performing component. For example, a wild reindeer area would be assessed as poor quality if human activity significantly restricts the herd, even if the population and grazing conditions are good.

The Norwegian Environment Agency identifies reindeer areas for classification under the quality norm and prepares a report explaining the assessed quality. Professionals carry out assessments supported by up to two local representatives familiar with the wild reindeer area. If the quality norm is not reached, or is at risk of not being reached, the Ministry of Climate and the Environment must prepare an action plan for improvement. Such plans consider activities in the area and balance social interests.

To date, the agency has appointed nine Wild Reindeer Committees following proposals from municipalities. These committees, among other things, approve stock plans and set annual hunting quotas. They also participate in spatial planning in counties and municipalities (according to the PBA), with a view to sustainable management of wild reindeer habitats.

2.5. Land-use planning

Best practice for spatial planning calls for an ecosystem approach to develop a multi-sector strategy that balances and achieves environmental, economic and social objectives. In an ideal scenario, spatial plans provide the environmental baseline and framework, including biodiversity targets, for strategic environmental assessments (SEAs) of proposed land-use plans, and EIAs for specific projects (Tucker, Quétier and Wende, 2020[40]).

Setting quantitative and time-bound biodiversity targets can help inform the design and sizing of mitigation and offsetting requirements for land-use plans. Spatial planning can, for example, identify target areas for ecosystem restoration, green infrastructure and offsetting. Norway is setting the stage with NiN ecosystem quality targets and quality norms for species and habitats as called for in the Nature Diversity Act. However, these targets are not fully integrated into planning. Norway is not alone in this regard. Only a few regions in the European Union develop large-scale terrestrial spatial plans that identify desired land uses with respect to environmental, social and economic needs. Moreover, not all countries explicitly address biodiversity in spatial planning by identifying areas of land with different levels of biodiversity importance and protection to achieve biodiversity objectives (Tucker, Quétier and Wende, 2020[40]).

The national government manages its activities related to spatial planning through five main mechanisms. These are marine management plans, river basin management plans (RBMPs) (for ecosystem-based management of marine and coastal waters, and rivers and lakes), sectoral legislation, the PBA and the system of national parks (Figure 2.20). In addition, the government may take direct statutory action to preserve important habitat areas or designated species. Sectoral ministries and agencies are systematically involved; it is a principle of Norwegian environmental policy that each sector deals with pressures and impacts resulting from its own activities.

Figure 2.20. Different domains have different approaches to spatial planning

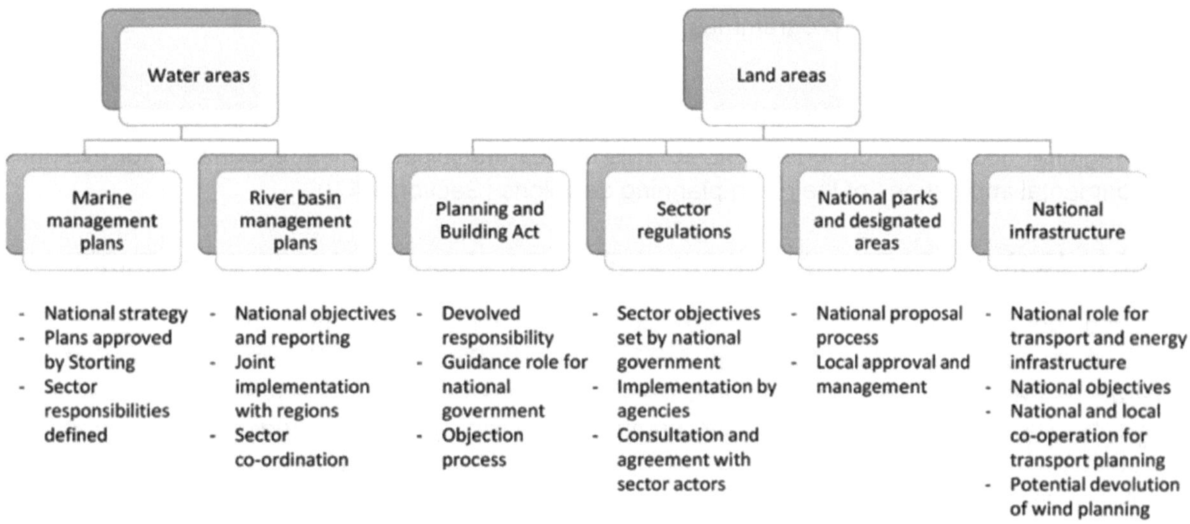

Source: Country submission.

Land regulation is seen as fragmented, with a complex division of authorities across sectors and between decision levels. A sector-based focus and division of responsibilities is in principle not a problem as long as authorities can co-ordinate. In many cases, however, one body's decisions will affect or interfere with another's areas of responsibility. Given interests are not always compatible or comparable, legislation allows broad discretionary assessments to balance conflicting interests. However, some sector bodies may face considerable pressure to deliver on sector-specific objectives at the expense of other important considerations (Ministry of Local Government and Modernisation, 2014[43]). For example, sector agencies may be under pressure to maintain timber or agriculture production levels, or complete transportation networks.

At the national level, the Ministry of Agriculture and Food (LMD), the Ministry of Climate and Environment (KLD) and the Ministry of Local Government and Regional Development (KDD) have the greatest responsibility for land management. KLD manages environmental legislation, including area protection, coniferous forest protection, game management, water management, inland fisheries management, motor traffic and nature supervision, and cultural heritage landscapes. The Norwegian Environment Agency and the Directorate for Cultural Heritage are government agencies under KLD but operate independently in many individual cases. The Norwegian Environmental Protection Agency is part of the umbrella agency and has more than 60 local offices. LMD administers agricultural legislation, while KDD is responsible for the municipal sector and the PBA (Box 1.2, Chapter 1).

The county governor is a national appointed entity with wide responsibility to represent national interests and act on behalf of the government. This includes:

- serving as an oversight and appeals body for a number of laws concerning wilderness (*utmark*) management
- managing certain stocks of inland fish
- managing area protection according to the Biodiversity Act
- handling area management of wild reindeer.

The county municipality (elected regional government) is responsible for:

- management of inland fish, except for vulnerable and endangered species and anadromous salmonids
- game management and hunting, except wild reindeer
- regional plans and action programmes, including for the wild reindeer herd
- outdoor recreation.

The municipality is responsible for planning and development. SEAs are linked to municipal master plans, although regional bodies also undertake SEAs. This makes municipal bodies responsible for evaluating the environmental implications of their own planning decisions (Section 1.4.2).

2.5.1. River basin management planning provides an example of good co-ordination

The national government sets out objectives and a national administrative structure, with different ministries and national agencies participating at different levels (Figure 2.21). This helps ensure that sector administrations harmonise their activities. Implementation responsibility is delegated to county and local governments. The county governments have primary responsibility for water regions (also termed river basin districts) and have been designated as *water region authorities*. Water regions may be divided into water areas. This is a devolved authority from the water region committee to allow for local participation.

The Norwegian Environment Agency is the national co-ordinating body. Its tasks include advising KLD, leading the Directorate Group, guiding water management authorities, co-ordinating water management with neighbouring countries and co-ordinating Norwegian participation in joint European water co-operation.

Water region authorities establish and lead water region committees. These committees are composed of representatives of the river basin district authority and other county governments, county governors' offices, and other affected sector authorities and municipalities. Representatives of affected licensees and private and public user interests advise the committee through a reference group.

All relevant authorities and stakeholders can participate in river basin work. The process helps ensure local anchoring by reflecting local knowledge and consent for environmental measures. In most river basin districts, a co-ordinator acts as an intermediary between the municipalities involved, the county municipalities and the state. As a planning authority, the municipality ensures that environmental goals and consideration for the aquatic environment are integrated into its local planning.

Figure 2.21. River basin management is co-ordinated and collaborative

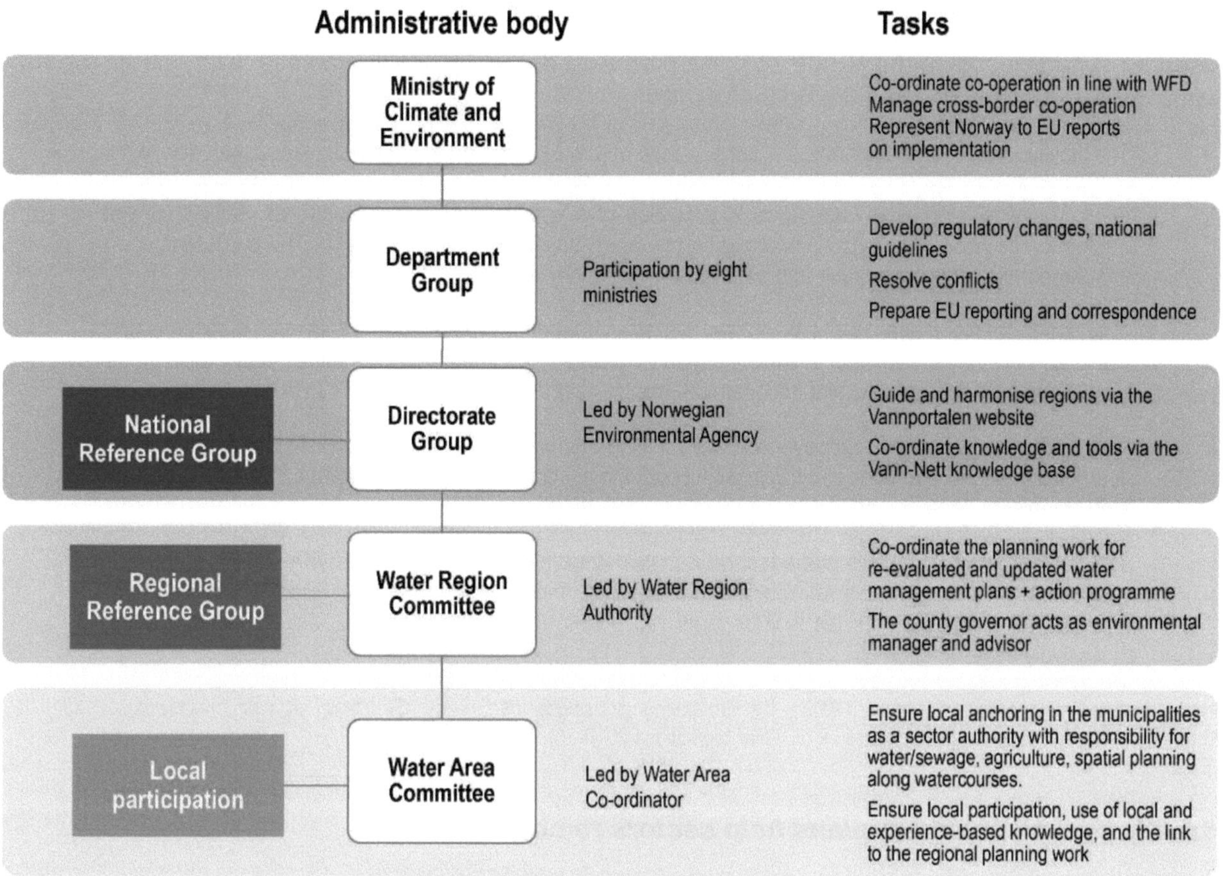

Source: Water Portal (2021), *Ministries and Ministries Group for Water Management*, www.vannportalen.no/organisering2/nasjonal-vannforvaltning/departementene-og-departementsgruppa.

The water region authority for each river basin develops RBMPs, which the national government approves. This forms the basis for the relevant planning and implementation activities by national, county and local authorities. The authorities concerned implement the necessary legislation and measures in line with their legal and administrative responsibilities.

These management plans describe the river basin and set environmental objectives for the water bodies. They provide an overview of protected areas and analyse human impacts. They set out an action programme and monitor results. The action programme part of the management plan includes all the measures to achieve national objectives and guidelines, including measures to protect and improve water quality, water management and use, including by controlling water extraction and discharge of pollution.

Box 2.6. River basin management planning works best with clear and realistic priorities

A survey of participants in the RBMP process produced generally positive results, with a few caveats. Some quotes from the survey sum up the results:

> "The holistic process strengthens the aquatic environment compared with sectoral treatment. The work brings together all the actors, influences are seen in context and all contribute to common environmental goals. The work increases awareness of the value of a good aquatic environment, as well as current problems. The knowledge base is improved, ecosystem-based and comprehensive. The process is open and democratic with participation and participation regionally and locally."
>
> "The work on the management plans can be strengthened by better prioritization of measures and distribution over planning periods, simplifying and clarifying instruments and measures and clarifying the relationship between regional and national priorities."
>
> "Authorities can do more to go beyond sector thinking and be more holistic. Priorities should be set more clearly according to theme or geographical scope, with associated allocation of funds. It is also important to communicate better the objectives and benefits of water management."
>
> "The risk is having unrealistic plans that do not yield concrete results, and leave unresolved issues and goal conflicts at a central level. Sufficient funding is needed for monitoring, process, staffing and implementation of measures, as well as clear processes, roles and responsibilities, without becoming excessively bureaucratic."

Source: Norwegian Environment Agency (2016), *Oppsummering av spørreundersøkelse: Evaluering av vannforskriftarbeidet 2010-15* [Summary of survey results: evaluation of work on water regulations 2010-15].

2.5.2. Marine management plans help sectors to co-ordinate

Marine management plans aim to facilitate value creation through the sustainable use of the sea areas' resources and ecosystem services, and at the same time maintain the ecosystems' structure, mode of operation, productivity and biodiversity. The management plans contribute to clarity in the overall framework, co-ordination and priorities in the management of the sea areas. Increased predictability for and better coexistence of marine-based industries is an important goal. Sector regulations form the basis for regulating activity in the management plan areas. Sector authorities also primarily implement measures in the management plans, in accordance with relevant laws and associated regulations (Kommunal- og moderniseringsdepartementet, 2021[13]).

Marine management plans are based on an integrated, ecosystem-based regime (Figure 2.22). Integrated, ecosystem-based ocean management balances conservation and sustainable use of rich, productive ecosystems. Ecosystem-based management uses available knowledge as a foundation, and considers ecosystems as a whole, including people, when decisions are needed on oceans and marine ecosystems. Marine management plans evaluate the cumulative effects of all human activities on the marine environment and by managing use of the oceans in a way that maintains the natural functions of ecosystems and ecosystem services.

Figure 2.22. Ecosystems-based ocean management balances conservation and use

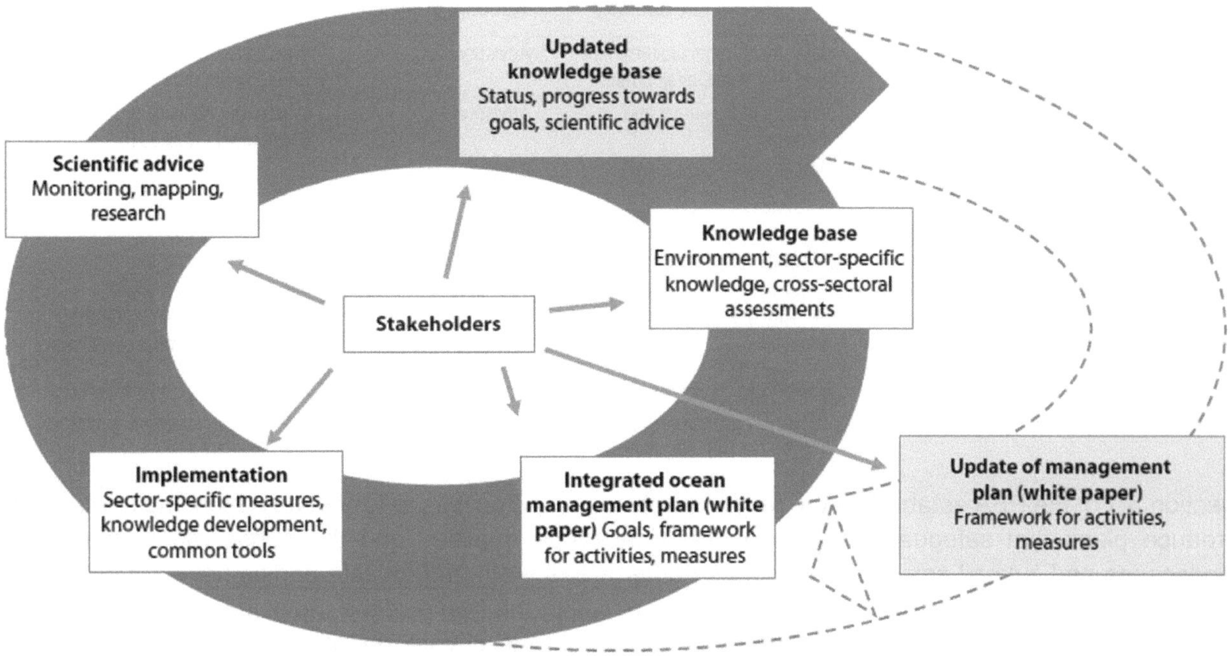

Source: Norwegian Ministry of Climate and Environment, (2019), *Norway's integrated ocean management plans*.

Work on the management plans is co-ordinated by an inter-ministerial Steering Committee for integrated ocean management, led by KLD. Other ministries represented in the committee are Labour and Social Affairs; Finance; Defence; Justice and Public Security; Local Government and Regional Development; Trade, Industry and Fisheries; Petroleum and Energy; Transport; and Foreign Affairs.

Scientific support for the plans provided by two advisory groups: the Forum for Integrated Ocean Management (headed by the Norwegian Environment Agency) and the Advisory Group on Monitoring (headed by the Institute of Marine Research). The former provides the overall scientific basis for updating and revising the management plans in co-operation with the latter. The Advisory Group also co-ordinates monitoring for marine ecosystems and reports on environmental status in the management plan areas.

2.5.3. The Planning and Building Act governs much of land-use decision making

The PBA provides a broad framework for planning and building in Norway, regulating co-operation of the public, municipalities, county institutions and national bodies. The law applies to the landmass of the country, all watercourses and marine areas up to 1 nautical mile from the baseline.

The Norwegian PBA is similar to the legislation of many of its Nordic neighbours (Table 2.3). The main differences are the ministry responsible and the binding or advisory nature of national guidance. All of the Nordics involve national, regional and municipal bodies to some extent in planning. Norway's system is unique in that private entities are the source of most planning proposals and that it specifies a set timeframe for the process.

Table 2.3. Responsibilities for planning legislation in Nordic countries

Country	Law	Responsible ministry	National guidelines	Notes
Norway	Planning and Building Act	Ministry of Local Government and Regional Development	Advisory	Was under Ministry of Climate and Environment until 2013
Denmark	Danish Planning Act	Ministry of Business and Growth	Advisory	Was under Ministry of Climate and Environment until 2015
Finland	Finnish Land Use and Building Act	Ministry of Environment	Binding	
Iceland	Planning and Building Act	Ministry of Environment	Advisory	Ministry of Environment must approve municipal plans
Sweden	Swedish Planning and Building Act	Ministry of Enterprise and Innovation	None	County Administrative Boards monitor enforcement of national policy

Source: Adapted from Fredricsson and Smas (2013), *En granskning av Norges planeringssystem* [Analysis of Norway's planning system].

Section 3.1 of the PBA establishes the responsibility for municipalities to formulate a planning strategy and produce plans that safeguard land resources, landscape qualities and the conservation of valuable landscapes and cultural environments, among other areas. As noted, private bodies have the right to put forward planning proposals (detailed zoning that are within the frame of the municipal plan's area part or a less detailed zoning plan), and indeed most come from the private sector. When a private body puts forward a plan, it must assess whether they must produce an EIA that meets established criteria, or whether it is sufficient to make an investigation without a formal EIA. These assessments are also generally produced by private firms. There is no certification process for firms that produce EIAs, but firms must ensure their assessments meet the requisite quality; they can be penalised for non-conformance.

The county (regional) council formulates a planning strategy, master plans and planning provisions for the region. Only the regional planning strategy is mandatory. These plans are intended to stimulate physical, environmental, health-related, economic, social and cultural development. The county council is required to establish a regional planning forum to bring together relevant government agencies, including the Sami Parliament, to discuss and co-ordinate. The outcomes of this forum are not binding. The public and civil society organisations are informed about the outcomes and may provide comments but do not participate directly.

National goals and objectives in the PBA are non-binding

In most cases, the national government does not set explicit or binding goals for land-use planning. It generally respects the principles of local autonomy and self-determination. The national government provides land-use guidelines for local authorities but can safeguard national or regional interests (mostly for infrastructure projects). This guidance forms the basis of national participation in the planning process. It includes multi-annual national expectations with regard to regional and municipal planning, and central government planning guidelines, planning provisions and land-use plans.

Every four years, the government issues a non-binding document that outlines its priorities and guidance to regional and municipal governments (Miljoverndepartementet, 2011[23]; Ministry of Local Government and Modernisation, 2019[44]). These national expectations cover many important policy areas, including climate, nature, cultural environment, transport, health and quality of life. Earlier versions provide clear guidance regarding the desired environmental outcomes of the planning process, for which the Environment Ministry was responsible. The latest version of this document, prepared by KMD, focuses much more on ensuring good processes at the local level rather than specific outcomes (Strand and Næss, 2017[45]).

The government has put much responsibility for achieving the SDGs on county and municipal governments. In its national expectations document, it says "The county and municipal authorities [should] base their social and land-use planning on the United Nations' Sustainable Development Goals." The national government contributes through co-ordination between stakeholders, sharing of lessons learnt to build local competence and development of indicators for all the SDGs (Kommunal- og moderniseringsdepartementet, 2021[13]; Ministry of Local Government and Modernisation, 2019[44]). In other words, the national government's role is enabling and supporting rather than leading.

The objection process

The national government and affected regional bodies, neighbouring municipalities and the Sami Parliament have the right to object to proposals regarding land use in the municipal master plan and the zoning plan in certain cases. These relate to issues of national or significant regional importance, or which are significant to the sphere of responsibility of the body in question.

Two principles have been set out for land-use decisions that affect biodiversity (Ministry of Climate and Environment, 2015[4]):

- The most valuable species, habitats and ecosystems should be safeguarded in connection with decisions on land conversion and land-use change.
- If a development or activity entails a risk of loss or of damage to valuable biodiversity, it should ideally be moved elsewhere.

With respect to area neutrality mentioned above, these principles should be seen as higher priority.

After 2013, the national government made efforts to reduce the number of objections raised by national agencies (NORUT, 2016[46]; Strand and Næss, 2017[45]). The number of objections sent to KMD between 2014 and 2019 dropped by one-third. The ministry (then the Ministry of the Environment) accepted about 50% of objections before 2014 but only 20% after 2014 (Figure 2.23).

Figure 2.23. Objections have declined significantly since 2014

Decisions by the ministry regarding objections, 2008-19

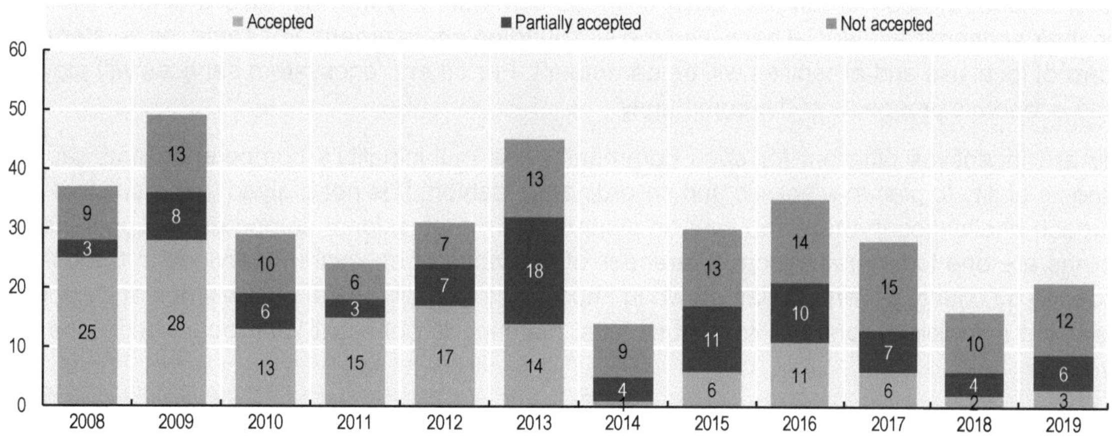

Note: Most objections are resolved without having to go to the ministry for final decision. Responsibility was moved from the Ministry of the Environment to the Ministry of Local Government and Modernisation in 2013.
Source: Country submission.

StatLink https://stat.link/3tquw6

It is unclear what is behind the reduced number of objections arriving at the ministry for decision. As noted earlier, the government signalled a preference for fewer objections, which could make county governors and national agencies more reluctant to produce them. During the same period, county governors and agencies also produced objections in a different way. They established a process that led to better dialogue between the county governors' offices and the state authorities, clearer and more predictable participation by government agencies, qualitatively better objections and fewer objections (NORUT, 2016[46]). Even though objections are deemed to be of higher quality, the ministry's rejection rate remains higher than in previous years.

Municipalities tend to view the objection process as needless bureaucracy that springs from a lack of trust in their capacity. From the perspective of county governors, this view reflects municipalities' lack of appreciation of their actual room to manoeuvre in the PBA. Governors note that between one-third and one-half of the objections are due to formal errors and not a challenge of local decision making (Ministry of Local Government and Modernisation, 2014[43]).

Local autonomy versus national priorities

Norway's land-use planning process is not exceptionally decentralised when compared to its neighbours (Fredricsson and Smas, 2013[47]) or to the OECD as a whole (OECD, 2016[48]). However, decision making is concentrated at the municipal level, which can lead to different outcomes in different municipalities. Most larger urban centres have ambitious environmental programmes, particularly with respect to climate change and the SDGs. Smaller communities with stable or declining populations struggle with ageing populations and feel pressure to provide economic opportunities to sustain their communities. Consequently, they may place a lower priority on environmental objectives (Kommunal- og moderniseringsdepartementet, 2021[13]).

Outside of major urban centres, there are four broad community types in Norway (Frisvoll, 2018[49]). Declining communities are those facing prolonged population decline, reduced employment opportunities and a limited economic base with a large share of public sector employment. Industry-dependent communities rely on resource-based businesses such as forestry, mining or energy. Recreation communities are attractive areas for outdoor activities, will have large numbers of leisure homes (secondary residences) and are close enough to population centres to make visiting practical. Bedroom communities are within commuting distance of larger labour markets and offer a good quality of life with a balance of rural and urban amenities. Each of these community types will have a different relationship between their economic and social basis and the surrounding environment. For some, ecosystem services in the form of local use and amenities will be paramount. For others, ecosystem services will play a minor role in the economic prospects of the community.

Not only are incentives different for each community, the municipality's competence and capacity will determine its ability to plan in a holistic and co-ordinated fashion. It is not a given that municipal planners will approach challenges in the same way as planners with professional competence. Local biodiversity action plans are one tool to raise local awareness of the value of ecosystem services to the community, and guidance by county governors has grown in importance. Building local competence and capacity is a necessary but insufficient condition to ensure local planning is coherent with local needs and national objectives.

Local opposition by landowners and municipalities has complicated the national objective to increase protected areas that are representative of all parts of Norway. On the one hand, this is reasonable, as local acceptability is important to the legitimacy and success of protected areas. On the other, more effort should be made to build local support for national objectives for biodiversity and landscape protection. Local acceptability should not imply a local veto when national interests are significant.

Use of exemptions

In 2019, more than 100 municipalities still lacked recently updated area plans (Rørholt and Steinnes, 2020[35]). Where area plans are out of date, developers may use the exemption or dispensation process to gain approval for development plans. The large majority of applications are approved through this exemption process each year (Table 2.4). However, this approach risks reduced transparency and making development activities inconsistent with overall objectives. For example, most applications for housing in the sensitive coastal zone area where special rules apply are made through the exemption process.

Table 2.4. Applications for new buildings along the coastal zone outside urban areas

	Total number of applications processed	Applications consistent with plans approved	Applications approved through exemption of regulation
2016	1 403	391	790
2017	1 384	446	720
2018	1 319	473	751
2019	973	278	606

Note: The Norwegian coastal zone, also known as the 100-metre belt, includes islands with mainland connection by bridge or ferry. In addition, the statistics include the 100-metre belt around the main rivers and lakes.
Source: Statistics Norway (2021), "Construction in the coastal zone", *StatBank* (database).

The exemption and dispensation practice is frequently used because the area part of the municipal plan is outdated. Ideally, the municipal plan is a strategic document that should inform development proposals and ensure harmony with municipal plans. Area plans cannot serve this function unless they are actively maintained. There need to be stronger incentives to update and modernise municipalities' plans.

The coastal zone has special protections

The coastal zone is a desirable area for development of holiday homes and other activities, and development pressure has reduced ecosystem quality in the coastal area. Coastal activities like dredging, and development of piers, marinas or artificial beaches can take place without any comprehensive plan and without any overall knowledge about cumulative consequences (Stokke et al., 2009[50]). Such measures can have negative consequences for marine biological diversity in the coastal zone. This is true for both spawning and rearing areas for important fish species and for fishing itself. The cumulative effects of such activity over time is of greatest concern.

To address this, development within the 100-metre belt along the sea has been banned (Kommunal- og moderniseringsdepartementet, 2021[51]). In this zone, it is not permitted to implement construction, demolition, alteration, changed use and other measures related to buildings, structures and facilities, terrain encroachment, or creation and alteration of property. The building ban applies to other activities and changes in land use in conflict with land purposes, planning regulations and consideration zones, or to older plans without a set building limit.

The building plan does not apply if the municipality has opened up a coastal area for development and set a building boundary in the municipal plan's area part or zoning plan. According to state planning guidelines, new measures can be approved to a greater extent in areas with little development pressure and a lot of accessible beach zone than in areas with the opposite conditions.

Avenues for action to improve outcomes of the planning process

Outside of the objection process, the national government mainly uses soft tools to influence the local planning process to achieve its objectives, such as for the SDGs. That is, it relies on guidance, advice, support and information to help shape local plans. These tools can be effective but may not be enough to ensure that national objectives are met. Sector regulations are stronger tools but are not always well co-ordinated. Most importantly, Norway needs to base measurable and time-bound national objectives on good scientific understanding of the state of land use, biodiversity and ecosystem services. In addition, it needs to measure and predict the cumulative effect of decisions on these ecosystem services. Such objectives and mechanisms would "close the loop" between planning and its cumulative outcomes.

Establishing frameworks for better horizontal and vertical co-ordination

Norway has used different approaches for planning and decision making in different contexts. These provide many examples of good practices that could help achieve more holistic land-use planning. For example, marine planning requires a long-term perspective and sectoral co-ordination to be successful, and Norway is generally seen as a role model in this area. River basin management is influenced by Norway's implementation of the WFD, which presupposes a certain national role. While this is not exactly a planning system like the PBA, it faces and solves many of the same problems as land-use planning. In particular, the WFD addresses the need for local acceptance and anchoring of projects in local communities, while balancing this local autonomy with national objectives. It also provides for better co-ordination of sector action and responsibility. Local land-use planning has not always been successful in this regard (Ministry of Climate and Environment, 2015[4]).

Better data and analysis connecting local decisions to national outcomes

The government has worked to reduce use of the objection process in the PBA. However, objections themselves do not appear to be causing serious problems. The motivation behind their use seems to be a desire to reduce conflicts by tipping the planning process in favour of local autonomy. Much of the population lives in peri-urban zones comprised mainly of forest and cultural landscapes with high biodiversity values. Consequently, conflicts between land use and conservation are inevitable and structural; eliminating conflict should not be an objective. The challenge is to develop institutions and practices that can handle conflict constructively. These should optimise development activity subject to environmental constraints as defined by the national government. Such constraints are broadly outlined in the Biodiversity Action Plan, and expressing them more concretely is an important next step.

Local decisions will add up to a certain overall impact, and this cumulative effect needs to be understood and kept within safe limits. The PBA does not systematically capture the accumulated consequences of land policy. Furthermore, local planning processes are not linked to national objectives and outcomes in a systematic and measurable way (Kommunal- og moderniseringsdepartementet, 2021[13]). This prevents an objective evaluation of the overall costs and benefits of proposed developments. Regional bodies, the county governor in particular, form the link between national objectives and local planning. They are the main providers of feedback to municipal planning and the source of most objections to submitted plans. Circular T-2/16 provides detailed guidance regarding issues of national significance (Klima- og miljødepartementet, 2021[52]). It sets out many important themes, but without clear indicators, it leaves much to the judgement of the county governor.

Having clearer metrics for evaluation can make this process more objective. While substantial work is already being done in this regard, several different tools are available to improve the situation. The Biodiversity Action Plan sets the stage for clear and measurable objectives that can serve as a benchmark to assess overall outcomes of the planning process. The NiN indicators provide a good overview of ecosystem condition and risk factors. These indicators could be combined with quality norms to quantify national objectives in more detail. The national planning database already contains details on planned development (Berglund and Kvifte, 2015[53]; Rørholt and Steinnes, 2020[35]; Steinnes, 2018[25]). This system could be connected to the EIA process for local plans and projects.

Ideally, improved information on the intersection of land planning, the value of ecosystem services and national objectives will help county governors do their jobs better. In addition, it will also provide municipal planners better tools to follow national guidelines, as well as a better overview of their own needs and options for housing planning. Municipalities can use the statistics and analyses in the municipal planning processes to both identify needs and solve challenges. At the same time, they can be used to evaluate how well private developers process submitted zoning plans (Berglund and Kvifte, 2015[53]).

Such a system of accounting for land-use change relies on accurate and timely data that are fit for purpose, a means to use that data to estimate the cumulative effect of planned changes and a way to feed this information back into the process so planners can make use of it. As both cumulative and local effects of planning decisions are important, a mechanism should ideally allow for optimal allocation of development opportunities within the overall constraints of the system. In this regard, municipalities should have a way to discuss and co-ordinate. Land-use changes outside this system must be limited if it is to function well. This means that use of exemptions or dispensations must be reduced to the extent possible. Improved and up-to-date municipal planning is the best way to achieve this reduction.

More specific guidance to local governments

National goals should be specific and actionable so local governments can evaluate their plans against them and measure progress. This requires information support and feedback at all stages of the process. Once again, the Biodiversity Action Plan can serve as a foundation for those national objectives within its domain. KLD is better placed to co-ordinate local planning with respect to national environmental objectives and is already responsible for most related tasks. On the other hand, KMD has greater expertise in the processes themselves. Sharing responsibility between the ministries can lead to more effective engagement with local planning. The governance of RBMPs is a useful model with the Norwegian Environmental Agency playing a co-ordinating role and communities undertaking most of the activity.

More targeted incentives

Providing proper incentives to municipalities to consider national interests is one way to align the incentives of local governments with national priorities. If the national government gives a mandate to local governments to achieve national objectives such as for climate change or biodiversity, local governments should not have to bear the full financial burden on their own. At the same time, the polluter-pays principle should be respected.

Financial support for biodiversity plans has been useful, but more can be done to incentivise action. For example, urban growth agreements for transport to achieve the zero growth objective for traffic are a successful example of cost sharing among governments. RBMPs provide incentives through clear national targets with more rigid requirements for implementation. *Ex post* assessment of actual versus expected results on a regular cycle can provide accountability that municipal plans are effective.

Better public consultation

The ideal of local participation and participation is strong among both politicians and planners. However, in practice, such participation is often limited to the minimum requirements for formal consultations. Community involvement depends in part on municipalities' willingness to involve part-time residents in the formulation of local policy (Ellingsen, Hanssen and Saglie, 2010[54]). There is great variation in political and popular involvement, competence and capacity in the municipalities, regardless of municipality size. This variation weakens the purpose and ambitions of the PBA (Hanssen and Aarsæther, 2018[55]).

The PBA has statutory requirements for public involvement. The municipal planning strategy must be made public 30 days prior to political consideration. There are also requirements for public consultation and scrutiny of the proposed plan. Municipalities are required to explain how they have considered comments received. However, the requirements are only to inform and consult. Local actors are not otherwise given a presence in the planning process. Moreover, municipalities are not required to provide a forum for dialogue or otherwise involve the public (Figure 2.24).

Figure 2.24. Requirements for public involvement in the Planning and Building Act

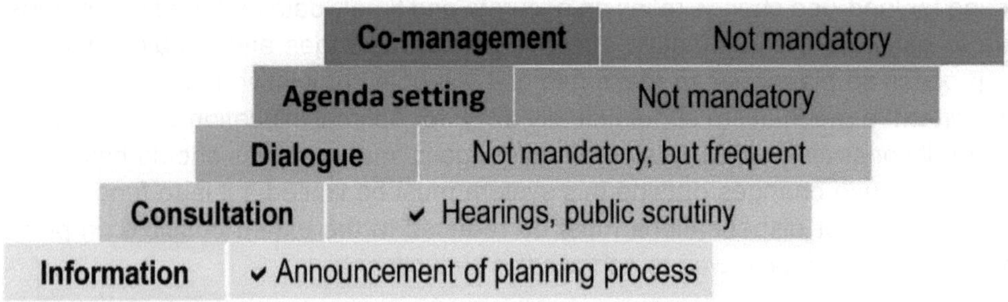

Note: The figure applies Arnstein's typology of citizen participation, which is presented as a metaphorical "ladder" representing increasing levels of public involvement.
Source: Ringholm, T, Nyseth T and Hanssen G (2018). *Participation according to the law?: The research-based knowledge on citizen participation in Norwegian municipal planning,* EJSD, vol. 67.

A national nature and environmental appeals board, following the Danish or Swedish model, can help ensure civil society has an effective means to engage in the planning process (Box 2.7). This extra venue to challenge decision making at all levels can help ensure the environment is given more "standing" in government processes. Norway already operates similar types of boards such as for real estate services and consumer complaints. Currently, civil society has little opportunity to do more than comment on planning proposals, except for the expensive and risky step of legal action. Such legal actions are more likely for "not in my backyard" issues like siting of waste management facilities or wind power generation than they are for environmental protection.

Box 2.7. Danish Appeal Boards give a stronger voice to citizens

Complaint boards are dedicated entities of ministries that process complaints of citizens relating to decisions of the administration. Members are usually appointed by the government or a municipal council. These boards are independent from local councils or ministers in processing cases, making their decisions, and launching or terminating an investigation.

Appeals boards enjoy independence from the rest of the public administration. No minister may give orders to an appeals board with regard to the outcome of decisions in order to commence or terminate an investigation. Nor can it interfere with the processing of an individual case. Decisions of appeals boards cannot be appealed to other administrative authorities unless granted by statute.

Most appeals boards are supervised by the parliamentary ombudsperson. This means the ombudsperson may, as a result of a complaint or on their own initiative, investigate decisions of an appeals board and assess whether the case processing or the decision is legal.

The Nature Protection and Environmental Board of Appeal is part of the Ministry of the Environment. Decisions by the boards may be brought before the courts and the boards are also supervised by the parliamentary ombudsperson.

Source: OECD (2010), *Better Regulation in Europe: Denmark 2010.*

Building capacity at the municipal level

The Norwegian commitment to local democracy is a strength of the system. It provides local anchoring that increases the legitimacy of decisions, and draws on local knowledge and experience. However, competence and capacity in small municipalities can be a significant problem in Norwegian planning (Hanssen and Aarsæther, 2018[55]). The government has taken steps to build local capacity for the planning system to work as intended. Consolidation of municipalities is a means to increase the scale of local government and the resources available to it. Promoting local biodiversity plans raises awareness of the value of ecosystem services to the local economy and the tools available to consider these benefits in local decision making. County governors increasingly serve a supportive role in the planning process and provide guidance at all stages.

More training for members of municipal governments can be helpful, especially for those newly elected. Ensuring that municipalities maintain permanent professional staff with responsibility for SDG implementation and other environmental issues of a national character (climate change, biodiversity) can also improve the quality of local decision making. In addition, it could be helpful to build support networks such as through professional development conferences where experiences and good practices may be shared.

References

Artsdatabanken (2021), *Endringer fra 2015 til 2021. Norsk rødliste for arter 2021 (Changes from 2015 to 2021: The Norwegian Red List for Species)*, (database), https://www.artsdatabanken.no/rodlisteforarter2021/Resultater/Endringerfra2015til2021 (accessed on 24 November 2021). [12]

Artsdatabanken (2021), *Resultater. Norsk rødliste for arter 2021 (Results. Norwegian Red List of Species 2021)*, (database), https://www.artsdatabanken.no/rodlisteforarter2021/Resultater (accessed on 24 November 2021). [10]

Berglund, G. and H. Kvifte (2015), *Sluttrapport – Statistikk og analyser av plandata (Final report - Statistics and analyzes of plan data)*, Asplan Viak AS. [53]

Centre, N. (2021), *The Norwegian Red List for Ecosystem and Habitat Types.* [63]

Chinners Reiss, K., E. Hernandez and M. Brown (2007), *An Evaluation of the Effectiveness of Mitigation Banking in Florida: Ecological Success and Compliance with Permit Criteria*, United States Environmental Protection Agency Region Four, https://floridadep.gov/sites/default/files/Final_Report_0.pdf. [42]

Ciglič, R. and D. Perko (2013), "Europe's landscape hotspots", *Acta geographica Slovenica*, Vol. 53/1, pp. 117-139, https://doi.org/10.3986/AGS53106. [57]

Climate Action Tracker (2021), *Climate Action Tracker*, website, https://climateactiontracker.org/countries/norway/ (accessed on 1 December 2021). [69]

Cowie, A. et al. (2018), "Land in balance: The scientific conceptual framework for Land Degradation Neutrality", *Environmental Science & Policy*, Vol. 79, pp. 25-35, https://doi.org/10.1016/J.ENVSCI.2017.10.011. [37]

Ellingsen, W., G. Hanssen and I. Saglie (2010), "Nye utfordringer i rurale kommuner. Fritidsboliger og lokaldemokrati [New challenges in rural municipalities. Holiday homes and local democracy]", *Kart og Plan*, Vol. 70, pp. 227-290. [54]

Faehn, T. et al. (2020), *Abating greenhouse gases in the Norwegian non-ETS sector by 50 per cent by 2030. A macroeconomic analysis of Climate Cure 2030*, Statstics Norway. [56]

Falleth, E. and S. Hovik (2009), "Local government and nature conservation in Norway: Decentralisation as a strategy in environmental policy", *International Journal of Justice and Sustainability*, Vol. 14/3, pp. 221-231, https://doi.org/10.1080/13549830802692849. [32]

Fauchald, O. and L. Gulbrandsen (2012), "The Norwegian reform of protected area management: A grand experiment with delegation of authority?", *International Journal of Justice and Sustainability*, Vol. 17/2, pp. 203-222, https://doi.org/10.1080/13549839.2012.660910. [27]

Framstad, E. et al. (2021), *Vurdering av økologisk tilstand for skog i Norge i 2020 (Assessment of ecological condition for forests in Norway in 2020)*, Norsk institutt for naturforskning, Oslo. [15]

Framstad, E. et al. (2010), *Naturfaglig evaluering av norske verneområder (Scientific evaluation of Norwegian protected areas)*, NINA Report 535, Oslo, https://brage.nina.no/nina-xmlui/handle/11250/2563864. [33]

Framstad, E. et al. (2012), *Naturfaglig evaluering av norske verneområder. Verneområdenes funksjon som økologisk nettverk og toleranse for klimaendringer*, [Scientific evaluation of Norwegian protected areas. The protected areas' function as an ecological network and tolerance for climate change], NINA Report 888, Oslo, https://brage.nina.no/nina-xmlui/handle/11250/2643056. [30]

Fredricsson, C. and L. Smas (2013), *En granskning av Norges planeringssystem (An examination of Norway's planning system)*, Nordregio, Stockholm, https://nordregio.org/publications/en-granskning-av-norges-planeringssystem/. [47]

Frisvoll, S. (2018), "Kommunereformen. Tabu og kontrovers (Municipal reform. Taboo and controversy)", *Samtiden*, Vol. 126/01, pp. 32-41, https://doi.org/10.18261/ISSN1890-0690-2018-01-06. [49]

Gundersen, I., G. Steinnes and M. Jostein Frydenlund (2017), *Nedbygging av jordbruksareal. En kartbasert undersøkelse av nedbygging og bruksendringer av jordbruksareal (Degradation of agricultural land. A map-based study of degradation and changes in the use of agricultural land)*, Statistics Norway, Oslo. [20]

Halvorsen, R. et al. (2015), "Natur i Norge (NiN). versjon 2.0.0. (Nature in Norway [NiN]. version 2.0.0.)", in *Artsdatabanken*, (database), http://www.artsdatabanken.no/naturinorge (accessed on 6 December 2021). [7]

Hanssen, G. and N. Aarsæther (eds.) (2018), *Plan- og bygningsloven 2008 (Planning and Building Act 2008)*, Universitetsforlaget. [55]

Hausner, V., G. Brown and E. Lægreid (2015), "Effects of land tenure and protected areas on ecosystem services and land use preferences in Norway", *Land Use Policy*, Vol. 49, pp. 446-461, https://doi.org/10.1016/J.LANDUSEPOL.2015.08.018. [26]

Henriksen, S. and O. Hilmo (2015), *Norwegian Red List of Species 2015: Methods and Results*, Norwegian Biodiversity Information Centre, Oslo. [11]

Hongslo, E. et al. (2015), "Decentralization of conservation management in Norway and Sweden – Different translations of an international trend", *Society and Natural Resources*, Vol. 29/8, pp. 998-1014, https://doi.org/10.1080/08941920.2015.1086456. [59]

Hough, P. and R. Harrington (2019), "Ten years of the compensatory mitigation rule: Reflections on progress and opportunities", *Environmental Law Reporter*, Vol. 49/10018, https://www.eli.org/sites/default/files/elr/featuredarticles/Jan19FA.pdf (accessed on 9 December 2021). [41]

Hovik, S. and E. Hongslo (2016), "Balancing local interests and national conservation obligations in nature protection. The case of local management boards in Norway", *https://doi.org/10.1080/09640568.2016.1176556*, Vol. 60/4, pp. 708-724, https://doi.org/10.1080/09640568.2016.1176556. [58]

Hovik, S. and E. Hongslo (2016), "Balancing local interests and national conservation obligations in nature protection: The case of local management boards in Norway", *Journal of Environmental Planning and Management*, Vol. 60/4, pp. 708-724, https://doi.org/10.1080/09640568.2016.1176556. [31]

Klima- og miljødepartementet (2021), *Nasjonale og vesentlige regionale interesser på miljøområdet – klargjøring av miljøforvaltningens innsigelsespraksis*, [National and significant regional interests in the environmental field - clarification of the environmental administration's objection practice], Klima- og miljødepartementet. [52]

Kommunal- og moderniseringsdepartementet (2021), *Meld. St. 40 (2020–2021) Mål med mening – Norges handlingsplan for å nå bærekraftsmålene innen 2030 (Goals with meaning – Norway's action plan to achieve the sustainability goals by 2030)*, Kommunal-og moderniseringsdepartementet, https://www.regjeringen.no/no/dokumenter/meld.-st.-40-20202021/id2862554/ (accessed on 15 September 2021). [13]

Kommunal- og moderniseringsdepartementet (2021), *Statlige planretningslinjer for differensiert forvaltning av strandsonen langs sjøen (State planning guidelines for differentiated management of the beach zone along the sea)*, Kommunal-og moderniseringsdepartementet. [51]

Kommunal- og moderniseringsdepartementet (2014), *Statlige planretningslinjer for samordnet bolig-, areal- og transportplanlegging (State planning guidelines for coordinated housing, area and transport planning)*, Kommunal- og moderniseringsdepartementet. [24]

Landbruks- og matdepartementet (2020), *Provided information*, Ministry of Agriculture and Food, Oslo. [14]

Landbruks- og matdepartementet (2016), "Endring og utvikling En fremtidsrettet jordbruksproduksjon (Change and development: A future-oriented agricultural production)", *Melding til Stortinget*, No. Meld. St. 11 (2016 –2017), Ministry of Agriculture and Food, Oslo. [17]

Landbruksdirektoratet (2020), *Årsrapport 2020 (Annual Report 2020)*, Landsbruksdirektoratet, Oslo. [22]

Lier-Hansen, S. et al. (2013), *Naturens goder – om verdier av økosystemtjenester (The benefits of nature – about the values of ecosystem services)*, Norges offentlige utredninger, Oslo. [6]

McKenney, B. and J. Kiesecker (2010), "Policy development for biodiversity offsets: A review of offset frameworks", *Environmental Management*, Vol. 45/1, pp. 165-176, https://doi.org/10.1007/S00267-009-9396-3. [39]

Metzger, M. et al. (2005), "A climatic stratification of the environment of Europe", *Global Ecology and Biogeography*, Vol. 14/6, pp. 549-563, https://doi.org/10.1111/J.1466-822X.2005.00190.X. [2]

Miljoverndepartementet (2011), *Nasjonale forventninger til regional og kommunal planlegging vedtatt ved kongelig resolusjon 24. juni 2011 (National expectations for regional and municipal planning adopted by royal resolution on 24 June 2011).* [23]

Ministry of Climate and Environment (2015), *Norway's National Biodiversity Action Plan Nature for Life*, Ministry of Climate and Environment, Oslo. [4]

Ministry of Justice and Public Security (2015), *Meld. St. 32 (2015-2016) Svalbard.* [62]

Ministry of Local Government and Modernisation (2019), *National Expectations regarding Regional and Municipal Planning 2019-2023*, Ministry of Local Government and Modernisation, Oslo, https://www.regjeringen.no/contentassets/cc2c53c65af24b8ea560c0156d885703/nasjonale-forventninger-2019-engelsk.pdf. [44]

Ministry of Local Government and Modernisation (2014), *Forenkling av utmarksforvaltningen: Rapport fra faggruppe oppnevnt av kommunal- og moderniseringsdepartementet (Simplification of outfield management: Report from a professional group appointed by the Ministry of Local Government and Modernisation)*. [43]

Mittenzwei, K. and W. Britz (2018), "Analysing farm-specific payments for Norway using the agrispace model", *Journal of Agricultural Economics*, Vol. 69/3, pp. 777-793, https://doi.org/10.1111/1477-9552.12268. [68]

NNV (2011), *Trønderlav*, Norwegian Society for the Conservation of Nature, Oslo, https://naturvernforbundet.no/truede-arter-i-norge/tronderlav-article25348-2625.html (accessed on 3 November 2021). [36]

NORUT (2016), *Samordning av Statlige Innsigelser (Coordination of State Objections)*, Northern Research Institute, Bergen. [46]

Norway's Government, Norwegian Farmers Union and Smallholders Union (2019), *Intentional Agreement between Agriculture and the Government about Reduced GHG Emissions and Increased Uptake of Carbon from Agriculture for the Period 2021–2030*, Norway's Government; Norwegian Farmers Union; Smallholders Union. [65]

Norwegian Biodivesity Information Centre (2021), *The Norwegian Red List for Ecosystem and Habitat Types*. [64]

Norwegian Environment Agency (2021), *Nature Index for Norway*, https://www.naturindeks.no/ (accessed on 20 January 2022). [5]

Norwegian Environment Agency (2021), "New national parks are proposed to be studied", 7 April, Norwegian Environment Agency, Oslo, https://www.miljodirektoratet.no/aktuelt/nyheter/2021/april-2021/nye-nasjonalparker-foreslas-utredet/ (accessed on 30 June 2021). [29]

Norwegian Environment Agency (2019), *Supplerende vern – fase 1 Miljødirektoratets oversendelse til Klima- og miljødepartementet (Supplementary protection – phase 1 The Norwegian Environment Agency's transmission to the Ministry of Climate and the Environment)*, Norwegian Environment Agency, Oslo. [34]

Norwegian Environment Agency (2017), *Forslag til plan for supplerende vern – Miljødirektoratets anbefalinger (Proposed plan for supplementary protection - The Norwegian Environment Agency's recommendations)*, Norwegian Environment Agency, Oslo. [28]

Norwegian Environment Agency (2016), *Oppsummering av spørreundersøkelse: Evaluering av vannforskriftarbeidet 2010 - 2015 [Summary of survey: Evaluation of the water regulations work 2010 - 2015]*, Norwegian Environment Agency, Oslo, https://www.vannportalen.no/sharepoint/downloaditem?id=01FM3LD2WKNNYNG4KOFVFJJYDZEO7XKPTB. [61]

Norwegian Ministry of Climate and Environment (2019), *Norway's integrated ocean management plans*, Norwegian Ministry of Climate and Environment, Oslo. [60]

OECD (2021), "Biodiversity, natural capital and the economy: A policy guide for finance, economic and environment ministers", *OECD Environment Policy Papers*, No. 26, OECD Publishing, Paris, https://doi.org/10.1787/1a1ae114-en. [8]

OECD (2021), *Policies for the Future of Farming and Food in Norway*, OECD Agriculture and Food Policy Reviews, OECD Publishing, Paris, https://doi.org/10.1787/20b14991-en. [19]

OECD (2021), *Policies for the Future of Farming and Food in Norway*, OECD Agriculture and Food Policy Reviews, OECD Publishing, Paris, https://doi.org/10.1787/20b14991-en. [21]

OECD (2016), *Biodiversity Offsets: Effective Design and Implementation*, OECD Publishing, Paris, https://doi.org/10.1787/9789264222519-en. [38]

OECD (2016), *OECD Regional Outlook 2016: Productive Regions for Inclusive Societies*, OECD Publishing, Paris, https://doi.org/10.1787/9789264260245-en. [48]

OECD (2011), *OECD Environmental Performance Reviews: Norway 2011*, OECD Environmental Performance Reviews, OECD Publishing, Paris, https://doi.org/10.1787/9789264098473-en. [3]

OECD (2010), *Better Regulation in Europe: Denmark 2010*, Better Regulation in Europe, OECD Publishing, Paris, https://doi.org/10.1787/9789264084551-en. [67]

PEFC Norway (2016), *Norwegian PEFC Forest Standard*, PEFC Norway, Geneva, https://cdn.pefc.org/pefc.org/media/2019-04/b017030b-c623-42b1-b494-d17f94bbd437/5706b1de-adae-596d-afb2-1d21060e9e08.pdf. [16]

Ringholm, T., T. Nyseth and S. Gro (2018), "Participation according to the law?: The research-based knowledge on citizen participation in Norwegian municipal planning", *European Journal of Spatial Development* 67, https://doi.org/10.30689/EJSD2018:67.1650-9544. [66]

Rørholt, A. and M. Steinnes (2020), *Planlagt utbygd areal 2019 til 2030 (Planned developed area 2019 to 2030)*, Statistisk sentralbyrå, Oslo. [35]

Simensen, T., L. Erikstad and R. Halvorsen (2021), "Diversity and distribution of landscape types in Norway", *Norsk Geografisk Tidsskrift – Norwegian Journal of Geography*, Vol. 75/2, pp. 79-100, https://doi.org/10.1080/00291951.2021.1892177. [1]

Statistics Norway (2021), *StatBank Norway*, (database), https://www.ssb.no/en/statbank/ (accessed on 11 October 2021). [18]

Steinnes, M. (2018), *Statistikk basert på kommuneplaner (Statistics based on municipal plans)*, Statistics Norway, Oslo. [25]

Stokke, K. et al. (2009), "'Bit for bit' utbygging i kystsonen (Development in the Coastal Zone)", No. NIBR/NIVA/HI 2009, Norsk institutt for by- og regionforskning, Oslo. [50]

Strand, A. and P. Næss (2017), "Local self-determination, process-focus and subordination of environmental concerns", *Journal of Environmental Policy and Planning*, Vol. 19/2, pp. 156-167, https://doi.org/10.1080/1523908X.2016.1175927. [45]

Tucker, G., F. Quétier and W. Wende (2020), *Guidance on achieving no net loss or net gain of biodiversity and ecosystem services*, report commissioned by the European Commission, Institute for European Environmental Policy, Brussels, July, https://ieep.eu/publications/achieving-no-net-loss-of-biodiversity-and-ecosystem-services-key-principles-and-best-practices. [40]

United Nations (2021), "Ecosystem Accounting: System of Environmental Economic Accounting", webpage, https://seea.un.org/ecosystem-accounting (accessed on 7 December 2021). [9]

Printed by Libri Plureos GmbH in Hamburg,
Germany

9 789264 182004